CRITICAL ETHICS

Critical Ethics

Text, Theory and Responsibility

Edited by

Dominic Rainsford
Lecturer in English
University of Aarhus
Denmark

and

Tim Woods
Lecturer in English and American Studies
University of Wales
Aberystwyth

First published in Great Britain 1999 by
MACMILLAN PRESS LTD
Houndmills, Basingstoke, Hampshire RG21 6XS and London
Companies and representatives throughout the world

A catalogue record for this book is available from the British Library.

ISBN 0–333–71885–2

First published in the United States of America 1999 by
ST. MARTIN'S PRESS, INC.,
Scholarly and Reference Division,
175 Fifth Avenue, New York, N.Y. 10010

ISBN 0–312–17533–7

Library of Congress Cataloging-in-Publication Data
Critical ethics : text, theory, and responsibility / edited by Dominic Rainsford and Tim Woods.
p. cm.
"Adapted from papers given at the Literature and Ethics conference at the University of Wales, Aberystwyth, in July 1996"–
–Acknowledgements.
Includes bibliographical references (p.) and index.
ISBN 0–312–17533–7 (hardcover)
1. Criticism—Moral and ethical aspects. I. Rainsford, Dominic, 1965– . II. Woods, Tim.
PN98.M67C75 1998
809—dc21 98–15289
CIP

10 9 8 7 6 5 4 3 2 1
08 07 06 05 04 03 02 01 00 99

Printed and bound in Great Britain by
Antony Rowe Ltd, Chippenham, Wiltshire

Contents

Acknowledgements

The essays in this volume are all adapted from papers given at the *Literature and Ethics* conference at the University of Wales, Aberystwyth, in July 1996. We would like to thank all of the speakers and other participants at the conference, for helping to make it such an enjoyable and intellectually challenging event. We are also grateful for the financial support which the conference received from the Humanities Research Board of the British Academy, from the University of Wales, Aberystwyth Research Fund, and the Department of English of UWA. We would also like to thank Joan Crawford and June Baxter for their secretarial help in the preparation of the conference and this volume. We are grateful to Dr Andrew Hadfield as one of the co-organizers of the conference, for his generous help and advice in editing the papers.

Dan Burnstone's essay was first published in *Philosophy and Literature*, Vol. 21, No. 1 (1997); it is reprinted here by kind permission of the Johns Hopkins University Press and *Philosophy and Literature*. Geoffrey Galt Harpham's essay is a shorter version of an essay that will appear in *In the Shadows of Ethics: Literature, Criticism and Culture* (forthcoming, Duke University Press, 1999). Steven Connor's essay includes material previously published in his recent book with Oxford University Press. We gratefully acknowledge these publishers' cooperation.

Notes on the Contributors

Michael Bell is Professor in the Department of English and Comparative Literary Studies at the University of Warwick. His publications include *Primitivism* (1972); *1900–1930 The Context of English Literature* (1980); *The Sentiment of Reality: Truth of Feeling in the European Novel* (1983); *F. R. Leavis* (1988); *D. H. Lawrence: Language and Being* (1992); *Gabriel García Márquez: Solitude and Solidarity* (1993); and *Literature, Modernism and Myth: Belief and Responsibility in the Twentieth Century* (1997).

Dan Burnstone is a Lecturer at the University of Cambridge and is writing a book on John Stuart Mill.

Steven Connor is Professor of Modern Literature and Theory at Birkbeck College, London. His books include *Charles Dickens* (1985), *Postmodernist Culture: An Introduction to Theories of the Contemporary* (1989; 2nd edn, 1996), *Theory and Cultural Value* (1992), *The English Novel in History, 1950–1995* (1996) and *James Joyce* (1996).

Simon Critchley is Reader in Philosophy at the University of Essex. He is author of *The Ethics of Deconstruction: Derrida and Levinas* (1992), *Very Little... Almost Nothing: Death, Philosophy, Literature* (1997) and *Between Ethics and Politics* (forthcoming).

Anne Cubilié gained her PhD from the University of Pennsylvania. She has taught at Penn and Swarthmore, and is now Assistant Professor in the Department of English at Georgetown University, Washington, DC, where she holds an appointment in Transnational Feminist Cultural Studies. She is currently working on a project that considers the relationship between women's testimonial literature from several different cultures and international human rights theory and practice.

Robert Eaglestone took his BA at Manchester, his MA at Southampton and his PhD at the University of Wales, Lampeter (1995). He is a lecturer in twentieth-century literature at Royal Holloway, University of London. His book, *Ethical Criticism:*

Reading after Levinas was published in 1997. He is currently working on a project entitled 'Modernism, Postmodernism and Ethics'.

Geoffrey Galt Harpham is Professor and Chair of the Department of English at Tulane University. His publications include *On the Grotesque: Strategies of Contradiction in Art and Literature* (1982); *The Ascetic Imperative in Culture and Criticism* (1987); *Getting It Right: Language, Literature, and Ethics* (1992); *One of Us: The Mastery of Joseph Conrad* (1996); and the new 'Ethics' chapter in the second edition of *Critical Terms for Literary Study*, edited by Lentricchia and McLaughlin (1995).

Colleen Lamos is Associate Professor of English at Rice University. She is the author of *Modernism Astray: Sexual Errancy in T. S. Eliot, James Joyce and Marcel Proust* (forthcoming). She has published articles in *Novel, Signs, Contemporary Literature*, the *James Joyce Quarterly*, the *National Women's Studies Association Journal, Feminist Economics, Pretext*, the *Lesbian and Gay Studies Newsletter*, the *Lesbian Review of Books*, and in the collections, *Engendered Perspectives: New Essays on 'Ulysses', Cross-Purposes: Lesbian Studies, Feminist Studies, and the Limits of Alliance, Joyce in Context, The Lesbian Postmodern, Lesbian Erotics* and *Quare Joyce*. She is currently co-editing a special issue of the *European Joyce Studies Annual* on 'Joycean Masculinities' and working on a book about homoerotic desire in the texts of modern British and American women writers.

Larry Lockridge is Professor of English at New York University. His publications include *Coleridge the Moralist* (1977), *The Ethics of Romanticism* (1989), *Nineteenth-Century Lives* (1989, as co-editor) and a biography of his father, *Shade of the Raintree: The Life and Death of Ross Lockridge, Jr., Author of 'Raintree County'* (1994).

Christopher Norris is Professor of Philosophy at the University of Wales, Cardiff. His books include *Deconstruction: Theory and Practice* (1982; 1991), studies of Empson, de Man, and Derrida, *The Contest of Faculties* (1985), *Spinoza and the Origins of Modern Critical Theory* (1990), *What's Wrong with Postmodernism?* (1990), *Uncritical Theory* (1992), *The Truth about Postmodernism* (1993), *Truth and the Ethics of Criticism* (1994), *Resources of Realism* (1997) and *New Idols of the Cave* (1997).

David Parker is Head of English at the Australian National University. His major publications include *Building on Sand* (1988, novel), *The Mighty World of Eye: Stories/Anti-stories* (1990), *Ethics, Theory and the Novel* (1994), *Shame and the Modern Self* (1996) and, as co-editor, *The Ethics of Literary Theory* (forthcoming).

Dominic Rainsford gained his PhD in 1994 at University College London. He has taught at universities in England, Wales, Poland and the United States, and now lectures in Denmark, at the English Institute of the University of Aarhus. His publications include *Authorship, Ethics and the Reader: Blake, Dickens, Joyce* (1997) and articles in *Contemporary European History*, *The Victorian Newsletter*, *English Language Notes* and *Imprimatur*. Current projects include a book on literature, national identity and the English Channel.

Leona Toker has an MA in English from Vilnius University, Lithuania, and a PhD from the Hebrew University, Jerusalem, where she has taught since 1978. She is the author of *Nabokov: The Mystery of Literary Structures* (1989) and *Eloquent Reticence: Withholding Information in Fictional Narrative* (1993); editor of *Commitment in Reflection: Essays in Literature and Moral Philosophy* (1994); and co-editor, with Shlomith Rimmon-Kenan and Shuli Barzilai, of *Rereading Texts/Rethinking Critical Presuppositions: Essays in Honour of H. M. Daleski* (1997).

Margaret Toye is completing her PhD at the University of Western Ontario, where she is the holder of a Fellowship from the Social Sciences and Humanities Research Council of Canada. Her thesis, written as a hypertext, examines contemporary ethics, pedagogy and electronic media, by concentrating on the ethics of Michel Foucault and the question of the contemporary ethical subject.

Lori Branch West is a PhD student in the Department of English at Indiana University. She is the holder of a five-year Fellowship for doctoral studies in the humanities from the Pew Charitable Trust. The title of her dissertation is 'Rituals of Spontaneity: Novelty, Repetition, and the Quandaries of Resistance in Eighteenth-Century Britain'.

Tim Woods is a lecturer in English and American studies in the Department of English at the University of Wales, Aberystwyth.

His publications include articles on the work of Louis Zukofsky, several articles on contemporary poetry in Britain, the theories of Emmanuel Levinas and Theodor Adorno, and on Paul Auster in Dennis Barone, ed., *Beyond the Red Notebook* (1995). He is currently writing a monograph on modern American poetics and ethics; a book, *Beginning Postmodernism*; and co-authoring with Peter Middleton a book on the representation of histories in post-war literatures.

Introduction: Ethics and Intellectuals

Dominic Rainsford and Tim Woods

The word 'ethics' has been used a great deal in the last few years by literary and cultural theorists. It is a controversial word. Some people are suspicious of it. Others would say that it represents a side of what it is to be a critic, theorist or intellectual that goes without saying. Two things are clear: that there is a process at work in the academy that is making many thinkers address the ethical simultaneously, and that, in doing so, they are pursuing a range of distinct and sometimes mutually contradictory projects. This volume is designed to explore both of these phenomena: the appearance of a common and timely endeavour, and the dispersal of thought along different ethical paths.

'Ethics' has tended to bring other words with it: sociable and optimistic words such as 'co-operation', 'community' and (although this one has a darker side) 'collaboration'. While there are a number of individual writers who have made themselves especially prominent in this new turn (or return) in criticism, much of the work has entailed an ideal of collectivity, and the anthology is perhaps its most appropriate vehicle. The essays in the present volume are themselves the echo of an earlier and much larger collaborative event: the conference, *Literature and Ethics*, held at the University of Wales, Aberystwyth in July 1996. To the satisfaction of its organisers, this conference attracted 68 speakers from a dozen different countries. Hundreds more made enquiries; many good abstracts had to be turned down.[1] The conference was marked by a very convivial atmosphere – as if, improbably, people interested in ethics were especially amiable – but there were plenty of underlying intellectual tensions, and some of these will be apparent in the conflicting emphases at work in this book.

There would be something wrong, of course, if all these people did not have varying ideas of what 'ethics' entails. As a branch of philosophy, ethics has been defined as the investigation of those systems which are the moral tenets intended to guide the lives of humans. However, within this spectrum, surveys such as Bernard Williams's *Ethics and the Limits of Philosophy* and Alisdair MacIntyre's *A Short History of Ethics* demonstrate that the history of ethical philosophy is not homogeneous. It has embraced a variety of terminologies, perspectives and debates which are often at odds with one another. Although ethical philosophy debates whether actions are to be viewed as right or wrong, there is large disagreement about the prior stipulation about what is to count as good. For instance, deontologists assume that some things are good in their own right, whereas consequentialists assume that some things are good because of what happens later as a result of them. Even the terms in which these arguments are couched cannot be agreed upon. The increasing complexity of modern life, as Williams argues, has led to new moral problems, so that arguments increase in sophistication without resulting in solutions. Lacking a common set of reference points, disputants go on arguing without altering moral dispositions or producing moral actions. This gap between ethical theory and practice haunts many of the contributors to the present volume.

While acknowledging these deeply rooted variances, certain broadly humanist interests and assumptions tend to be shared by ethical philosophers working in analytical and empirical philosophy. For example, many philosophers presuppose that ethical actions and dispositions are the free choice of discrete 'subjects'. Williams concludes his conspectus by stating that 'in one sense, the primacy of the individual and of personal disposition is a necessary truth'.[2] Beyond this, the definition of what is 'good', 'moral' or 'ethical' has frequently been treated as fundamental to a common human essence, irrespective of social, racial or gender differences. The influential G. E. Moore, for example, argued in his *Principia Ethica* that ethics is 'undoubtedly concerned with the question of what good conduct is',[3] where goodness appears to be a quality which is directly experienced by a kind of moral intuition: it has only one true form, and you know it when you see it.

This sounds a dogmatic and out-of-date position, but it is not easy to do without a quasi-metaphysical recourse to an idea of truth or goodness that can be shared, and that can make a coming-together of different voices between one pair of covers more than a self-advertisement pact. In fact, most of the contributors to this volume are at pains, one way or another, to minimize 'self'. In several cases, this involves tracing and embellishing the work of Emmanuel Levinas, whose appeal to alterity, to 'otherness', makes his position at first sight the opposite of an ethics which leans on the conception of a personal, individual good.

For Levinas, ethics is the sphere of transactions between the 'self' and 'Other', and is not to be construed as a naming of conduct within a branch of philosophy. Therefore, it cannot look to the broadly humanist discourse of a G. E. Moore, rooted in a fixed idea of self and subjecthood, for its perspective. Levinas suggests, in fact, that the ethical relationship between 'self' and 'Other' is *constitutive* of the social fabric. It is only as a result of one's relationship with another that any sense of self can emerge, which in turn suggests that one always 'owes' one's 'identity' to another. 'The ethical language we resort to does not proceed from a special moral experience, independent of the description developed until then. It comes from the very meaning of approach, which contrasts with knowledge, of the face which contrasts with phenomena.'[4] Or, to put it another way, one's sense of self derives from turning to another, and the self is thus always divided, always finding its source elsewhere.

The essays in this book move in the area of discussion mapped out by these different parameters of ethical approach, while ranging across many subjects and disciplines, from queer theory to the philosophy of science. For although the revival of 'ethics', like other large theoretical developments of the last 30 or 40 years, has perhaps been most conspicuous in literary and cultural studies, it has extended throughout the humanities, and even beyond. But is it indeed a new development? It can be taken as a flight from newness. The ethical is a category that was neglected for a considerable period, throughout the 1960s, 1970s and 1980s, in part because it was felt to have been surpassed and discredited. The Left regarded ethics as a liberal humanist apology for the bourgeois subject, while poststructuralists tended to treat most ethical discourse as contaminated with metaphysics. If the new turn is simply reactionary – a retreat to a critical environment undisturbed by poststructuralism – then it is nothing to be excited about.

One of our contributors, Geoffrey Harpham, writing elsewhere, has suggested that the new emphasis on ethics has indeed occurred, in part, as a direct reaction to some poststructuralist/postmodernist tendencies. In particular he singles out the exposure in 1987 of the collaborationist war-time writings of Paul de Man, whereupon 'heated but still decorous debates about the nature of literary language, the role of metaphor in the discourses of rationality, the functioning of discursive regimes, the relevance of philosophy to literary study, the dominance of "Western metaphysics," abruptly gave way to charges of personal immorality, collaboration in the Holocaust, opportunism, and deception'.[5] What happened with de Man was an opportunity for those who wished to resist 'theory' to say that it was all a lot of posing, a kind of sophistry that glossed over questions of right and wrong conduct. The de Man affair was part of a much wider pattern of exposure and revulsion which has afflicted the reputations of other philosophers and theorists (Heidegger, for example), and of many modern literary authors, such as T. S. Eliot (the alleged anti-Semite), Conrad (the colonial racist) and Virginia Woolf (the snob). So we can see this case as just one more instance of a strong tendency in the second half of the twentieth century for ethics to be applied to literature and philosophy negatively, through the attribution of moral blindness and failure. But there has also been a sense that the specific kinds of theory practised by de Man and many lesser figures in poststructuralism and allied movements just did not allow for discussion of some of the aspects of texts which are really most important to the majority of their readers, including various positive kinds of ethical content or valency. At least, such allowances were not made openly.

In fact, the critical practices of de Man, Foucault, Lacan, Derrida *et al.*, have been enlisted over the last few decades in projects that are overwhelmingly motivated by ethical concerns – above all, in attempts to expose and rectify the oppression or marginalization, through culture, of individuals and groups on the basis of race, class, sex and/or gender, or sexuality.[6] These identity-centred projects are all about the dismantling of ethics, in a sense, because they cast doubt on the validity of an ethical system that presents itself as speaking for everybody (such a system will just be speaking for some people, in effect, at the expense of others), but to participate in these projects, putting forward arguments against oppression, delivering one's discontent through books and journals, telling one's readers that earlier critical claims have been erroneous, misplaced, biased or unfair, is to participate in a discourse that is all about right and wrong (however much the earlier applications of those categories may be revised) and hence thoroughly in the field of ethics.

So it seem that the time has come to move away from a crude distinction between old-fashioned critical practices which allowed one to talk about truth and goodness, for example, and new ones that have seen through such concepts and left them far behind. What is at stake here is not a conflict between ethical and non-ethical criticism but between different ethical approaches – at their most basic, the universalist, and the differentialist or other-oriented; and the conflict between these approaches is itself one of the most difficult and enduring ethical cruxes.

For while our day-to-day judgements about how to live our lives and interact with others are generally the result of our having internalized the norms of a particular community, our interactions are inevitably engagements with 'otherness', meetings or non-meetings with those who, to some extent, will not share our beliefs and cultural history. All moral claims are likely to strike my interlocutor differently from the way that they strike me: the difference may be minor, and we may muddle through, but it could easily be quite radical. And if we emphasize difference beyond a certain point, the attempt to communicate at all, in matters of value, will begin to seem quite useless.

Colleen Lamos's essay, in this volume, provides a good example of an attempted *rapprochement* between identity politics and an idea of the ethical that extends beyond specific groups. She describes 'two competing theoretical paradigms', namely 'lesbian and gay theory' and 'queer theory'. The first of these concentrates on lesbian and gay texts on the principle that they are equal in value and interest to the writings of straight authors. There is an ethical imperative here: treat gay and lesbian texts as significant, because that is what they deserve. 'Queer theory', on the other hand, exposes the cultural nature of the heterosexual/homosexual binary, and consequently 'queers' all kinds of texts. It has its origins in gay and lesbian theory but inevitably exceeds those origins. In doing so, it draws attention to the limits or conservatism of 'lesbian and gay theory'; that is, to the ways in which it 'calls upon so-called universal human values and upon historically respected notions of the individual and the social good'. 'Queer theory is thus unethical in the Nietzschean sense because it belies accepted ethical truths and pursues a negative critique.' However, Lamos goes on to argue that queer theory has positive, constructive, communitarian implications. One is concerned with others, it seems, because one recognizes that one is other, oneself; that is, one does not necessarily recognize oneself. This entails a changing, adaptable, 'pragmatic', non-prescriptive ethics.

A different version of ethical criticism which likewise manages to acknowledge and profit from postmodernism occurs in Robert Eaglestone's paper. Eaglestone uses deconstructive theory, but tries to escape from its potential passivity. He concentrates on moments of unreadability or 'flaws' in Henry James's *The Golden Bowl*, in a way that could easily be compared to the poststructuralist J. Hillis Miller. But whereas Miller's 'ethics of reading' is so exacting that the connection between texts and the ethics of real-life situations, or of interaction with 'others' outside books, seems indefinitely postponed, Eaglestone tends to locate his aporetic moments in the words and presentation of characters, the 'people' in books, moving from this to an idea of the literary character as other, ultimately unknowable, and therefore ethically problematical and significant, in a way that is exemplary of all interpersonal transactions. If one wished to position this mode of reading in relation to ethics beyond literature, within the discourse of philosophy, one would say that it is in conflict with the narrativists, who consider moral reflection as a search for social identity (this is the approach that underlies Martha Nussbaum's less open literary readings, which Eaglestone criticizes), and in accord with the postmodernists, who regard moral obligation as a feeling of being bound to another person through a recognition of his or her capacity to suffer, which cannot be reduced to understanding or a coherent narrative. Eaglestone reasserts the impossibility, beyond a certain point, of speaking for anybody else, but finds the dramatization of this predicament in literature ethically compelling rather than nullifying.

So there is plenty of evidence, in this collection, of ethical thought beyond postmodernism or involving postmodernism, but the problems addressed all have a long philosophical history. As Dan Burnstone demonstrates, there may be striking parallels between the 'latest' difficulties in ethical theory, and those of a quite different time. Burnstone discusses the significance of style in John Stuart Mill. 'Style' sounds like an old-fashioned critical term, suggesting undivided authors and univocal texts. But Burnstone's 'style' – and Mill's – is more than this. It is a matter of moral self-comportment as well as linguistic expression. It clothes communications, but at the same time draws attention to idiosyncrasy and incommensurability. Ethical positions may be *nothing more than* style; that is, a pose, an avoidance of collective, political questions: this shows the value of the 'commensurabilist' position which Burnstone takes from linguistic theory, whereby there is a belief that concepts (including moral ones) can, with the right words, be conveyed uncorrupted from one person to another. On the other hand, style may suggest elements of insuperable individualism, and of incomplete self-understanding, a lack of transparency to self and others. Mill combines these different aspects, making 'style *exemplary* rather than narrowly personal so that it manifests a public virtue – of political integrity – and not simply a personal peculiarity'. So it is as though style (and, by extension, literature) forms the medium through which different subjectivities, and ethical claims, are negotiated – while drawing attention to the difficulty of such negotiations, their resistance to a simple calculus of the utilitarian type. Many of Burnstone's concerns seem very close to those of Derrida and other recent theorists – style as *différance* – but he is also suggesting that these were live issues in the mid-nineteenth century.

However, despite the good use that many of our contributors make of much earlier texts and ideas, it is clear that there is something peculiar about the climate that makes this book possible, and it is worthwhile to try to historicize ourselves. One might wonder, for example, whether the current resurgence of explicit reference to ethics in the humanities is attributable (or at least related) to specific developments in the wider world, bigger moral crises than the de Man affair. Certainly, the Gulf War has been a strong, recent stimulus to this debate, with many cultural theorists finding themselves impelled to comment on an event that was real, political, massively destructive and intensely violent, but which was also a cultural performance, mediated for the vast majority of us by a great deal of calculated manipulation of texts and images. Before that, events such as the State of Emergency in South Africa in the 1980s, the Eastern European revolutions of 1989, the massacre in Tiananmen Square, and the war in Bosnia have raised the stakes of being a committed intellectual – people have been dying for the sake of ideas, while others with ideas have found themselves in situations of executive power. A greater understanding of the aesthetic and performative elements in politics and ideology has made real events seem very much the humanities' business. Tobin Siebers, for example, in his *Ethics of Criticism* of 1988, ends by holding up literary forms of value as the antithesis and possibly the antidote to the 'bird's-eye view' of nuclear missiles and cold-war rhetoric.[7] And since then, we have had the case of Salman Rushdie, where a book, a novel, was suddenly a matter of international relations, riots, terrorism, life and death.

Of course there are always frightening things going on in the world for intellectuals to worry about, but there is a particularly strong sense, now, that intellectuals' worries may have consequences. Thus, Christopher Norris writes in this volume about scientific debate, which might at other times have been thought of as invulnerable to quirky developments within the humanities, as being in danger of infection with bad postmodernism. Starting with Heideggerian and other ideas of the limited truth-content of science and technology (their alleged dependence on language games, their remoteness from primal Being, and so forth), and with the ethical consequences of these ideas, Norris draws parallels with structuralist and poststructuralist ideas of the limited, strictly relative (or even non-existent) truth-content of texts. He presents these approaches as misguided and dangerous: they undermine political autonomy, and fail to account for the limits that we tend to experience (and which seem to indicate some truth beyond linguistic structures), however much we may desire to imagine our own worlds for ourselves. Thus, Richard Rorty, among others, is seen as drifting into a solipsism which is reprehensible from Norris's public-spirited point of view.

Here we have not just an intellectual thinking about ethics in the abstract, but rather an intellectual assessing the moral usefulness of other thinkers' work, and, by extension, his own. This 'return to ethics' reflects the enduring desire, among scholars and teachers in the beleaguered humanities, to feel that what they are doing is important, honourable and even *good*. Even those who, in the wake of poststructuralism, would be least inclined to believe in such terms, testify to their meaningfulness through their own conspicuous desire to work, to argue, to have certain effects on their students. In fact, it is through teaching that most people in the humanities are likely, most often, to find themselves consciously in a moral predicament.

'Given the vast attention now paid to the performativity of gender, sexuality, race, ethnicity, nation, literature,' writes Biddy Martin in a recent *PMLA*, it is surprising that there is not more writing about pedagogy and the construction of knowledge in our classrooms and in our daily interactions with one another and with undergraduates and graduate students.'[8] In fact, this has to be one of the biggest growth areas in the theoretically advanced,

American-oriented, self-consciously professional field of literary/cultural debate that *PMLA* exemplifies. Thus, Margaret Toye's timely paper, in this collection, attempts to make the transition to pedagogical practice from literary and cultural theory, and to do so in an ethically responsible way. Again, this involves the dilemma of whether it is best to emphasize difference or to seek some sort of equivalence or commensurability between moral agents – such as the teacher and his or her pupils. Like Norris, Toye draws attention to some of the dangers in treating the other as absolutely different, unknowable, beyond any kind of common understanding or experience. As an alternative, she mentions ethical systems which place the emphasis on the self. For instance, Toye suggests that Foucault's self-orientation is ultimately to do with performance in a social context, and hence relates intelligibly to communal life, while a Levinasian concept of absolute alterity, which seems to respect the Other, risks making real others invisible and community an illusion. Derrida is put forward as thinking beyond the Levinasian Other to a sort of other-as-a-version-of-the-self, an 'alter ego' who is worth taking into account insofar as he/she, *like me*, is a self with his/her own other(s). However, Toye is not entirely happy with either of the two main categories of approach that she has traced, privileging the other and the self respectively, and alludes to a wide range of theoretical models for an 'elsewhere', conceived as mediating (with what is perhaps a necessary element of mysteriousness) between interiority and exteriority: from the Kantian sublime to *écriture féminine*. Ending as she does with a series of questions, it might seem that Toye is suggesting that the healthiest thing for a teacher to do is to raise doubts – but this obviously risks being rather flat and disempowering. Students tend to value teachers who put forward a strong position, who seem to believe in things, who have – to purloin Dan Burnstone's word – a certain style.

This desire for a pedagogy of performance and example, with all its dangers, underlies Michael Bell's discussion of that much-maligned proponent of an earlier form of ethical criticism, F. R. Leavis. Bell presents Leavis as an exemplary mentor who did not disseminate his opinions so much as show what it is like to have opinions, provoking his students into thinking for themselves – so that his pedagogical method carried its own health-warning. However, Leavis reached the limits of his own activity, according to Bell, when he hoped to extend his methods of reading, criticism and teaching into a wider vision of society. Hence his isolation within Cambridge, which Bell compares to Rousseau's exclusion from Geneva. For Bell, there is a lasting incommensurability between the type of individualistic, oppositional collaboration practised by Leavis and the larger political collaboration of a social contract. The individualism of Leavis and Rousseau is here linked to the European tradition of *Bildung*, of self-cultivation: something which has been attacked in Modernism, and which continues to be attacked in postmodernist views of the Subject. Bell concludes thus: 'As members of the academy we can pursue a residual ideal of *Bildung* only in so far as this has itself become a specialism, and we collaborate in an institutional sense which, from the individual's point of view, is as close to Kundera as to Leavis.' The Kundera reference relates to his discussion, in *The Art of the Novel*, of collaboration with Nazism in the 1940s, a version of 'collaboration' which Kundera and Bell both see as more or less applicable to everybody's status in a modern society. In particular, Bell finds this sense of 'collaboration' operative within the humanities in contemporary Britain, where 'individuals pursuing activities in which they believe have implicitly to endorse conditions which run counter to them'. So, this paper suggests that it is becoming more and more difficult to be a *Leavisian* collaborator, but that we ought to try; if we collaborate more in a Leavisian sense, perhaps, we will collaborate slightly less in a darker one.

Bell and Toye, in their different ways, draw attention to an ethical crisis in the public status and management of the humanities, not just in the humanities' response to problems in the world outside the university. Indeed, there is plenty of other evidence of academics worrying about whether they are personally doing the right thing, in their professional lives. The self-scrutinizing moral tone that now prevails in the most powerful body in literary and cultural criticism, the Modern Language Association, has already been mentioned; but the MLA has recently found itself confronted by a rival movement, the Association of Literary Scholars and Critics, whose claim, as an alternative collectivity or collaboration of academics, is essentially an ethical one. The ALSC implies that the MLA has been doing wrong to authors and students alike by privileging certain specific kinds of reading (above all, differentialist and identity-based critiques) above all others. And there is a wider concern about the possible illegitimacy or fraudulence of what we write, publish and teach – as in the recent spectacular case of Alan Sokal, the physicist who successfully submitted for publication in a journal of cultural studies an article that he knew to be nothing but jargonized drivel, just to make the point that frauds and buffoons can flourish in the current academic world, if they use the right terminology.[9] (No big surprise to many of us in the trade.) Similarly, one could cite the regular and highly popular Bad Writing Contests now held by the journal *Philosophy and Literature* ('searching for the world's ugliest academic prose') as further evidence of a kind of fervour in sections of the academy for rooting out nonsense and making ourselves presentable.

When it comes to talking about ethics, the danger of putting ourselves forward as sanctimonious charlatans – 'the chattering classes' as Margaret Thatcher used to say – seems particularly acute. For who are we to talk of such things? This is something like the feeling that underlies Geoffrey Harpham's paper in this collection. More particularly, Harpham is exercised by the way in which contemporary intellectuals put themselves across, not just as politically and ethically powerful, but as heroic in their self-imposed marginality and 'dissent' from the benighted institutions that surround and silently support them. Intellectuals, in Western democracies at least, may be provocative towards this or that state institution, Harpham argues, but are only able to be so within an orderly social structure that ultimately depends on forces such as the police and the army. Thus, Harpham attacks what he sees as the falseness of intellectual positions like that of Edward Said, who seems to claim the liberated and heroic status of an 'exile' while enjoying tremendous respectability and acclaim; or of Homi Bhabha, who seems to think that by privileging the marginal, theoreticians can effectively disrupt and defuse the oppressions of centralized power. In general, Harpham suggests that high theory has led influential thinkers away from a clear perception of their real status in society, and their real helplessness (or responsibility) when it comes to ethical issues. Postmodern reactions to the Gulf War are a focus here, and Harpham sides with Christopher Norris's attacks on Baudrillard, for example. But Harpham challenges Norris, too, suggesting that criticizing the critics is not enough: after a while, you have to say what ought to be done in the real, political moment. The essay ends with praise of the Czech playwright/president Václav Havel, who, according to Harpham, unites genuine flexibility and originality of thought with the courage to take a clear stand on pressing issues – in a way that inevitably exposes him to risks of error and opposition.

So the question of personal status is an important one when it comes to talking about ethics, and we have made a point, in this collection, of assembling a range of contributors whose current professional standing varies greatly: from leading figures in this 'revival' of ethics to scholars right at the start of their teaching careers, or still at work on their doctoral dissertations; from critics who may have felt required to assess themselves, ethically, in response to the public prominence (as far as academia allows) that has gradually accrued to them, to beginners for whom alternative career-paths are still not out of the question, and who may well want to feel that what they are letting themselves in for is something decent.

In other words, this is a collection in which personal concerns (am I doing the right thing?) and public, professional ones interact with one another constantly, just as, on the theoretical level, issues of the self and the other, the different and the collective, are continually in negotiation. There are efforts, here, to take account of the speaker's own historical, economic and institutional circumstances, and to compare these with the conditions endured by the others of whom we speak. But there are efforts, too, to get beyond what Steven Connor refers to as the 'proprietary ethics' in which 'voice' – one's own or someone else's – can be denied, suppressed or taken away. Connor points out that the widespread theoretical concern with a person's self-presentation through voice, and with possible interferences with this self-presentation, sits oddly with a postmodern understanding of the instability of the subject. He is interested, rather, in an ethics of voice that does not tie it down, does not attach it to a specific, fixed speaker. Voice, for Connor, is the medium, beyond the subject, in between and around subjects, where ethics happens. Voice 'signifies at every moment the inescapability of a *Mitsein*, or being-for-others; signifies itself as the occasion of such a *Mitsein*'. That is, to give voice is to commit oneself to a kind of ethics, and vice-versa. 'To count as an ethical partner, one must be a potential interlocutor.'

For Tim Woods, the possibilities of ethical interlocution extend not just into the collectivity of living intellectuals, but into the past and the future. In contrast to Bell, for example, who sees the scholar or thinker's role in modern society as inevitably compromised, if not corrupted, Woods describes a postmodern condition in which the ghosts of other times – in Derrida's 'hauntological' sense – enrich the present; where, just as the instability of subjecthood (as

Connor argues) makes for a 'being-for-others' that is more real and trustworthy than any fixed identity, so the instability of our apprehension of the 'now' frees us, to some extent, from the fear that the present is set in its ways, for good or ill. Woods argues that ethics is firmly tied to a Levinasian concept of responsibility for the other; and that the viability of an ethics depends critically upon our notions of history: 'a politics of temporality appears to be intricately connected to the ethical and judicial structures of society'.

However, these gestures towards an ethics beyond individual identity, or beyond the current state of the world, have some frightening aspects. They threaten to disrupt the sense of integrity that most of us experience and tend to rely upon. Thus Simon Critchley, discussing the ethics of Levinas, notes the requirement for a 'conception of the subject' which contains a 'disposition towards alterity' – a disposition that is manifested when consciousness is exceeded and challenged, or traumatized, by some sort of 'impossible', unknowable transaction with otherness; i.e. this liberating, open, non-proprietary, postmodern 'ethics' arises through a kind of violence overtaking consciousness. Critchley concludes that 'without a relation to trauma, or at least without a relation to that which claims, calls, summons, interrupts or troubles the subject . . . , a summons that is experienced as a relation to a Good in a way that exceeds the pleasure principle and any promise of happiness (any *eudaemonism*) there would be no ethics'. For ethics and non-totalizing politics to function, there has to be a perpetual move to re-experience the inexperienceableness of alterity, traumatically. It seems that Critchley is saying, with Levinas, that ethics arises in the pain of being sundered from an earlier, larger subjecthood, comprising an impossible-to-realize union of self with alterity. There is the implication that, although you cannot know the other, you can know that you do not know the other, and that this produces a disorienting, enriching fall into ethics.

Thus, in his different way, Critchley can be seen as arguing, with Harpham, for the necessity of a kind of self-exposure, a putting-oneself-at-risk, in ethics. So that to be ethical has something tragic about it, or at least, to use Critchley's word, something melancholy. A similar conclusion is hinted at by the most self-referential and perhaps self-jeopardizing paper in this collection, Larry Lockridge's discussion of biography and autobiography. Lockridge puts himself at stake in this paper by discussing his own career as critic, and, particularly, his recent role as biographer of his father. This self-referentiality interacts significantly with Lockridge's discussion of the ethics of narrating lives – one's own or others'. He is clearly uncomfortable with some recent approaches to literary criticism and biography, and to the relation between these two kinds of writing, that seem to sense little in the way of an ethical bond or obligation between the writer and the individual whose life or texts provide the matter for discussion. On the other hand, Lockridge is aware of the impossibility of telling the whole truth in any critical/biographical or autobiographical account. Furthermore, he is sympathetic to a view of autobiography which holds it to be a development of the life it purports to narrate, and hence, in a way, self-justifying, or incapable of being wrong. So this is a paper which is thoughtful and discursive, favouring a 'weak' line (as Lockridge himself suggests) rather than imposing a strong model of what biography or criticism or autobiography should be. Its drift is to encourage us to think about the ethical difference it makes if we are reading the narrative of a life written by the liver of that life, or by somebody else, and hence to think of the characters found in 'non-fiction' texts, and of ourselves, the readers, as being, in part, real people – which is to say, creatures of the realm of ethics, entities which we treat as having an extra-textual presence and hence capable of being affected for better or worse by our behaviour.

Lockridge is encouraging us to think of writing in relation to its living, or once-living, author – the thing that much recent theory has encouraged us not to do – and hence to re-introduce ourselves to an ethical valency of literature that links it to the joys and worries of our real lives. Or perhaps, still more, to the tragedies of our real lives. For, just as in Critchley's talk of 'melancholy', or Bell's presentation of a kind of pathos in Leavis's awkward and anti-social exemplariness, Lockridge leaves us with a sense of the author as vulnerable and exposed, paying a high price, potentially, for being ethically significant.

Anne Cubilié, in the essay that concludes this collection, raises the stakes of authorial risk-taking and of the critic's claim to ethical reading by discussing texts in which the real and often appalling suffering formerly endured or witnessed by the author is the main concern – the testimonial writings of survivors of the war in Bosnia. Cubilié takes us again into ethically motivated forms of postmodern identity politics, arguing that testimonial writings by women, such as the texts of the Bosnian authors Slavenka Drakulić and Elma Softić, resist a hegemonic discourse on the part of international Human Rights bodies by stressing their gendered origins, i.e. their difference from a universal humanist subjecthood, and by presenting a fragmented, multiple, postmodern subjectivity. The paper looks forward, consequently, to a new kind of Human Rights discourse which values difference – indeed, links *rights* to difference – rather than universality or sameness.

There is a strong contrast, here, with Leona Toker's point of view in the preceding paper. Toker is also concerned with prose descriptions of life in real situations of extreme oppression – specifically in the Gulag, as described in the short stories of Varlam Shalamov. Toker maintains that the testamentary presentation of facts combines with the aesthetic function in these texts to produce a whole that has a special ethical value. She argues that the reader of these works is allowed to achieve a limited insight into the life of the Gulag: an insight that depends on the foregrounding of *attitudes* as distinct from either facts or ideas. It is an argument that presents literature as an arena in which readers can address their own moral sympathies and limits through the staged ethical concerns of the characters and, implicitly, the author. Toker is implying that literary texts have a thickness – a density of human experience beyond finite ideas – that facilitates ethical thought in a way that texts that do not aspire to literariness cannot; and hence, that the aesthetic dimension of texts like Shalamov's does not represent any belittlement of the horrific realities to which they allude, but rather the opposite. Toker's readings suggest the possibility of considerable identification, on the part of the reader, with individuals in circumstances very different from his or her own – quite a different situation, in the end, from that put forward by Cubilié, for whom testamentary writers seem to achieve a kind of power through exposing their own difference, an otherness that is partly born of the trauma of real endured and witnessed violence, and is partly the kind of ontological or epistemological trauma that Critchley describes.

The differences between Cubilié's paper and Toker's are to some extent typical of this whole collection, and of the ongoing rift between an ethics that is designed to further the good through consenus or commensurability (which requires that we are not all, ultimately, entirely 'other'), and an ethics that hesitates to say what someone else's good might be, for fear of misconstruing and oppressing them. By translating these problems into the field of recent historical atrocities, Cubilié and Toker make the dangers of each approach all the more apparent. Toker might be thought to run the risk of domesticating the Gulag – of encouraging readers to think that they know what was going on in the minds of its victims, and hence collaborating in their own small way in the stifling of those victims' other, unknowable voices. Cubilié, on the other hand, could seem to be suggesting that a kind of exemplary strangeness, a distressed authority that has parallels with Lockridge's self-revelations, with Critchley's melancholy, with Bell's version of Leavis as rebarbative mentor, and even with Burnstone's account of style, can be achieved through the real experience of terrible violence, and hence that this violence is empowering – almost a good thing. It is the risk that any attempt at a non-prescriptive (or, in the broadest sense, queer, or, one might also say, anarchist) ethics has to run: if I disavow your values, because I am *other*, how can I claim that you should care for me?

The ethical dangers in the discourse of *difference* are pursued further in David Parker's paper, which also deals with literary material linked to the most extreme human rights violations. Through a discussion of the scandal and moral confusion surrounding Helen Demidenko's novel, *The Hand that Signed the Paper* (1994), this essay argues that identity politics, or certain critical approaches that revolve around the idea of 'recognition', have entailed an emphasis on a particular kind of ethical problem, and have encouraged blindness to other kinds. The blatantly anti-Semitic and callous elements of Demidenko's novel, according to Parker, have been overlooked by some critics because it seems admirably to recognize the 'difference' of Australia's Ukrainian immigrants. The Nazi treatment of the Jews was also based, Parker implies, on an idea of 'difference' – one group seeing the other as so different as to be beyond the concerns of morality. Parker effectively exposes the dark side of a mode of 'ethical' thinking that is all about not presuming to speak for others – because one cannot necessarily know them – but not really about having respect for others (which must involve some kind of identification). There is an epistemological dimension to Parker's argument, here, which echoes Christopher Norris's paper: both are concerned with the ethically dangerous consequences of limiting concepts of knowledge, of other social groups in Parker's case, and of the workings of the natural world in Norris's. Parker is also concerned, given the odd facts of the Demidenko case, with the authenticity of an authorial standpoint – in a way that links his argument with

Lockridge's account of the ethics of autobiography, and with the wider debates about intellectual charlatanism, presumption and fraudulence which have already been mentioned in this introduction. The most postmodern of our contributors are of course trying not to make claims that pre-empt and colonize another person's truth, but we have Norris's insistence that there are times when truth is single, verifiable, not a matter of point of view, and we have Harpham's observation that too much difference puts you uselessly at the margins.

But Harpham's prescription for the modern intellectual – that she or he should not linger as a privileged pseudo-exile on the margins, but move towards the centres of power and acquire dirty hands – has a disturbing side to it, perhaps. It raises the spectre of the darker form of collaboration talked about by Bell: the immoral collaboration that Kundera sees as inescapable in modern Western life. What, in fact, must we do, to get it right? And will we know that it was right when we have done it? And why do we care anyway? There is some kind of mystery here. For all the Levinasian flexibility that most of the contributors to this volume demonstrate – their willingness to find new ethics in new places, among different constituting social groups – there is a level on which all are working within a shared system of values. We are all carrying on as though something really matters. Toye, for example, comes across as being admirably in doubt about most things, but never about the desirability of being a 'good' teacher, finding a pedagogy that furthers our students' interests, however 'other' they may be.

This earnest doubtfulness leads us to the reading and rereading of Lori West, who begins her essay by linking Lyotard's 'differend' with Derrida's concept of 'iterability'. Both theorists are seen to be talking about a relation to the Other which is ongoing, interminable – where the Other is ultimately unknowable, but where I affirm a belief in or desire for that Other through again and again listening to what they seem to be saying, asking 'am I now hearing this Other', or, as West asks, after Lyotard, '*Arrive-t-il?*' West uses Derrida's concept of 'eating well' usefully here: by 'eating well' Derrida means not just consuming, but allowing for others' consumption, being hospitable, enacting a kind of ritual, attesting to a kind of faith in the Other's unknowable presence, that must go on to infinity. Thus, West advances an idea of repetition as ethically wholesome ritual, or of repetition or a kind of habitual thinking as the very stuff of ethics in itself, providing a matrix for all our intellectual/academic work. She turns then to religious liturgy, which involves a practice of endlessly repeated readings, affirming a faith in the existence of the unknowable (deity) while simultaneously drawing attention, *ad infinitum*, to the impossibility of grasping that entity in any finite phrase. West does not have to apologize for bringing religion into the debate, she says, because the structure of literary studies already has an analogous principle of faith at its core: we testify, in reading, to a desire to believe in something beyond ourselves that can be approached through words. Except that we don't really ever achieve this approach, and so we go on reading and rereading as an act of faith that is intrinsically ethical, giving 'the benefit of doubt' to the Other. From this, West concludes that a new kind of academic practice might be in order, involving more rereading and less haste to make a statement (i.e. publish): a strong poststructuralist argument, in effect, for an old-fashioned-seeming, diligent and rather priest-like approach to scholarship.

This ethical diligence, this willingness to attend to the difference of others, is one thing that we are left with by West's essay and by many others in the collection. On the other hand, we have Harpham's imperative to make statements on matters of pressing concern. There might seem to be a contradiction here that is ultimately hopeless: as if we have to settle for one or the other. But perhaps we can have both.

The essays in this collection can easily be read in such a way as to place them in conflict with one another. Some seek to identify shareable truths as the basis for ethical action; others imply that the assumption that one could share is oppressive. Some imply the need to commit oneself promptly and unequivocally on moral questions; others imply an ethical imperative to hold back, reconsider, think yourself uncertain, read again. But all of these positions seem to operate within a meta-ethics whereby thinking and arguing one's way through to a right mode of thinking, acting, interacting with and influencing others is *a priori* a thing worth doing. None of the work within this collection would make any sense, in other words, to someone who had not already bought into an approach to the world that is basically affirmative, seeing and attributing value. It is as though ethics has to be grounded in a form of epistemological naivety and a basic liking for life. Once this commensurable state has been recognized we can proceed to act on the recommendations of both critical camps: for diligent reading will be justified, finally, by the active promotion of respect for other people's differing wishes or rights; and forthright moral and political campaigning will be less likely to go wrong and do harm if it happens within a culture that habitually pauses, reflects, and re-reads the mobile texts through which it constitutes its self or selves.

Notes

1. Versions of another 15 papers from the same conference appear in *The Ethics in Literature*, ed. Andrew Hadfield, Dominic Rainsford and Tim Woods (London: Macmillan; New York: St Martin's Press, 1998).
2. Bernard Williams, *Ethics and the Limits of Philosophy* (London: Fontana, 1985) 201.
3. G. E. Moore, *Principia Ethica* (Cambridge University Press, 1903) 2.
4. Emmanuel Levinas, 'Language and Proximity', in *Collected Philosophical Papers*, trans. Alphonso Lingis (Dordrecht: Martinus Nijhoff, 1987) 124.
5. Geoffrey Galt Harpham, 'Ethics', in *Critical Terms for Literary Study*, ed. Frank Lentricchia and Thomas McLaughlin, 2nd edn (Chicago University Press, 1995) 387–405 (389).
6. The work of Jacques Derrida himself has increasingly shown an explicit engagement with current ethical issues, such as nuclear disarmament, Algerian immigration, European collective politics, apartheid, the pedagogy of philosophy, and anti-Semitism.
7. Tobin Siebers, *The Ethics of Criticism* (Ithaca: Cornell University Press, 1988) 239.
8. Biddy Martin, 'Introduction: Teaching Literature, Changing Cultures', Special Topic: 'The Teaching of Literature', *PMLA* 112 (1997) 7–25 (23).
9. See Dennis Dutton and Patrick Henry, 'Truth Matters', and Alan D. Sokal, 'Transgressing the Boundaries: An Afterword', *Philosophy and Literature* 20 (1996) 299–304 and 338–46.

Part I
The Politics of Ethics

1

What Price Collaboration? The Case of F. R. Leavis

Michael Bell

I THE IDEA OF COLLABORATION

In his Preface to *The Common Pursuit* (1952), F. R. Leavis described the practice of literary criticism as a constructive collaboration: '"The common pursuit of true judgement": that is how the critic should see his business, and what it should be for him. His perceptions and judgements are his, or they are nothing; but, whether or not he has consciously addressed himself to co-operative labour, they are inevitably collaborative.'[1] Such an ideal of critical collaboration is problematic, as the Leavises' own careers demonstrated. But their difficulties have too often been seen in terms of personality, while the true interest of the case is the other way round: the Leavises' strong-minded conception of their own integrity throws light on the tensions of collaboration as such.

An obvious question concerns the limits of the collaborative circle. What common premises are required, and to what extent do the shared premises already foreclose significant disagreement? And where premises are not shared, are there individuals who should be actively excluded from collaboration? The last question has been more darkly posed by Milan Kundera: 'in the course of the war against Nazism, the word "collaboration" took on a new meaning: putting oneself voluntarily at the service of a vile power. What a fundamental notion! However did humanity do without it until 1944? Now that the word has been found, we realize more and more that man's activity is by nature a collaboration.'[2] Kundera extrapolates a universal recognition from a particular historical politics and his remarks have a special pertinence to present-day Britain. In the Nazi occupation of Europe, or the cold-war period of

Russian domination, the daily fact of collaboration was self-evident although, as Kundera himself would be the first to agree, it did not have the simple moral sign that might be inferred from this passage. Merely to live under an oppressive regime, even without actively supporting it, is a degree of collaboration; and if you wish to resist it, or to mitigate its effects, you often *have* to work within it. By one of those dramatic ironies of which history is so fond, just as the overt conditions of collaboration have been dismantled in Eastern Europe, Britain has become a more obviously divided society in which individuals have been increasingly, if not always consciously, placed in precisely this position. As public institutions of humanistic education adopt commercial and mutually competitive assumptions, individuals pursuing activities in which they believe have implicitly to endorse conditions which run counter to them. The comparison is grotesquely melodramatic, of course, in that no Gulag awaits the dissenters here, but the condition is important to recognize precisely because it lacks such dramatic visibility. We are all collaborators.

The question is whether Leavis's and Kundera's accounts of collaboration apply to different contexts, and are therefore different *meanings*, or whether they are inescapable *aspects* of the same meaning? Must every positive collaboration have this dark shadow? Is this the necessary price of collaboration? Leavis's embattled relations with the literary and academic 'establishments' of his day have rightly been discussed in biographical and institutional terms, but the personal and local dimensions have obscured the level of principle which his case supremely highlights. Whether or not his unwillingness to compromise was ultimately preferable, morally or politically, to other postures, it reveals with unusual starkness the principled tensions which are obscured by more average accommodations. What was at stake for Leavis was not just the institutional and political context, but existential judgements of individuals. As this question is considered more closely in the next sections of this essay, it becomes apparent that there is also an historical dimension to it. Leavis is a boundary stone dividing us from an earlier era. Or at least he should be; in practice he remains as a stone, just beneath the surface, to 'trouble the living stream' in ways that need to be examined first.

II COLLABORATION AND THE INDIVIDUAL

The last two decades have seen a periodic rediscovery of the ethical dimension of criticism.[3] Those who write on this theme face a tactical difficulty in that it is as impossible to ignore Leavis as it is dangerous to mention him. No one wants to be in the invidious position of simply espousing the Leavisian conception, of having nothing more up-to-date and sophisticated to say than that. Yet he so obviously occupies the ground. And so a minor convention has grown up of using a reductive account of Leavis as a way of warming up the topic, and clearing the supposedly cruder conceptions out of the way. This topos of contemporary criticism brings out both the principled problems of collaboration and their epochal transformations. Bernard Williams provides a conveniently condensed example in a *Times Higher Education Supplement* article of 1987.

At the height of Thatcherism, Williams was arguing a case for governmental support of the humanities as a vital resource in a civil society. To make the case stick, he had first to dissociate himself from the naive view, attributed by him to Leavis, that the frequenting of great literature has, *per se*, a morally beneficial effect on the individual.

> [A]ccording to Leavis . . . the study of literature was necessary because it was associated with certain central and stern virtues, of sensibility, honesty and truthfulness.
>
> If that claim is applied directly to individual people, it seems that good readers and sensitive critics will be noticeably better people than a lot of other people, and that is extremely hard to believe. But more important than that is the point that even if the claim were true, it would still say nothing about the relation of such people to the rest of society. It is also very important that such a view cannot give any account of the significance of *research* in the humanities.[4]

Williams then develops his own case to argue that a knowledge of the cultural past is vital to a proper understanding and direction of the present:

> The classic error of thoughtless conservatism is to forget that what is old is merely what used to be new. Another, and at the present time more destructive, error is to forget that anything has

> any history at all, and to suppose that the social world simply consists of a given set of objects to be manipulated by go-getting common sense. No such views are likely to survive unchanged by the enquiries of a fruitful and imaginative history, or of other humane studies.

The striking aspect of this claim is that, although it does not have to be confined to the specifically Leavisian conceptions and values, it was precisely Leavis's great theme and, in offering a more sophisticated version of it, Williams has succeeded in the strict etymological sense of the word: the sustaining cordial he offers us is Leavis and water. Meanwhile the problems of this critical historical activity at the institutional level, which the case of Leavis actually serves to highlight, are obscured; they are implicitly left behind as merely the peculiarities of the Leavisian posture dismissed in the opening movement of the essay. If the smooth confidence of Williams is in striking contrast to Leavis's often tortuous prose, this is perhaps because something is missing. Williams's Leavis is, in the proper sense, a scapegoat ritually incorporating, and thereby removing, the problems of the literary academy in so far as this seeks to perform the function of criticism.

A more startling example of the burial and reinvention topos occurs in Wayne Booth's *The Company We Keep: An Ethics of Fiction* (1988). In an early chapter, Booth raises, in order to exorcise, the necessary ghost of Leavis by quoting, as representative, a passage in which Leavis appears to be rather crudely ranking several poems.[5] In fact, this is from an early piece in which Leavis was discussing an exercise developed by I. A. Richards and others, in the early years of the Cambridge English School, of giving students for comparison several anonymous poems including acknowledged masterpieces and recent magazine verse. No doubt there are problems in Leavis's critical procedure, and perhaps a discussion of them could be initiated by considering the nature of this exercise, but no such discussion follows: the tendentiously chosen passage is merely the millstone by which Leavis is removed from the surface of the discussion. Having dismissed Leavis, Booth goes on to develop his own model of critical activity. For this purpose, and perhaps to emphasize the originality of his thought, he coins the term 'coduction':

> [W]e need a term that suggests . . . the reliance . . . on the past experiences of many judges who do not have even a roughly

> codified set of precedents to guide them. The term must imply a communal enterprise rather than a private, 'personal' calculation logically coercive on all who hear it.
>
> Since I find no term that meets these demands, I must for once reluctantly resort to neologism: *coduction*, from *co* ('together') and *ducere* ('to lead, draw out, bring, bring out'). Coduction will be what we do whenever we say to the world (or prepare ourselves to say): 'Of the works of this general kind that I have experienced, *comparing my experience with that of other more or less qualified observers*, this one seems to me among the better (or weaker) ones, or the best (or worst). Here are my reasons.' Every such statement implicitly calls for continuing conversation: 'How does my coduction compare with yours?'[6]

As with Bernard Williams, the most casual knowledge of Leavis reveals the derivativeness of Booth's 'coduction'. But in this case his laborious neologism seems a direct echo of Leavis's 'collaboration', and he even goes on to cite Michael Polanyi in support. Assuming that this extraordinary recycling of Leavis is unconscious, it raises the question of to what extent 'coduction' is an unconscious memory or an unconscious suppression of memory; and particularly because a centre-piece of Booth's subsequent argument is a recognition of his earlier failure to read Lawrence properly, and he credits a rereading of Leavis as partly instrumental in his born-again conversion.[7] In fact, Booth might usefully have reread Lawrence and Leavis on 'impersonality' since his book is essentially a conversion narrative in which the confessional dimension comes over, to an outsider, not as a courageous necessity of the case but as a coy self-importance based on his assumptions about his own status. It is not so much the fact that he has changed his mind, as that *he* has changed his mind, which is assumed to be telling. But that can only be so within a specific collaborative circle; and its effect is to make one wonder indeed about the company he has kept; about the nature of some academic collaboration. Meanwhile, it is precisely the question of personality, the relation to the self, which is at the problematic heart of collaboration; and which is passed over in Booth's strange formulation of a 'private, "personal" calculation logically coercive on all who hear it'. I confess that I do not understand what could be meant by this, or what degree of irony may be intended, but its terms bear on the essential problem in a way that Bernard Williams's essay illuminates.

Williams implicitly acknowledges that a social defence of the humanities must rest on criticism as well as scholarship since knowledge of the past is to be brought to bear on the decisions of the present. And the conception of a neutral knowledge, although disinterestedness is an important regulative principle within the academy, cannot be the grounding principle of a humanistic discipline. Not only the subject-matter, but the activity itself, is value-laden and depends on the quality of the person doing it. It is not clear, therefore, that Williams's defence of research in the humanities can afford so completely to dismiss the question of the moral quality of the individual who performs it. In raising the notoriously difficult question of the moral effect of art *on* the individual, he obscures the necessary involvement *of* the individual. The first point to make here is that Leavis did not claim to be a better person himself so much as to affirm the significance of great writers such as Blake, George Eliot and Tolstoy; who were themselves, of course, not necessarily better people in their everyday lives. Leavis saw the critic's skill as the ability to respond and acknowledge. Yet, of course, response is inextricable from responsibility, and to that extent it is necessary briefly to revisit the hoary question of the moral effect of art.

In effect, Williams offers a less dramatic version of George Steiner's repeated claim that, after Auschwitz, there can be no belief in the moral efficacy of even the greatest art; and Steiner, too, has repeatedly offered Leavis as his straw man despite this being in such startling contradiction of Leavis's life-work. Steiner and Williams pose this important question at an inappropriate level of generality. In their respectively political and philosophical emphases, they elide or marginalize the category of the individual. Indeed Williams is explicit in dismissing Leavis not totally, but because his claims only apply 'to the cultivation of the individual'. And to that extent, of course, he is right. For Leavis, the individual was the vital term. He always insisted that the recognitions at stake in art, as in any other evaluative realm, can only be realized by individuals and the quality of the individual response is therefore a necessary premise. Neither connoisseurship nor scholarship are guarantees of such a response, and may well be the signs of its absence. Just as the adage that travel broadens the mind depends on your having a mind in the first place, otherwise travel can be a great reinforcer of bigotry, so Leavis was the last person to trust the supposed efficacy of great literature, per se, on some generalized reader. He deeply distrusted most readers, including the academic professionals of his day, many of whom might be like Henry James's highly cultivated villains and self-deceivers, and his criticism was always an attempt to produce, and to draw the reader into, an exemplary personal response. That is what made it at once so compelling to some readers and unacceptable to others. Leavis's focus on the individual does not just make a claim that Williams can afford to dismiss, it identifies the inescapably problematic nature of the claim that Williams, and perhaps many of us, would wish to make.

The oxymoronic idea of an exemplary personal response, rather than Booth's 'logically coercive', is the principled tension underlying the Leavisian notion of collaboration. In a notorious instance, he could not even collaborate with his own earlier self who had once thought differently of Dickens.[8] The tension can be seen in the writing itself. Leavis's circuitous, self-qualifying prose constantly tests the reader, each parenthetic clause beating the boundaries of the inner sanctum, fending off any merely reductive, uncomprehending agreement. Leon Edel records Henry James telling his brother William's children that the great rule of life was to be kind, and one way of understanding the involutions of James's prose, particularly in his criticism, is as a way of serving at once the interests of truth and of kindness.[9] The point gets made as part of a larger, slowly unfolding, recognition, so that its force sinks in as an after-effect, and as part of the whole view. Leavis's prose bears some analogy with James's, but its moral sign is opposite. With Leavis, the motive is not kindness, nor unkindness, so much as the fear of kindness, in both its senses. His prose communicates a suspicion of the easy relation; while the reader, if sympathetic, is drawn into the inner sanctum by the same kind of subliminally enactive participation that Leavis saw in the reading of poetry. Leavis's own language enacts; it enacts the dangerous necessity of that form of collaboration we call being understood.

Comparison with James suggests that the collaborative conflict in Leavis's prose has a more general pertinence for the early twentieth century when there was a suspicion of ideas as such and when the category of the individual was being put, as we now know, under terminal strain. Earlier European culture provides landmark instances of the refusal to collaborate. Molière's Alceste experienced something of the Leavisian predicament, and the play allows us to see it as a real one even if the overall comic structure, and the underlying social conception, finally encourage us to see him in the light of an absurd extremity.[10] In the following century, however, France was to see in Rousseau a more powerful disturbance for whom neither social containment nor exclusion were adequate strategies. And for Rousseau himself the tensions of the collaborative relation eventually shaded into paranoia. An analogy between Rousseau and Leavis is not fortuitous since Rousseau represents the first full impact of the idea of the individual in the modern sense which underlies Leavis's rearguard insistence on it. The individual is necessarily a martyr, in the strict sense of being a witness, and the slide from that to the market-place sense of the term, as an object of persecution, and then to being a 'martyr' as a self-conscious posture, is fatally easy.[11] Rousseau and Leavis both recognized that the price, and therefore perhaps the badge, of integrity may be isolation, and that hostility may be the index of a necessary non-collaboration.

The intrinsic instability of Rousseau's model is reflected in the ambiguous relation of *Émile* to *The Social Contract*. The two works were conceived as complementary: one suggesting the proper political order and the other seeking to produce the individual citizen through a process of education. But the fact of their *being* two separate works is as telling as their intended complementarity. Is education the internal correlative *of* the proper political order or is it rather a substitute *for* it? And this is not just a matter of a gap between the two works, since the tension is evident within *Émile* itself. The preceptor's manipulation of Émile's experience is not directed only towards his positive formation, its primary function is to provide a *cordon sanitaire* protecting the pupil, in his formative years, from the outside world. The attempt to change the world is premised on an initial separation from it. Correspondingly, within the social world, Rousseau's home city of Geneva was his enabling myth: it was a real place exemplifying an ideal possibility, although, in the event, Rousseau found himself excluded even from Geneva, which became the home of his arch-enemy, Voltaire. So too, Leavis's ideal Cambridge of educational collaboration was contradicted by the real Cambridge of those whom he saw as opposing his ideals. Even at the level of a small city state, or of a university, the gap between individual education and social transformation was not to be closed for either of them although a belief in this possibility remained the motivating force of their lives and work. For both, there was an absolute requirement that personal response have a universal and exemplary force but, in so far as they sought to enforce this requirement at different historical moments, Leavis can be seen to close the age which Rousseau inaugurated. To appreciate this it is helpful to consider the fate of an important post-Rousseauvian conception of personal education for wholeness: the idea of *Bildung*.

III COLLABORATION AND *BILDUNG*

The gap between *The Social Contract* and *Émile* suggests that the educational process is in some measure a separate domain, and that in turn suggests two different forms of intellectual collaboration: the political and the pedagogic. The spatial image of collaborative circles contrasts with a chronological model of mentor and pupil at different stages of personal development. Rousseau's influence on conceptions of education was given a different inflection through Goethe and the sub-genre of the *Bildungsroman*. The great *Bildungsromane* are not simply realistic, although they do not fully depart from realism either, and this formal balance reflects, among other things, their recognition that in organized education true psychological developments are enabled by artificial means. The form is quite consciously emblematic in contrast to the literalism of Rousseau, and of the eighteenth-century novel of sentiment generally. This relates to the further fact that, although in the Wilhelm Meister novels as compared with *Émile*, Goethe shifts the viewpoint from the mentor to the pupil, the function of the mentor, as in later *Bildungsromane*, remains crucial. The departure from verisimilitude is largely to focus the ghostly interventions and backstage perceptions of the mentor figures. I say 'backstage' because their emblematic function is frequently not to impart understanding, so much as to withhold it, or even to demonstrate its present incommunicability. The mentor is often a deliberately grudging collaborator.

In this regard, a central recognition of the form is the educational principle of what might be called the open secret. Goethe was a great lover of fictional mystification: the secret society, tower, room, or casket. But when you get there, the cupboard is always bare: the secret does not lie in the object but in the process. Hence, contrary to the usual meaning of the phrase, the open secret here means one that may be told over and again while remaining a secret. I once taught a semester of 'Introduction to Poetry' in America in which the last session was devoted to the students' own summary and critique of the course. Several cardinal principles were identified leading the students to claim that if I had given these principles at the beginning of the course everything would have been much easier. I replied that, funnily enough, I had done just that on the very first day. They confidently denied this and when the class left I found myself with that familiar figure, the note-taker, the universal amanuensis to life, the student who, on being told not to take notes, solemnly inscribes the instruction. Having lingered to consult his record he came up with a wondering expression saying 'You did say it. Look, it is here in my notebook.' In a sense, the students were quite right because my first enunciation of these principles was an example of the open secret. They understood the words but did not yet possess the experience to which the words referred. And therefore the words disappeared completely from memory. If they had not disappeared, a reductive and illusory understanding might even have blocked the longer, more circuitous, process of eventual recognition. The enemy of true understanding is not ignorance, but banality. Yet it is not meaningless to enunciate general principles, as long as this is understood, by the mentor, as a stage in a process rather than the end of it. And when the end of the process is reached, the statable principles are still not in themselves knowledge, only an *aide-mémoire* for referring to it. So when Wilhelm Meister is taken into the Society of the Tower at the end of his apprentice years, and is given a scrip of moral aphorisms, the scene has a mixture of solemnity and absurdity for it is only in a ceremonial sense that understanding can be imparted in this way.[12] Such narrative topoi of the *Bildungsroman* point to the delicate art of conducting education as one of leading others to see something for themselves so that the moment of recognition may actually be experienced as an independent insight. You can tell when some students have finally understood when they come to tell you of their bright idea.

The topos of the open secret in the context of *Bildung* throws a further light on the modern topos of the reinvention of Leavisian thought, for his life's work was centred in teaching, and it had the pedagogical relation as its implicit form. It may be that the wheel is such a handy item that when cultural memory of it dies someone always reinvents it, but Wayne Booth's recreation of the Leavisian collaboration seems much more like an instance of the slow process of recognition expressed emblematically in the *Bildungsroman*. When he finally understands, it feels to him like a new recognition, and he is genuinely unaware that a mentor has once set him on the path by telling him something he could not at that time appreciate. Yet it may also be that there is some historical shift, some epochal interference, which by the latter part of the century has made Leavis hard to see even when he is being directly invoked.

IV *BILDUNG* VERSUS MODERNITY

Against a larger background of European thought, typical discussion of Leavis is painfully provincial and, as I have indicated elsewhere, to be properly understood he needs to be run alongside major thinkers like Heidegger whose essential thinking about language and creativity Leavis, in his later years, worked out for himself.[13] Leavis developed a similarly collective sense of the creative process of language in a living culture. But Heidegger was less attentive to the individual critical responsibility to which Leavis still gave essential emphasis, and indeed Heidegger was notoriously a collaborator in Kundera's sense. But moving Leavis onto this larger stage of European thought invites the more general reflection that the relation of art to life has always eluded analytic definition or philosophical grounding. If Leavis's thought has been occluded, the same applies to one of the greatest of all discussions of the meaningfulness of art: Schiller's *Letters on the Aesthetic Education of Man*.[14] Schiller has often been sidelined as an aesthete just as Leavis has been taken for a simple moralist.

And to see how we get from the moment of Rousseau to that of Leavis, Schiller, along with Goethe, provides an analytic bridge. For Schiller was writing contemporaneously with Goethe's composing of *Wilhelm Meister's Apprenticeship*. The contemporaneity of these two works reflects an important, but still little recognized, fact about the notion of *Bildung*. The moment at which the ideal of *Bildung* as an achieved personal wholeness reached its apogee was also the moment of its essential dissolution. Schiller's powerful case for placing the category of the aesthetic at the centre of an understanding of education is partly reflected in *Wilhelm Meister's Apprenticeship* but the novel already treats the ideal of personal *Bildung* with a deconstructive irony and, in the successor novel, *Wilhelm Meister's Journeyman Years*, the whole conception of personal wholeness is renounced, with extraordinary prescience, in favour of specialization; which was indeed to be the modern educational form. This shift between the two novels arose partly from Goethe's recognition of developments in European culture, but just as importantly it arises from the internal instability of the *Bildung* ideal itself. Goethe recognized in this ideal the danger of dilettantism; and Nietzsche was to see the more radical possibility of nihilism. Nietzsche's memorable definition of modern man as a 'wandering encyclopaedia' had already been countered by Goethe's acceptance of 'wandering' as a necessary and fruitful condition for which he can still invoke the old trade term of 'journeyman'.[15] The individual could find a personal, but socially oriented, fulfilment by renouncing an earlier conception of personal wholeness.

Schiller argued an analytic case based on the nature of aesthetic experience as such. He was not therefore so concerned with the question of individual reception or understanding; although he recognized well enough that art can only address those who have ears to hear. But when we jump to Nietzsche, at the other end of the story of *Bildung*, the question of the individual is central. Nietzsche's hostility to Rousseau focused on the question of sentiment, and the pathos of personality, both of which are caught in the term *ressentiment*. In heralding the shift from an earlier ethics of sincerity to a modern ethics of authenticity, Nietzsche signals the end of the Enlightenment's project of moral sentiment, which was closely linked to the category of the individual.[16] For both Rousseau and Leavis the individual response was crucial, and their own personalities were inextricable from their 'thought'. Of course, Nietzsche was supremely aware that self-presentation was central to the expression of his thought too, but he understood this in a crucially different way. For Nietzsche's modernity lay in his simultaneous deconstruction of the category of the individual. The self Nietzsche presents in his writing is always, in the first instance, a textual one. It takes a while to realize this, and it could hardly have been realized until a general change in culture made it comprehensible, which is why Nietzsche has truly come into his own only in the late twentieth century. But the period of modernism was an important chapter of that history and, as I have indicated elsewhere, it was Leavis who most comprehensively worked through the relevant thinking.[17]

To put the point briefly, a central preoccupation of several modernist writers, both creatively and critically, was the question of sincerity. Superficially, this was a matter of rejecting the very notion of sincerity as a critical criterion and of stressing the significance of artistic impersonality. And this was indeed an important motif in the period's frequent attacks on a debased romanticism and sentimentalism. But what was really at stake was a more complex meditation on impersonality whereby 'sincerity' and 'authenticity', both dangerously limited notions in themselves, were reworked into a conception of responsibility. Lawrence, who was perhaps most directly concerned with responsibility, began his mature career by rejecting the 'old stable ego'.[18] Jacques Derrida has recently followed a similar trajectory in drawing a notion of responsibility out of the dissolution of the substantive subject: 'There neither can, nor should be, any concept adequate to what we call responsibility. Responsibility carries within it, and must do, an essential excessiveness.'[19]

This throws a final light on the continual reinvention of Leavis's thought. Leavis insisted on the category of the individual, not to defend a naive essentialism, but as a centre of responsibility. Whereas Nietzsche accepted the risks of relativism, Leavis had a teacherly concern for holding together a world which he knew had no external grounding but whose inner nature could be learned. Or rather one could learn to participate in the collective, critical and creative process of world-making itself. Hence whereas Nietzsche was leaving the Rousseauvian era behind, Leavis attempted, on the same premises, to hold it together. Likewise, Nietzsche was relatively indifferent to political or social programmes, and thought a *Bildungsanstalt*, an institution of humanistic education, was a contradiction in terms, while Leavis still wished to create a new order through public education. Such a sense of common purpose, at the level of a public institution, has since become inconceivable, while many cultivated individuals no longer believe either in *Bildung* or in the category of the individual. Yet that must be precisely why individuals continue to reinvent Leavis's thought without recognizing it. For collaboration, in Leavis's sense, remains a practical necessity even if it can only be conducted by ideological sub-groups, not by the literary academy as a whole. The problem he represents does not go away. As members of the academy we can pursue a residual ideal of *Bildung* only in so far as this has itself become a specialism, and we collaborate in an institutional sense which, from the individual's point of view, is as close to Kundera as to Leavis.

Notes

1. F. R. Leavis, *The Common Pursuit* (London: Chatto and Windus, 1965) v.
2. Milan Kundera, *The Art of the Novel*, trans. Linda Asher (London: Faber, 1988) 125.
3. Apart from those discussed in this paper see, for example, J. Hillis Miller, *The Ethics of Reading: Kant, de Man, Eliot, Trollope, James, and Benjamin* (New York: Columbia University Press, 1987); Martha Nussbaum, *Poetic Justice* (Boston: Beacon, 1995); David Parker, *Ethics, Theory and the Novel* (Cambridge University Press, 1994).
4. Bernard Williams, 'Necessity Disguised as Luxury', *Times Higher Education Supplement*, 23 January 1987, 4.
5. Wayne C. Booth, *The Company We Keep: An Ethics of Fiction* (Berkeley: University of California Press, 1988) 50. His reference is to *A Selection from Scrutiny*, 2 vols (Cambridge University Press, 1966) I, 248–57.
6. Booth, *The Company We Keep*, 72–3.
7. Ibid., 286.
8. The change occurs between the chapters on *Hard Times* in F. R. Leavis, *The Great Tradition*, revised edition (London: Chatto and Windus, 1960) and F. R. and Q. D. Leavis, *Dickens, the Novelist* (London: Chatto and Windus, 1970).
9. Leon Edel, *Henry James*, 2 vols (Harmondsworth: Penguin, 1977) II, 557.
10. See Judith Sklaar, 'Let Us Not Be Hypocritical', *Dedalus*, 108 (Summer, 1979) 1–26.
11. See Jean Starobinski, *Jean-Jacques Rousseau: Transparency and Obstruction*, trans. Arthur Goldhammer (University of Chicago Press, 1988) 47.
12. Johann Wolfgang von Goethe, *Wilhelm Meister's Years of Apprenticeship*, trans. H. M. Waidson (London: Calder, 1979), Book VII, Ch. 9, pp. 66–7.
13. I discuss this in *F. R. Leavis* (London: Routledge, 1988), esp. pp. 62–9.
14. For an excellent account see the Introduction by Elizabeth M. Wilkinson to Johann Christoph Friedrich von Schiller, *On the Aesthetic Education of Man: In a Series of Letters*, ed. Elizabeth M. Wilkinson and L. A. Willoughby (Oxford: Clarendon, 1967).
15. Johann Wolfgang von Goethe, *On the Uses and Disadvantages of History for Life*, trans. Peter Preuss (Indianapolis: Hackett, 1983) 24.
16. On this see Charles Taylor, *The Ethics of Authenticity* (Cambridge, MA: Harvard University Press, 1991) and Lionel Trilling, *Sincerity and Authenticity* (London: Oxford University Press, 1972).
17. See Bell, *Leavis*, 27–130.
18. *The Letters of D. H. Lawrence*, vol. II, ed. James T. Boulton and George Zytaruk (Cambridge University Press, 1981) 184.
19. See 'Eating Well: On the Calculation of the Subject: An Interview with Jacques Derrida', in *Who Comes After the Subject?*, ed. Eduardo Cadava, Peter Connor and Jean-Luc Nancy (London: Routledge, 1991) 108.

2

Imagining the Centre

Geoffrey Galt Harpham

Can a work be overread? Can it be so thoroughly picked over by generations of readers that it is replete with its own interpretations, drained of contemporary pertinence, debarred from a future? If so, one such text might be Kant's brief essay, 'An Answer to the Question: "What is Enlightenment?"'[1] Its main claim, that people should think for themselves rather than simply accepting the doctrines they inherit and inhabit, seems so obvious today that it is difficult to imagine it as ever having been controversial, and therefore difficult to see why anyone should return to Kant for instruction on this point. Even worse, when one does return to Kant, one finds that the summons to reason is nested in other notions that have become scandalous. Crystallized in the notorious injunction to 'argue as much as you like, but obey', a chilling emphasis on civil order is backed up by ominous references to the 'numerous and well disciplined armies' that properly secure the stability of a disputatious culture. Moreover, Kant's fawning deference to his sovereign seems a relic of a pre-democratic era, a mark of what he himself characterized as 'immaturity', a political and intellectual position from which we can learn nothing. In short, Kant's essay is both contemporary to the point of banality, and immured in its own relatively unenlightened context.

But if this little essay has lost its power to inspire, perhaps it retains other, undiscovered powers. Let us begin with an hypothesis: Kant's 'answer to the question' of enlightenment, I will suggest, expresses not only the reigning cliché in the self-description of the modern intellectual, especially literary intellectuals – that they think for themselves and are answerable to no one – but also, in its forthright compact with the authorities, a blurted confession that today's intellectuals would make if only they had the insight and the honesty. In effect, Kant says that enlightened critique is acceptable or even possible only when it occurs within a politico-conceptual space demarcated and secured by the police. Thus constrained, 'free' thought must be a kind of group hallucination, an agreed-upon game with a conservative programme that remains hidden despite its manifest success. This programme, I will begin by proposing, is a truth denied by many but disproven by none.

One who has certainly tried to disprove it is Edward Said, whose recent book, *Representations of the Intellectual*, sketches out a portrait of the activist thinker meant to confound what he sees as a dangerous and cowardly conception of the intellectual as a mere entrepreneur, someone who reflects on and is reflected in a postmodern culture with no 'outside', and therefore no true politics.[2] Indeed, Said's own career as an outsider, an iconoclastic and committed public intellectual, could be taken as a model for the kind of fiercely independent intellectual activity he advocates. The true intellectual, Said argues, is able to 'speak the truth to power' because he or she is an 'exile', an 'amateur', unimplicated in its structures of security and so unintimidated by its threats. Only from the margins, Said insists, can one perform one's ethico-political duty as an intellectual, in part because one's duty is to represent and advocate the interests of the marginalized, the dispossessed, the underrepresented. It is implicitly on behalf of these people that the intellectual undertakes to attack class privilege or social injustice and, in general, to interfere with the untroubled self-regard of the dominant group. Necessarily, the intellectual is a loner, a singular if not exactly friendless individual heedless of the personal consequences of his activities. As should already be apparent, Said's book can be read not just as an attack on postmodernism, but as a crystallization of certain tendencies in cultural Modernism. Said is seeking, one might argue, to purify Kant by liberating the intellect from the false securities offered by armies and patrons; he is trying to complete Kant's work by emancipating the injunction to use your own reason from the crippling burden of obedience.

His account labours, however, under a couple of burdens of its own making. The first is the burden of inconsistency. In one bewildering passage, Said seems to take two opposed views virtually at once, claiming first that real intellectuals try 'to uphold a single standard for human affairs', and then adding, as if it were a clarification, that 'there are no rules by which intellectuals can know what to say or do' – so the intellectual is both a stern partisan of the unwavering law and a figure of unprogrammed anarchy. In another instance, Said argues for partisanship and passionate commitment over disinterestedness – but then, a few pages later, urges a 'universalist' perspective that 'forbids calling one side innocent, the other evil'. Throughout, Said argues, with no discernible sense of the problems involved, that the intellectual must be both affiliated and independent, a cross between Gramsci and Tiresias, Sartre and St Simeon Stylites. In such moments, which are frequent, he seems to be approaching a kind of twist, a paradox in his conception of the intellectual, but not to have worked through it, or even perhaps to have apprehended it.

The argument's second burden is even more difficult to negotiate: it is Said's own eminence. Can Said be serious when he speaks of cultivating 'one's rare opportunities to speak', or when he assures his audience that being an intellectual is 'a lonely condition', or that the intellectual ought to risk personal security as the cost of truth? These are, after all, the Reith Lectures, broadcast over the BBC and reprinted for the mass market to an audience long familiar with their author as one of the most recognizable and distinguished public intellectuals in the world. What risks has Professor Said run? Or rather, what proof can he offer that anything has been risked, given the cascade of honours that has descended upon him? And given his eminence, how, precisely, does Said stand 'on the side of' the weak and oppressed? When everything one touches turns to gold, when all one's courageous acts redound to one's personal credit and secure one's eminence, when – to put the matter in the most vulgar and offensive way possible – one makes a decent tenured living doing this, how can one claim to stand in the danger zone? The unasked question is whether one's public and professional stature modulates or inflects in any way not just one's ideas or judgements, but also what might be called, with productive ambiguity, one's *position*, which is to say one's actual (as opposed to claimed) affiliations. Has Said truly identified the nature of the risk run by the eminent intellectual; or is he facing down a non-existent enemy, pretending or ventriloquizing a circumstance of dispossession he does not experience, his back turned to another enemy whose subtler subversion he does not suspect?

Here we confront a third burden, which takes the form not of inconsistency but of uniformity. Said is speaking to and for intellectuals and their fans. One reason his account seems such a *welcome* statement is, I submit, that it accords beautifully with the fonder and more traditional self-conceptions of such people. The fact that his book is 'stimulating' rather than, say, 'controversial' as it seems to want to be flags the possibility that some fugitive principle of self-regard, whose enjoyment in the dominant group the intellectual spoils, has found its way into the group of dominant intellectuals as they rehearse their own most heroic attributes. Since Kant, these attributes have gathered, especially among those on the left, into a pose of narcissistic oppositionality. When we – that is, professional intellectuals – hear that the mission of the intellectual is to disturb or disrupt, to risk ostracism, to be 'embarrassing, contrary, even unpleasant', do we not feel a certain antique *frisson*? Do we not say to ourselves, and not for the first time, 'Yes, that's me – a royal pain'?

The issue at this point is the relation of the intellectual to the site of real power – the power to determine actual policy, actual legislation, actual priorities, actual goals, actual action in a democratic culture, which is to say a culture in which the majority rules and the rules must serve the majority as well as protect the minorities so that they may, if they choose, try to influence or even become the majority. When they define themselves as both amateurs and partisans, dead-set 'against the prevailing norms' as Said puts it, intellectuals fashion *themselves* a minority; they protect *themselves* not from injustice but from the responsibilities and uncertainties of authority, towards which they sustain a strictly negative relation. Absent a compelling or immediately obvious reason to do so, the Saidian intellectual – in fact a bourgeois professional – imagines himself undefined by profession or class. He imagines himself, moreover, as a person who chooses to affiliate with those who do not have the power to choose their affiliations, the disempowered and dispossessed; and who chooses *not* to affiliate with those who do have the power to choose their affiliations, those who enjoy power in general. The true risk such an intellectual runs is that oppositional negation may become not just a position or an attitude, but a form, a style, a haven, and ultimately a low-security prison. To be against power and prevailing norms, to resist worldly temptations, to refuse accommodation, to operate without rules or guarantees – how can one do all this, and do anything at all? An element of fantasy and what might be called poetic invention seems to be at work here. It is not just that the agency of the intellectual seems unreal, but that the very idea of the intellectual is modelled on fiction, a discourse produced by experts in 'negative capability' or the 'extinction of personality', by people who stand at a reflective distance from the power centre and who, as a consequence, nothing affirmeth.

In Said's final essay, the problem exfoliates anecdotally. Here, Said recounts his relationship with an unnamed Iranian acquaintance over a period of about 15 years. A sophisticated intellectual, this man had found himself forced to make a series of painful choices, beginning with a wary but dedicated support for the Ayatollah's theocracy, which eventually rewarded his service with persecution. The toughest call of all, however, was the Gulf War, which Said's friend saw as a conflict between fascism and imperialism, in which he chose – out of battle-hardened principle – the latter. Dismayed, Said declares this decision 'unnecessary': 'I was surprised,' he writes, 'that none of the formulators of this, in my opinion, unnecessarily attenuated pair of choices had grasped that it would have been quite possible and indeed desirable on both intellectual and political grounds to reject both fascism and imperialism.'

Said is surprised, that is, that nobody had thought of the intellectual's way out, which is not to choose at all, but to complain about the choices, or perhaps to construct another set of choices, more abstract, more nuanced, more undecidable than the original ones. His friend had reluctantly signed on to service in a government run by fanatics and bullies – but might there not, Said asks, be 'some more discreet – but no less serious and involved – way of joining up without suffering the pain of later betrayal and disillusionment?' Might there not, in short, be some way of joining up by not joining up? 'Not being a joiner or party member by nature,' he says in sentences that sound almost confessional, 'I had never formally enlisted in service. I had certainly become used to being peripheral, outside the circle of power, and perhaps because I had no talent for a position inside that charmed circle, I rationalized the virtues of outsiderhood.' His role in the politics of the Middle East was confined to being an 'independent member of the Palestinian parliament in exile', a group dedicated not to formulating policy but rather 'to resist Israeli policies'. Said himself 'refused all offers that were made to me to occupy official positions; I never joined any party or faction.' While he refused to 'collaborate' with Jews or American supporters of Israel, he 'never endorsed' the policies of Arab states either. Clearly, what finally separates Said from his friend is precisely this, that, caught in a snarl of history and forced to choose between imperfect alternatives, his friend had risked, and suffered, disillusionment and betrayal and worse; while Said had been fortunate enough to be able to resist everything without the anxieties and disappointments that beset joiners.

While Said is too capacious and singular a figure to be typical of any group or movement, many scholars and critics – especially leftist, minoritarian, postcolonial, cultural-studies types who are concerned not only with political but with broadly social issues or issues of identity – look to him as model and guide. For all these, social and political marginality is simply presumed: a certain 'critical' distance from what Lacan calls the Master Signifier, taking a step back from actuality into possibility, is a prerequisite for both the classical philosopher and the contemporary intellectual. Calling the centre into question constitutes, indeed, the central and unquestioned project of an entire class of intellectual work today, and it is this project, rather than the character of individuals, that I am trying to assess. One mark of this project is an emphasis on theory: the margin is the place, it seems, for that superior form of intelligence capable of formulating general principles from the ground-level swirl of phenomena. It is also, as Said would undoubtedly agree, the very site of independent judgement, of that acute or unexpected angle of vision that penetrates through conventional thinking to the core of things. Intelligence as such seems to flourish more freely, to shine more brightly, when it is distanced from the scene of action, when it decamps on the alternative terrain of scientific knowledge so that it can be, in a certain sense, irresponsible or unresponsible, so it can operate without concern for the worldly consequences of its operations, consequences that might force compromises or even denials of theoretical necessities. A certain 'otherness', a 'nowhere' quality, appears to be built into the very nature of modern critical thought.

But this otherness can take various forms, and what I am drawing attention to is the tendency of contemporary thinkers to think *about* otherness *from the point of view of* the other. What might be called the *thought of the other* has effectively displaced traditional paradigms and fertilized whole fields of inquiry, especially those in which questions of identity are at stake. To measure the contributions, and to mark the limits, of this thought we can consider one of the most influential and productive research projects in recent years, Homi Bhabha's interrogation of the relation between colonizers and the colonized. Imposing Christianity and Eurocentrism all over the globe, the great colonial powers also, Bhabha argues in *The Location of Culture*, exposed themselves to the continual possibility of counter-appropriation, deflection, parody, mockery that inhabited the very gestures of deference and obedience.[3] In the colonial circumstance, the presumption of effective hegemony was continually compromised by the uncontainable possibility of inauthenticity: a virus of 'sly civility' infected the discourse of the colonized and threatened the ease of the colonizer, and the ponderous, oppressive, insecure centre was made constantly vulnerable to the supple and insidious agency of the margin.

Unexpected and illuminating as it is, this argument is just the beginning. From the claim that the margin is a freer and somehow more intelligent position than the centre, Bhabha proceeds to the further claim that the margin is actually more central than the centre. The dutiful but insincere subaltern utterance, Bhabha points out, is 'split' in that the 'content' of the utterance is at variance with 'the structure of its positionality'. Although emerging on the periphery of power, this split indicates 'the general conditions of language', the splitting of *all* utterances: rightly apprehended, the margins, and the margins alone, display the hidden law of the centre, a secret division that structures and *de*centres everything. The margin becomes, as Bhabha puts it, a 'paradigmatic place of departure' for a study of identity and utterance in general. With the discovery of decentring as the rule rather than the exception, we have arrived, Bhabha suggests, at a conception that could found a progressive rethinking of all identity as hybrid, open, ambivalent, discontinuous, in-between. And it is this second claim that constitutes the real point. If the margin were merely more interesting than the centre, that would be curious but politically neutral. If, however, the law of the margin could be shown to regulate the entire field, including the centre – where, because of repression, it could not 'appear' – then a certain dominant configuration of forces would be overturned and the world would become open to new kinds of agency. It would become possible to think, for example, not just of the 'foreign' language of the colonized, but of the 'foreignness of languages', all languages. The playing field would be levelled at last.

And the levelling agent would be theory. There is no surer sign of the marginality of Bhabha's discourse on marginality than the extraordinary prestige it accords to theory. For Bhabha, the political potential of marginocentrism is realized when the condition of the margin is made general by applying it as a template to the entire field – by reconceiving the realia of subaltern identity as the basis for a theory of identity *tout court*. Bhabha fully understands that the general project of theory – in particular the theory of cultural difference – has worked to 'foreclose on the Other' by depicting it as a 'good object of knowledge, the docile body of difference'. Still, he insists that theory can and must be reclaimed as a matter of political principle. In a post-realist age, theory arises from the ashes of ontology. 'I want to take my stand,' he says, 'on the shifting margins of cultural displacement – that confounds any profound or "authentic" sense of a "national" culture or an "organic" intellectual.'

I cannot claim to be culturally displaced, but the place I have lived for ten years, Louisiana, is rapidly disappearing into the Gulf of Mexico, and the river that gives my city, New Orleans, its distinctive character as 'the River City' constantly threatens to shift course abruptly somewhere upriver, which would make us 'the River-Bed City'. These disquieting facts give me, perhaps, some sensitivity to shifting margins, enough at least to know that they are hard to stand on for persons, buildings and cities alike. And this is the problem. Identity as hybridity, as in-betweenness, liminality, other-than-itself – these notions, while issuing from a 'committed theoretical perspective', are emancipatory in a strictly theoretical sense, a sense that Said (saluted by Bhabha for his 'pioneering *oeuvre*') might fault for being insufficiently committed. Said might wonder, as I do, what the 'commitment to theory' (the title of Bhabha's essay) actually entails. 'Committed to what?' Bhabha asks proleptically; 'at this stage in the argument, I do not want to identify any specific "object" of political allegiance – the Third World, the working class, the feminist struggle.' All these, while 'crucial', do not exhaust the options for 'intellectuals who are committed to progressive political change in the direction of a socialist society'. More urgent – at this stage in the argument – is the theoretical project.

So urgent, so complex, so interesting is this project that it eclipses all possible 'objects of political allegiance'. The question of what is to be done gives way, in Bhabha, to the question of 'the force of writing, its metaphoricity and its rhetorical discourse, as a productive matrix which defines the "social" and makes it available as an objective of and for, action'. Social praxis is thus humbled before its grounding circumstance and enabling condition; and theory, or 'ideological intervention', acquires political credentials as the partner of praxis, existing with it 'side by side'. But, one might ask, isn't theory sufficiently distinct from praxis that its pursuance must come at the expense of its partner? Could it not be said that the insistence on theory is a way of keeping all options open, and all hands clean, even while promising that some positive determination – strictly in keeping with 'socialist' commitments, of course – will arrive some day, not today? Is not praxis here *itself* foreclosed as a docile body of difference, a good object of knowledge? If theory makes the social realm 'available' as an objective of action, why do intellectuals hold so little power? Why are all the ropes in the hands of theoretical naïfs or primitives? The cost of marginality, for Bhabha, may well be the verso of its analytical power: the principled unwillingness, for the present moment, to specify, to decide, to particularize, to commit oneself to a recognizably political statement becomes, without transformation, an inability to do so. Having opened up the field of identity, having deconstructed a false and non-necessary structure, having exposed the agency of writing, Bhabha seems unable to spell out ways of re-closing the field in a new, more positive and productive configuration. The emancipation from the Master Signifier has not, at least not yet, produced any new determination of the post-colonial subject or polity. Everything is, for the moment, suspended, weightless, in a protracted state of indecision. Bhabha is able to imagine and desire forms of freedom, especially in the mode of 'freedom from', but uninterested, it seems, in the project of imagining a 'freedom to', in any but the most general sense. 'Socialism' functions in this context as a general oppositionality, the prospect of whose realization generates a vague sense of jubilation that could only be spoiled by the declaration of an allegiance to a particular candidate, strategy, piece of legislation, political party, initiative. The point in the present context is that marginality may be the site of insight; but it may also be the place, or non-place, of those who are simply out of it. Today, intellectuals, most of whom are weirdly secure in a world where volatility is the rule, a world that has not made a commitment to theory, are, in general, out of it. Their imagining of the world lingers on the edges. They can thus offer no way of deciding hard cases where interests clash, no way of ranking interests, no principle of decision; nor do they conceive of such principles of resolution in any but oppressive terms. To the extent to which they urge such traditional values as 'openness', or 'participation', they remain committed to form rather than content, and thus are liberals rather than radicals.

I have considered only a few examples, and these not at length; but each one can stand for a class, and together they summon up an ethos. It is not a specifically postmodern ethos, although postmodernity (whose presiding spirits are perhaps Jean-François Lyotard's stranded Martiniquans, mistreated by French law and yet unable to secure justice because the only courts available to them are French) is congenial to it. But the presumptions and intellectual habits to which I am drawing attention originated in the very roots of modern critical thinking and now extend beyond postmodernity to postcolonial studies, gender studies, some versions of feminism, post-Marxist political theory, on out to the governing presumptions about intellectual work, especially literary intellectual work, today. It spreads, as it were, from the power-phobia of the classic Left to the analysis of social, psychoanalytic and gender identity. Within this ethos, the place of privilege is occupied by the cognitive virtues of subversive insight and critical analysis, which are typically opposed to what is represented as the reactionary and stupid arrogance of the hegemonic class. Obsessed with power and force, contemporary critical theorists of the kind I'm describing cannot seem to imagine what it would be like actually to possess or exercise them; for them, power and virtue are natural antagonists. Thinkers in this mode see power either as an instrument of specific oppression, beaming out from a centre in the manner of Foucault's Panopticon, or as a circumambient force of local coercions, to be resisted in the manner outlined in Foucault's *History of Sexuality*. In the first model, power is elsewhere; in the second, it is here, but not possessed by 'us'.

Surely, one would think, there must be exceptions. As, for example, the work of Christopher Norris, a towering figure in contemporary critical theory who has boldly proclaimed the vitality of the Enlightenment heritage as the cornerstone of a leftist critique of postmodernist anti-rationalism. If many on the left seem to take a sceptical heretic's pride in remaining outside the mainstream of an essentially conservative political culture, Norris does not; he speaks from the centre of a theoretical and ethical rule based on reason and accurate representation that empowers the critic to make positive judgements and statements about the real world. While Laclau and Mouffe might cheerfully offload 'the discourse of the universal and its implicit assumption of a privileged point of access to "the truth"' as an obstacle to achieving radical democracy, Norris insists that only the truth will set us free.[4] And while many sustain a non-committal commitment to theory, Norris urges the overriding importance of the political as such.

Nowhere are these commitments more aggressively pursued than in *Uncritical Theory: Postmodernism, Intellectuals, and the Gulf War*, a book inspired, if that's the word for it, by the flaccid urbanity of the 'intellectual' response to the Gulf War.[5] The immediate insult, an anticipatory article by Jean Baudrillard suggesting that the proliferation of images generated by the media that would cover the war would so block the reality of the situation that the Gulf War would never 'happen' – followed in due course by another piece after the war claiming that it did not in fact happen – epitomized for Norris virtually every moral and intellectual shortcoming of postmodern intellectualism. Go along with the epistemological arguments of Lyotard and his ilk, Norris declares, and you will play yourself off the field by removing any grounds you might have for deciding between better and worse arguments, true and false statements, right and wrong actions. Reject the distinctions made available by enlightened thought, and you cannot protest when reason is infected by morality, or when politics becomes aestheticized. You cannot, for example, raise your voice even in the event of a hugely destructive war, justified with demonstrably false statements and flawed premises. The general silence of postmodern intellectuals when the Gulf War did break out in fact confirmed Baudrillard in one respect: for them, at least, the war did not exist.

Norris offers as a bracing counter-balance to the examples set by Baudrillard, Lyotard, Fish, and Rorty, such contemporary heroes as Chomsky, Habermas and, conveniently for me, Said, whose book *Orientalism* mounts, Norris says, a powerful argument for rejecting shoddy and biased scholarship about the Middle East coming from the imperial nations in the nineteenth century.[6] What impresses Norris is that Said proceeds in a spirit of '*getting things right*', a powerful phrase that implies a faith that bad research – myths, pseudo-histories, propaganda, revisionism – can be checked and rejected in favour of a '*better* knowledge' of fact and a '*better* grasp' of the ideological issues. But Norris's own knowledge and grasp do not enable him to make positive statements about the actual conduct of the war. While he can point to specific facts about the drawing of boundary lines, the true history of American commercial and political interests in the Middle East, the actual responsibility for reported oil spills, accurate body counts, and so forth, the burden of his argument is negative and critical: he asserts that the United States was not justified in making war on Iraq, and that the war it fought was not the war it said it was fighting. He does not take the side of Iraq, or of Kuwait's ruling class. A partisan of truth and justice, he maintains a virtually Swiss neutrality with respect to the actual military conflict. One of the most committed defences of critical commitment in recent years, *Uncritical Theory* is noncommittal on the question of what ought to be done in a situation where all options are imperfect, if not equally so. Keeping the idea of truth and reason pure, enlightened critique is reluctant, perhaps even powerless, to prescribe actions that must necessarily bear the smudges of compromise, interest and destructive force.

As the phrasing of the last sentence suggests, I am not truly criticizing Norris, with virtually all of whose stated commitments and arguments about and against the Gulf War I agree, and only wish I had expressed with such lucidity, force and detail. I want, rather, to foreground the 'intellectual' component in his project, a commitment to theory that inflects the very form of his judgements and statements by restricting them to negative formulations. Negation is such a force in Norris's discourse that it structures his most basic and fundamental point, which is, broadly, that we should *not* abandon Enlightenment distinctions and premises. The passage in *Uncritical Theory* on Said is especially rich in examples of negative argumentation. To be sure, he concedes, Said's persuasiveness in *Orientalism* derives not just from the truth of his arguments but also from the affective force of his impassioned rhetoric and his compellingly vivid narrative style – but 'one can readily concede these debating-points...and still hold on to the crucial premise: that there is a difference between truth and falsehood'. If we abandoned that distinction, 'there would simply be nothing to choose between the various competing narratives'; moreover, if one gave up the notion of verifiable truth, 'one might as well accept the post-modern-pragmatist line...', a line that leads, for Norris, directly to perdition. The persistence of truth claims in everyday discourse suggests, however, that people do not accept this line, for to make any truth-claim at all is to invoke as a necessary entailment all the terms associated with 'enlightened truth-seeking discourse, even if those terms are perceived as tainted by their involvement in a history of [oppression]'. So while ideas of reason may be beyond our attainment in the real world, 'they none the less offer a crucial yardstick' by which claims may be measured. What all these concessions and warnings have in common is a strategy of 'negating the negation': arguments for enlightenment may be flawed (negatable), Norris says, but the alternatives are far worse. Norris is against postmodernism, against aesthetic ideology, against US action in the Gulf War, against 'end of ideology' thinking. But he is silent on the question of what – Kuwait having been invaded – one ought to do or even to have done. In the Middle East, critique falls silent, exhausted by the task of identifying erroneous premises, false statements and inadequate understanding.

If there were a visual symbol of the cognitive style I am describing, it might be the Romanian flag, displayed at the overthrow of Ceausescu in 1989. As Žižek recounts this incident in *Tarrying with the Negative*, the red star had been cut out so that the flag had 'nothing but a hole in its center'.[7] This evacuation of the locus of power represents, for Žižek, the very object of modern critical philosophy, which is to 'render visible' the '"produced", artificial, contingent character' of the Master Signifier. For only if the Master Signifier is seen as 'nothing' can thought truly be free. Žižek presumes, rather than argues, that the intellectual is most effective when he or she 'stays in the hole', maintaining a critical distance from the centre of power. But this is a prescription for purity rather than effectiveness. Indeed, as the people of Romania – who believed that the hole was truly empty and that they were free at last, only to discover that they were in fact 'serving unrecognized ends' – could instruct us, it is a prescription for radical ineffectuality. To be truly effective, to contribute to the production of positive and predictable consequences, an intellectual would have to embrace, to an undetermined extent, another principle, whose symbol Žižek discovers, but relegates to an inconsequential footnote. This symbol is a 'monument' at the university campus in Mexico City, composed of a jagged ring of concrete encircling a 'formless black undulating surface of lava'. This unmonumental monument, this monument to unmonumentality, suggests a different project, 'Mexican' rather than 'Romanian', in which thought seeks not the laws of its own freedom but the full-frontal apprehension and even a sober and unillusioned embrace of what is theoretically unassimilable, irreducible to thought. With this project, contemporary academic-critical thinking has virtually nothing to do.

The appeal of the margin to the intellectual is clear. The margin is the site of theoretical consistency, for identity organized in clear and distinct ideas ('unfixity', 'hybridity', 'imitation', etc.) and for a secure – exclusively critical – relationship to the powers that be. Advertised as the ethical position, the margin is actually in flight from ethics, which is centred in the centre where conflicting imperatives meet and mingle. It is only when one accepts responsibility – especially the responsibility for making decisions that affect a plural totality – that one appreciates the true difficulty of decision. For responsible action, as all who are in a position of responsibility understand in their bones, exposes one not just to unjustified attacks but, what is harder, to justified attacks, attacks typically launched from the margin, where intellectuals congregate to celebrate their uncompromised rectitude. As the example of Said suggests, intellectuals celebrate above all their autonomy and independence, which they characterize in terms of disobedience to repressive power. It was Kant's subtle genius to recognize the kernel of obedience that lay at the heart of autonomy.

I am not advocating the abandonment of enlightened critique, nor am I suggesting that enlightened individuals have a monopoly on docility. One only needs to consult Robert von Hallberg's book on East German writers and intellectuals, *Literary Intellectuals and the Dissolution of the State*, to be reminded of the dangers of intellectual conformism within institutions.[8] Rather, I am probing the limitations of marginal thinking, and urging thinkers today not to discover some more effective means of resisting power or normative configurations but to begin forming some other, more familiar, confident and productive relations with them. If thinkers today would leave the ghetto, they must, I argue, strive to overcome not their lower but their higher natures; they must surrender their fastidiousness, their desire to be blameless; they must come up with more effective ways to join up with some positive set of interests than by not joining up. To do this, thinkers must acknowledge that a pluralist democracy requires the maintenance of numerous and well disciplined armies of various kinds, with their terrible capacity for devastation; they must concede that they live in a world of norms and centres as well as edges and margins, a world in which principles must occasionally be enforced by force, a world that sometimes demands to know the answers to such questions as: whose side are you on? what must be done? which action is best? which principles and whose rights should prevail? and, who are you?

What is needed is not – I wish to be clear on this point – a new boldness on the part of intellectuals in prescribing to the world as philosopher-kings or -queens, but rather a more general willingness to 'imagine the centre', to see things from the point of view of a democratic and plural polity that needs on occasion to act as if it were a single integrated entity, to grasp the moment of identity and normativity that secures and dignifies culture's differences. To do this, one would have to be willing to live with that dimension of worldly life irreducible to theory and incommensurate with strict principle, willing to choose among flawed alternatives. Intellectuals who would imagine the centre must be prepared to suspend for a time both their fascination and their revulsion with centrality; they must learn to regard power and identity as dangerous but necessary allies, snarling guard dogs that might turn on them at any moment no matter how well they are treated.

They might turn, for a model, to Václav Havel, who, in a speech given in May 1996, positioned Europe in a particular historico-metaphysical moment, and offered, with the specificity of one accustomed to governance, an immediate project.[9] Beginning with the statement that Europe has traditionally been defined by 'shared values', Havel urges his audience to affirm a new political structure in which the whole of Europe, including such countries as the Czech Republic, would be included as equal partners. The European Union, he insists, 'should formulate a clear and detailed policy of gradual enlargement that not only contains a timetable but also explains the logic of that timetable'. I cite this bracingly specific moment because it so markedly contrasts with the species of intellectualism I have been discussing. As a Czech, Havel is one who, with respect to Europe, really is on the margins. Still, while speaking the truth to power, he is concerned for the identity of the totality: as he argues, 'if democrats do not soon begin to reconstruct Europe as a single political entity, others will start structuring it in their own way, and the democrats will have nothing left but their tears'. One of the many things that makes Havel so inspiring a figure is that he has discovered a way of being an intellectual that includes such projects as running a nation, and even a continent. He has, in short, learned to imagine the centre.

Admittedly, Havel's talk of 'shared values', 'solidarity' and 'universalism' does not inspire everyone. At the end of his talk, he urges Europeans to 'follow the example of Him in whom [Europe] has believed for two thousand years, and in whose name it has committed so much evil'. Are Jews, Gypsies, secular humanists, Muslims, Hindus, atheists and the metaphysically challenged, then, not truly Europeans; are they outcast from the universe of the universal; is this universe the property of missionaries and crusaders? One would like clarification. But this problematic patch underscores the element of risk that accompanies all attempts to imagine the centre. I do not have an answer to this problem, and have in fact argued that there is no answer. If, however, anyone who reads these words should discover a way of formulating principles that actually guide action in specific contexts, and carry with them no downside risk, I urge them to call me, collect, any time of the day or night.

On second thought, e-mail me.

Notes

1. Immanuel Kant, 'An Answer to the Question: What Is Enlightenment?' in *Kant's Political Writings*, ed. Hans Reiss, trans. H. B. Nesbit (Cambridge University Press, 1991) 54–60.
2. Edward Said, *Representations of the Intellectual* (New York: Vintage, 1996).
3. Homi K. Bhabha, *The Location of Culture* (London: Routledge, 1994).
4. Ernesto Laclau and Chantal Mouffe, *Hegemony and Socialist Strategy* (London: Verso, 1985).
5. Christopher Norris, *Uncritical Theory: Postmodernism, Intellectuals, and the Gulf War* (London: Lawrence & Wishart, 1992).
6. Edward Said, *Orientalism* (New York: Pantheon, 1978).
7. Slavoj Žižek, *Tarrying with the Negative: Kant, Hegel, and the Critique of Ideology* (Durham, NC: Duke University Press, 1993).
8. Robert von Hallberg, *Literary Intellectuals and the Dissolution of the State: Professionalism and Conformity in the GDR* (University of Chicago Press, 1996).
9. Václav Havel, 'The Hope for Europe', *New York Review of Books*, 20 June 1996, 38–41.

Part II
Ethics and History

3

Ethics, Hermeneutics and Philosophy of Science

Christopher Norris

I

In this essay, I shall be comparing developments in Anglo-American philosophy of science over the past four decades and changes in the currency of *avant-garde* thinking among cultural and literary critics. These projects have little in common, it will surely be argued, aside from their each having started out with certain strong methodological commitments, and having then abandoned these in the face of accumulating problems that eventually led to such doctrines as ontological relativity, semantic holism, the 'linguistic turn', and the discursive construction of reality. Beyond that there is a great difference – I would readily concede – between the aims of philosophy of science in the broadly analytic mode and the kinds of thinking that claimed 'scientific' warrant during the period of high structuralism. Where they differ most sharply is on the issue of language, discourse, or representation, that is to say, the extent to which language may be thought of as affording referential access to a domain of real-word (extra-discursive) objects, processes, and events. For structuralists – and even more so for poststructuralists – the notion of our having such access can only be a product of those current (perhaps deeply naturalized) signifying codes that constitute 'reality' so far as we can possibly know it. Hence Foucault's structuralist premise, that all kinds of knowledge, in the natural and the human sciences alike, can be shown to take rise from some particular (purely 'arbitrary') arrangement of signs or discursive representations.[1] Clearly such an argument is worlds apart from anything envisaged by philosophers of language and science in the Anglo-American analytic tradition. And this applies even to those – Quine among them – whose outlook of sturdy commonsense physicalism sits oddly with their otherwise wholesale talk of ontological relativity.[2]

Nevertheless, having entered these necessary caveats, I would still maintain that structuralism and analytic philosophy of science have both run up against similar problems and for much the same reason. That is to say, they each yield ground to the sceptic's arguments at precisely that point where (in Quine's terminology) a gulf opens up between 'word' and 'object', or again – following Saussure – where 'signifier' and 'signified' are conceived as standing in a purely arbitrary relationship, and the referent simply drops out as a notion devoid of explanatory content. For it is then a very short distance to those other, more extreme variants of the linguistic, hermeneutic, or textualist 'turn' which reject the appeal to any meta-language – any higher-level discourse of method or theory – that would somehow place limits on the possible range of first-order signifying systems. This is what happens with the passage from structuralism to poststructuralism. It is also the starting-point of Foucauldian genealogy, of Lyotard's radically nominalist approach to issues of meaning and truth, and of Rorty's idea – drawing upon these and a promiscuous variety of other sources, from Wittgenstein to Heidegger, Quine, Kuhn, and Feyerabend – that 'truth' *just is* whatever we take it to be according to our current interpretive lights.[3] Indeed, the very fact that Rorty can mix these sources with at least some show of justification is enough to suggest that they do, after all, have certain premises in common.

Those premises can be stated very briefly as follows. The legitimate business of theory – whether in philosophy of science or the various extensions of structuralist method – is *not* to give a justificatory account of how knowledge comes about or how truth-claims are properly unwarranted. Rather, it is to analyse the languages, narratives, modes of inferential reasoning, etc., which make up the field of accredited 'knowledge' at any given time. From which it follows, on the sceptical (poststructuralist or ontological-relativist) view, that in principle there can exist as many such schemes as there exist languages or ways of picking out objects in accordance with this or that Rortian 'final vocabulary'. For there is (so it is claimed) no fact of the matter that decides which objects correspond to which statements in our observation-language, nor again any core set of logical entailment-relations or putative 'laws of thought', which could ultimately serve to adjudicate the issue between different (incommensurable) theories. And this because statements are not true in virtue of how things stand in reality, but only – as Quine and Foucault both argue – in virtue of their fit with the entire range of statements (discourses, language-games, conceptual frameworks, etc.) that decide what shall count as a veridical utterance in relation to this or that going ontological scheme. Hence the demise of those erstwhile 'strong' methodologies – like classic structuralism or the deductive-nomological programme in philosophy of science – which equated theoretical rigour with the move to a higher (formalized or meta-linguistic) level of enquiry. For at this stage there appeared to be nothing – no ground-rules of method, no logical constraints, observational checks, or empirical validity-conditions – that could save those programmes from the more extreme consequences of their own ontological-relativist position.

Hence also the currently widespread idea that the only alternative to a minimalist (or deflationary) account of truth is the turn toward hermeneutic models of depth-understanding that dispense altogether with such outworn conceptions of logic, method, and truth. 'Another way to put this,' Joseph Rouse suggests, 'is that for there to be things of any particular kinds, there must be a world to which they belong. But the reality of that world is not a hypothesis to be demonstrated; it is the already given condition that makes possible any action at all, including posing and demonstrating hypotheses.'[4] This claim is borne out, so he believes, by Tarski's 'disquotational' theory which manages to dispense with all those ideas of truth-to-the-facts, 'correspondence', or science as a project supposedly aimed toward deeper explanatory hypotheses which can then be tested against the evidence.[5] For such talk simply fails to make sense once we grasp the point that 'truth' is a redundant term which can always be made to cancel through. This in turn suggests to Rouse – as similarly to others in the 'post-analytic' camp – that there must be something more to the issue of truth, and that the best place to look for that 'something more' is in the region of depth-ontological enquiry opened up by Heideggerian hermeneutics.

Thus (to repeat): '[t]here cannot be things that cannot interact with the things disclosed within a meaningful world (as there cannot be truths or falsehoods that cannot be expressed in a language)'.[6] All the same, Rouse argues, we should not be misled into thinking that this can become a charter for anti-realism in philosophy of science. Nor is it in any sense a pretext for those forms of wholesale ontological-relativist doctrine that treat the objects of scientific enquiry as so many optional contracts out of this or that language-game, Rortian 'final vocabulary', or whatever. On the contrary: 'the language we speak does not determine which of its sentences are true'. Moreover, '[t]he practices that constitute our "world" likewise do not determine which things exist, with what properties'.[7] The realist may suspect that what is involved here is a thoroughgoing version of the linguistic or cultural-conventionalist 'turn', combined with a depth-ontological (hermeneutic) jargon that counts 'reality' a world well lost for the sake of such profound revelations. But according to Rouse, quite simply, '[w]hich things there are, what properties they have, and what relations they enter into are determined by the things themselves and "how things stand" with them'.[8]

So one can carry on talking about the world and all its furniture – from quasars to quarks – just so long as one takes the Heideggerian point that those 'things' can only emerge against the horizon of intelligibility that constitutes the 'world' of meaningful practices and life-forms. However this argument will appear less than convincing if one asks how the properties of *x* can be determined *both* by its intrinsic nature – as revealed through scientific investigation – *and* by its role within some given context of linguistic or cultural preunderstanding. For in the latter case nothing could count as an object – or as evidence for that object's nature and properties – except in so far as it showed up among the range of presently accepted practices and beliefs. That is to say, there could be no escaping the 'hermeneutic circle' which Heidegger – and Gadamer after him – have raised to a high point of interpretive principle.[9] Rouse is quite happy to embrace this idea, on the one hand because he thinks that we have no choice in the matter, and on the other because it involves not a 'vicious' circularity, but a way of rendering science more accountable to the range of human needs, values, and social priorities. For if, following Quine, 'there is no nonlinguistic, pre-theoretical fact of the matter to which we could appeal to resolve disagreements about how the world is', and if moreover – as he takes Tarski for example to have shown – 'truth is a metalinguistic predicate' devoid of substantive content, then surely nothing is lost (and a great deal gained) by acknowledging the hermeneutic circle.[10] What we lose is just a set of mistaken, residually positivist ideas about the logic of scientific enquiry and its bearing on first-order observation statements. What we stand to gain, as Rouse sees it, is a much enhanced sense of science's social and ethical responsibilities, along with a suitably scaled-down conception of its claim to determine how things stand 'in reality'.

However, this Heideggerian line of argument sits awkwardly with Rouse's attempts elsewhere to placate his typecast 'realist' opponent by adopting a liberal attitude with regard to the various entities turned up in scientific research or in our everyday dealings with the world. More precisely: it brings out the strain of implicit anti-realism which attaches to such talk of 'things' (or entities) once subject to reinterpretation in the depth-ontological or hermeneutic mode. Thus when Heidegger asks 'What is a Thing', he questions both our everyday ('ontic' or 'factical') notions of thinghood and that entire history of philosophico-scientific thought which has always been captive to 'metaphysical' ideas of knowledge, truth, and representation, this latter conceived on the model of a perfect correspondence (*homoiosis*) between the knowing mind and the objective order of things.[11] This is why, in Heidegger's estimation, 'science does not think'. What it fails to think is the 'question of Being' (or the 'ontological difference' between Being and beings) which first found expression in the thought of the pre-Socratics, and whose subsequent withdrawal – with the advent of 'philosophy' as we know it from Plato to Descartes, Kant, Husserl, and beyond – is coterminous with the epoch of 'Western metaphysics'.

Hence Heidegger's brooding on the 'question of technology' where the epoch of Western post-Hellenic 'metaphysical' thought is defined – in brief – by its somehow 'predestined' forgetfulness of Being, by its exclusive concern with the beings (or objects of cognitive and technologico-scientific grasp) that henceforth lend themselves passively to treatment in this fashion, and by its fall into a mode of epistemological (or representationalist) thought which sets a gulf between subject and object that cannot be bridged but only 'dammed up' by the ever more exploitative uses of nature as a 'standing reserve' or an 'object on call'. Such is the very 'essence' of technology, whose manifestations include – as Heidegger notoriously listed them – mechanized agriculture, factory production-lines, and the mass-slaughter of human beings in the death-camps at Auschwitz and elsewhere. If there is indeed such an 'essence' whose origins lie far back in the history of Western metaphysical thought, and which was thus predestined to manifest itself in this range of latterday forms, then it becomes pointless to moralize on the subject or suggest that there is an all-important difference between Auschwitz on the one hand and on the other such 'monstrosities' as mechanized agriculture. What these have in common is their belonging to an age of metaphysico-technological 'enframing' when everything is reduced to the dead level of instrumental or calculative reason. Mere 'correctness' (or accurate representation) henceforth becomes the sole aim of thought, which in turn gives rise to that epistemological – or technocratic – will-to-truth whose manifestations are everywhere around us.

And yet, he continues, 'in order to be correct, this fixing by no means needs to uncover the thing in question in its essence'.[12] For to think the 'essence' of technology is also to open a space where technology appears in its true character as the simply inescapable destiny of thought for an epoch whose horizon has so long been configured by those same (metaphysical or representationalist) ideas of knowledge and truth. In which case the ontic/ontological difference has its equivalent in two ways of thinking about technology. There is the kind of superficial denunciation which never gets beyond protesting its effects upon this or that aspect of our contemporary life-world. But there also remains the possibility for an authentic (depth-ontological) thinking-back into the 'question of technology', a thinking that would reveal those various stages in the epochal declension – the 'concealment' of Being – which began with the theory of truth-as-correspondence. Thus:

> [w]hen we consider the essence of technology, then we experience Enframing as a destining of revealing. In this way we are already sojourning within the open space of destining, a destining that in no way confines us to a stultified compulsion to push on blindly with technology or, what comes to the same thing, to rebel helplessly against it and curse it as the work of the devil. Quite to the contrary, when we once open ourselves expressly to the *essence* of technology, we find ourselves unexpectedly taken into a freeing claim.[13]

This apparently more relaxed, open-minded and receptive approach to the 'question of technology' goes along with the famous 'turn' (*Kehre*) in Heidegger's later work, his belief that thinking can best comport itself through a kind of wise passivity (*Gelassenheit*), an attitude of unforced acceptance in response to whatever may yet be revealed of Being and truth. Still there is the danger, as he warns, that 'in the midst of all that is correct the true will withdraw'.[14] However we shall not be any better equipped to avert that danger if we suppose that simply by denouncing its particular causes or effects – say industrial pollution, the destruction of animal species, or the depletion of the ozone-layer – we have thereby confronted the 'essence' of technology as a challenge to thought.

Not that Heidegger altogether ignores these specific matters for concern. 'Agriculture is now the mechanized food industry. Air is now set upon to yield nitrogen, the earth to yield ore, ore to yield uranium, for example; uranium is set upon to yield atomic energy, which can be released either for destruction or for peaceful use.'[15] Yet such concerns are of secondary importance when set against the question of technology and its demand for an authentic (depth-ontological) thinking that would address that question in its very essence. 'What is dangerous is not technology,' Heidegger writes. 'There is no demonry of technology, but rather there is the mystery of its essence.'[16] And again, in a passage that offers at least some degree of clarification:

> The threat to man does not come in the first instance from the potentially lethal machines and apparatus of technology. The actual threat has already affected man in his essence. The rule of Enframing threatens man with the possibility that it could be denied to him to enter into a more original revealing and hence to experience the call of a more primal truth.[17]

What this passage clarifies, it seems to me, is not so much the logic or the justifying grounds of Heidegger's argument but the sheer amount of deep-laid verbal mystification – 'bewitchment by language', in Wittgenstein's phrase – which befogs his thinking about the 'question' (or the 'essence') of technology. For technology has no such 'essence'; only a diverse range of applications and purposes, some of them beneficial, others harmful, and others again – like genetic engineering or certain branches of 'peaceful' sub-atomic or particle research – as yet very largely untested as to their social and ethical consequences. To think of them all as possessing some 'mysterious' (though not necessarily 'demonic') essence is just another version of that moral obtuseness which led Heidegger to compare mechanized agriculture with the gas-chambers at Auschwitz, or – in his correspondence with Marcuse – to equate the treatment of the Jews in Nazi Germany to the post-war suffering of displaced populations in Soviet-occupied Eastern Europe.[18]

Nor is there much improvement to be noted in his habits of moral judgement when Heidegger undergoes his mid-life 'turn' to a non-assertive ethos of *Gelassenheit*, waiting-upon-truth, or letting-be. What this change amounted to in ethico-political terms was a switch from the language of 'resoluteness', *Dasein*, 'being-unto-death', 'the self-assertion of the German university' (with Heidegger as its self-appointed philosopher-Führer), etc., to a language of wise acquiescence in the given (predestined) occurrence of events which effectively absolved him of all responsibility for his words and actions during that earlier period. And there is a parallel shift in his thinking about the 'question of technology', one that emerges most clearly when Heidegger writes about technology as 'no mere human doing', but as a 'revealing that orders', that 'sets upon man to order the actual as standing-reserve in accordance with the way it shows itself'.[19] For in this case the question would be posed at a level far deeper – and historically much further back – than could be grasped by any merely 'ontic' or 'factical' dealing with particular problems in the nature of our current technologically oriented life-world. That is, it would require us to contemplate the 'essence' of technology as having somehow been set in place from the ancient Greek beginning, from that moment when philosophy and science took their destined turn toward an epistemological (or representationalist) mode of being-in-the-world. On this view it is the merest of anthropocentric illusions to think that we might come up with particular remedies for particular aspects of our current technological fix, or indeed to suppose that *we* – as individuals or co-ordinated action-groups – could affect its outcome in any significant way. This presumption errs on the one hand by mistaking accident (or localized symptom) for essence, and on the other by attributing to human agents a power of judgement and choice over questions of ultimate (primordial) import.

II

I shall cite one further passage from 'The Question of Technology' which brings out this close relation, in his later work, between Heidegger's thinking about techno-science and his attitude to issues of ethical, historical, and political responsibility. 'The essence of modern technology', he writes,

> starts man upon the way of that revealing through which the actual everywhere, more or less distinctly, becomes standing-reserve. 'To start upon a way' means 'to send' in our ordinary language. We shall call the sending that gathers (*versammelnde Schicken*), that first starts man upon a way of revealing, *destining (Geschick)*. It is from this destining that the essence of all history (*Geschichte*) is determined. History is neither simply the object of written chronicle nor merely the process of human activity. That activity first becomes history as something destined. And it is only the destining into objectifying representation that makes the historical accessible as an object for historiography, i.e. for a science, and on this basis makes possible the current equating of the historical with that which is chronicled.[20]

One could find no better example of that *echt*-Heideggerian 'jargon of authenticity' whose effect is to obfuscate those very issues – of science, technology, historical understanding, the ethics (and the politics) of environmental concern – which it purports to address at a level of depth-ontological enquiry beyond the merely 'ontic' or 'factical'. Thus history in the authentic sense of that word should be thought of as proceeding from (or answering to) the summons of a destiny whose 'sending' may be heard – for those wise enough to hear – in the etymological link between *Geschick* and *Geschichte*. In so far as we persist in ignoring that summons (as for instance by seeking to ascertain the facts of history or consulting 'written chronicles') we thereby demonstrate our incapacity for 'thinking' at anything like the requisite depth. All the more so – presumably – if we carry this refusal to the point of contrasting Heidegger's *ersatz* mystique of origins, destiny, truth-as-unconcealment, etc. with the prime imperative to get things right as a matter of ethical and socio-historical justice. This merely shows that we are still in the grip of that 'objectifying' (representational) mode of thought that 'makes history accessible' (in Heidegger's words) 'as an object for historiography, i.e. for a science'. But if so, then this error is itself predestined and in no sense a matter of 'our' responsibility. For it belongs to the horizon (or the 'world-picture') of an epoch that has witnessed the withdrawal of Being and the giving-over of thought to the reign of metaphysics, of instrumental reason, and of modern science as the technocratic will-to-power in its latest – possibly terminal – phase.

All of which suggests that philosophers like Rouse should at least take pause before enlisting Heideggerian depth-hermeneutics, along with Foucault's Nietzschean genealogies of power-knowledge, as an alternative resource in thinking about present-day science and its discontents. In both cases there is a failure to conceive how ethical values could possibly be reconciled with cognitive or knowledge-constitutive interests. That is to say, what Foucault takes over uncritically from Heidegger is his notion of the subject – especially the Kantian transcendental subject – as a mere figment of the humanist imaginary, a point of intersection between (on the one hand) the order of objectifying representations and (on the other) a sphere of 'suprasensible' precepts, dictates and values which lies altogether outside and beyond the realm of phenomenal cognition. Hence Foucault's well-known description, in *The Order of Things*, of the insoluble antinomies to which this illusory conception supposedly gave rise. Thus Kant's chief bequest to the nineteenth-century natural, human, and social sciences was the idea of 'man' as a curious 'empirical-transcendental doublet', a hybrid creature whose existence was purely an artefact of this short-term (soon to be mended) rift in the fabric of discursive signs and representations.[21]

Foucault follows Heidegger very closely in his reading of Western metaphysics as the history of an error, one that issues most visibly in Kant and the aporetic 'discourse' of a project which strives to reconcile the claims of understanding and reason, epistemology and ethics, determinism and free will, phenomenal cognition and reflective judgement. For Heidegger it is manifest in that entire tradition of thought – from Plato to Husserl – whose history bears witness to the forgetfulness of Being and the retreat of thinking into a realm of merely 'ontic' (as opposed to depth-ontological) concern.[22] This tradition had substituted notions of a truth-as-correspondence (*homoiosis*, etc.) and of the knowing subject as its privileged locus for that originary wisdom whose truth is obscurely to be glimpsed in the pre-Socratics. For Foucault it is less a matter of some long-lost primordial truth than of the sheer contingency – the range of always shifting discursive or epistemic formations – that come to light through an applied archaeology of 'knowledge' in its manifold guises to date. But in one crucial respect – as Foucault acknowledged – his thinking was deeply and lastingly indebted to Heidegger. This had to do with Heidegger's questing-back into the history of the root 'metaphysical' illusion, which opened up the cleft between subject and object, or which conceived of truth on the order of an adequate correspondence between ideas (or accurate representations) and the various real-world objects, entities, or events to which those ideas had reference.

In Heidegger's account this notion takes hold with the passage of a metaphor from the Greek *hypokeimenon* ('substance'; 'foundation'; 'that which supports from beneath') to the Latin *subiectum* and thence – via Descartes – to the range of modern post-Kantian variants on the mind as a more-or-less clear or distorting mirror held up to reality. At which point the way appeared open for Foucault to dissolve this entire problematics of language, truth, and representation into a field of open-ended discursive possibility where subject and object are likewise conceived as products of a specular (imaginary) 'fold' in the fabric or representation. To thinkers of a more pragmatic mind Heidegger has likewise seemed to offer a welcome escape-route from the travails of old-style epistemological (and new-style analytic) thought. Thus all one need do, according to Rorty, is play down Heidegger's portentous jargon of 'Being', 'ontological difference', 'Western metaphysics' and so forth, and interpret him as headed toward the sensible pragmatist conclusion that truth is pretty much what we make of it at this or that stage in the ongoing cultural conversation. From which it follows that the truth-claims of the natural as well as of the human and social sciences are best regarded as so many language-games, discourses, 'final vocabularies' or elective metaphors, adopted for no better (and for no worse) reason than their happening to fit with the current self-images of the age.

Thus analytic philosophy has beaten a rapid and somewhat dishevelled retreat from its early (verificationist) idea of truth as consisting in a one-to-one match between truthful propositions and observationally-warranted states of affairs. In so doing it has espoused a whole range of contextualist strategies, among them – most notably – the Wittgensteinian appeal to 'language-games' or cultural 'forms of life'; Quine's idea of truth as a predicate capable of redistribution in as many ways as there exist alternative ontologies or conceptual schemes; and various forms of so-called 'internal realism' (like Hilary Putnam's latest candidate) which seek to head off the more disabling consequences of a full-fledged relativist approach but which still define truth as immanent – or relative – to this or that particular context of enquiry.[23] What these arguments all have in common is their assumption that philosophy of science has to do with the linguistic structures (whether sentences, statements, propositions, Rortian 'vocabularies', or entire 'fabrics' of belief) which alone make it possible to analyse the various orders of scientific truth-claim. In other words they all adopt some version of Carnap's doctrine of 'semantic ascent', i.e. the idea that philosophy (as a formal, second-order or 'meta-linguistic' mode of analysis) should concern itself *not* with questions of *de re* truth or causal explanation but with questions in the realm of meaning, logic, and strictly *de dicto* necessity. And this despite what has mostly been perceived – by Quine, Davidson, Putnam and others – as the collapse of Carnap's logical-empiricist programme and the hopelessness of any such attempt to devise a formal metalanguage for the analysis of empirical (first-order) statements of scientific truth.[24] All that is left, it then appears, is a Tarskian semantic or formalized conception of truth whose function is exhausted – or which cancels right through – when applied to every sentence of the canonical form: '"Snow is white" is true if and only if snow is white.'

So one can see why recent commentators (Rouse and Malpas among them) should argue that there must be *something more* to scientific truth – more substantive, interesting, or profound – than is anywhere allowed for on the Tarskian account.[25] Davidson expresses a similar conviction in his 1990 series of lectures on 'The Structure and Content of Truth'. 'My own view', he writes, 'is that Tarski has told us much of what we want to know about the concept of truth, and that there must be more. There must be more because there is no indication in Tarski's formal work of what it is that his various truth predicates have in common, and this must be part of the content of the concept.'[26] But if this sounds promising then it has to be said that Davidson's lectures don't live up to their promise. In fact, like so much of his work, they simply veer across at a certain point from acknowledging the problem – the apparent vacuity of Tarski's semantic formula – to proposing a 'solution' that consists in little more than the unreconstructed empiricist idea that what makes our sentences true or false is the pattern of sensory stimuli that impinge upon our nerve-ends from time to time and thus (supposedly) decide the issue quite apart from all talk of paradigms, languages, theoretical frameworks, 'conceptual schemes' or whatever. It is the same sort of strategy – a fallback to 'commonsense' empiricism as a counter to their own more sceptical arguments – that one finds in certain passages of Quine's 'Two Dogmas' and in Thomas Kuhn's attempt to placate his critics on the issue of paradigm-incommensurability.[27] Its *locus classicus* is the closing sentence of Davidson's essay 'On the Very Idea of a Conceptual Scheme': 'In giving up the dualism of scheme and world,' he writes, 'we do not give up the world, but re-establish unmediated touch with the familiar objects whose antics make our sentences and opinions true and false.'[28] One need not be a card-carrying Hegelian to detect in this passage what Hegel diagnosed as the hallmarks of naive sense-certainty; all the more so given its occurrence at the close of an essay which has gone some lengthy and elaborate ways around to address precisely the issues that are here brushed aside with such breezy assurance.

So there would seem good reason to suppose that the 'something more' is not to be had by recourse either to a formalized semantic conception of truth in the Tarskian mode nor again – at the opposite extreme – to a radical empiricism adopted in default of more adequate conceptual resources. At this point, as Rouse and Malpas would argue, the only way forward is to seek some alternative conception of truth that doesn't reduce to mere tautology on the one hand or, on the other, to Davidson's kind of bluff no-nonsense empiricism. What is required is a Heideggerian (or depth-ontological) approach that preserves the basic structure of Tarski's theory – that is to say, its purely formal system of notation for capturing the intuitive idea of truth across each and every sentence held true in a given language – while at the same time introducing a new dimension of truth as 'unconcealment', *aletheia*, 'opening', 'horizontal preunderstanding', etc. For Malpas, indeed, this is the realization toward which – did they but know it – Davidson, Quine, Putnam, Kuhn, Rorty and company have long been travelling. Just as Rorty sees Deweyan pragmatism at the end of every philosophical road (including Heidegger's, once shorn of its grandiose ontological pretensions) so Malpas sees Heidegger as the one philosopher to have worked his way through and beyond the vexing antinomies of present-day analytic thought.

Of course Malpas has to recognize the deep resistance that such an argument is likely to encounter. After all, '[s]o radical is this shift that we may well wonder why we should use the term "truth" to refer to this fundamental opening'. And again: '[w]hy call this opening, this unconcealing/concealing, truth? Why should we even pay attention to such opening?'[29] Especially – one might add – since Heidegger has so long been held up by philosophers in the 'other' (analytic) tradition as a cautionary instance of what goes wrong when thinking is seduced by the fake profundities of a language that trades upon obscurantist rhetoric and an *ersatz* jargon of authenticity.[30] Malpas, however, is undeterred by the odds stacked against him in making this argument. Had the objectors come up with anything more useful or substantive in the way of 'truth' then their criticisms might have carried some weight. As it is he finds nothing bar a fixed aversion to Heidegger's style and a range of place-filler substitutes – Tarski's included – which satisfy only the barest requirements for a formal theory.

Hence, he argues, the signal importance of Davidson's work as an enterprise that presses all the way with this current 'post-analytic' trend in philosophy of mind and language. What Davidson brings out is the sheer *impossibility* of giving any genuine (i.e. non-trivial or informative) content to the idea of truth so long as one remains within the terms laid down for such debate by the tradition that runs from logical empiricism to its various latterday offshoots. For if these schools of thought have one thing in common it is their failure to produce any viable alternative to the logical-empiricist dichotomy between first-order 'facts', observation-statements, or matters of empirical warrant and the second-order logic of scientific or philosophical enquiry. Where they differ is on the question as to whether such a programme can be carried through with success. Thus the holists and pragmatists concur in thinking that this project was foredoomed to failure since it rested on a number of untenable assumptions – like the two last 'dogmas' of Quine's essay or (in Davidson's variant) the 'very idea of a conceptual scheme' – which collapsed under sceptical scrutiny. But the first and most crucial stage in this chapter of developments was that whereby philosophy took the turn toward a formalized language where issues of material (*de re*) causal or explanatory truth were supplanted by issues of metalinguistic (*de dicto*) veridical warrant. For the way was then open to other, more thoroughgoing versions of the 'linguistic turn' which relativized truth no longer to particular sentences, statements, or propositions, but rather to the entire existing 'web' or 'fabric' of beliefs held true at some given time.[31] At which point the Heideggerians can claim that such conceptions of truth are manifestly either circular, redundant, or trivial, and that only a depth-ontological approach can save thinking from this dead-end predicament.

III

It may be felt that I have skewed the issues here by taking just a few of Heidegger's more questionable statements and presenting them as typical or symptomatic instances of a much wider trend in present-day 'post-analytic' philosophy. After all, there would appear to be little enough in common between (on the one hand) Heidegger's notorious remarks about the death-camps, technology, and 'Western metaphysics' and (on the other) the genial suggestion by various pragmatically minded liberal thinkers that philosophy should henceforth take its place as just one language-game or cultural life-form among others, those others including science – or technology – once shorn of its domineering will-to-truth and restored to a decently scaled-down sense of its role in the ongoing cultural conversation. Nevertheless it seems to me that there remain some worrying implications about this current desire to demote science – along with philosophy of science and epistemology – to the point where it possesses no greater claim to truth than the language-games of, say, religion or literary criticism. Where the confusion comes in, I have argued, is with the idea that *any* conception of science as aimed toward a better, more adequate understanding of real-world objects, processes, or events must *always and inevitably* carry along with it a doctrine of absolute 'cognitive privilege', or a technocratic drive to exclude or devalue ethical, social, and political concerns.

This idea takes various forms according to its various inter-disciplinary contexts and sources. It finds expression in the 'strong' sociology of knowledge, an approach that avowedly collapses all distinctions between context of discovery and context of justification; in Lyotard's notion of a postmodern science given over to 'performative' rather than 'constative' criteria of suasive efficacy; in Paul Feyerabend's kindred ('anarchist') idea that we should lift all constraints of method, consistency, and truth, thus allowing a thousand speculative flowers to bloom and deciding between them on purely social and ethical grounds; in Rorty's neopragmatist view that science *just is* whatever counts as such by the lights of some given cultural community with its own preferred metaphors, language-games, narratives of scientific 'progress', etc.; in Wittgensteinian resorts to language and social context as the furthest one can get by way of justifying scientific or other orders of truth-claim; and lastly, in the Heideggerian (depth-hermeneutical) appeal to a dimension of truth as concealment-revelation whose import precedes all mere determinations of 'ontic' or 'factical' concern.[32] To which might be added the more moderate or circumspect anti-realist contentions of philosophers such as Michael Dummett and the arguments of a 'constructive empiricist' like Bas van Fraassen who sees no reason to adduce 'laws of nature', intrinsic properties, causal dispositions or other such extravagant hypotheses when we can get by just as well on the modest assumption that scientific theories are justified solely by their pragmatic, instrumental, or predictive yield.[33]

Roy Bhaskar has pursued some of the consequences of such thinking in his book *Philosophy and the Idea of Freedom,* most of which is taken up with a critique of Rorty's neopragmatist position.[34] His argument – in brief – is that Rortian talk of creative 'redescription' is misleading when applied to epistemology or philosophy of science in so far as those disciplines cannot be construed as creating or inventing the various objects that constitute their proper ontological domain. To adopt this extreme anti-realist line is to invite all manner of antinomies, paradoxes, or aporias when it comes to explaining how science could possibly afford us knowledge of the world, or again, how we could ever have reason – cultural–linguistic preference aside – for counting certain theories more adequate (better borne out by argument or evidence) than others of notionally similar scope. Indeed there is something decidedly myopic about Rorty's idea of freedom, construed as it is in such wholesale world-transformative terms as to leave no room for any irksome constraints upon the human will to redescribe 'reality' in response to an ever-shifting range of interests, values, or desires. For there can then be no accounting – no making due allowance – for those various factors of a physical, causal, environmental, or psychological nature that do place limits – whether we like it or not – on our freedom to refashion ourselves and the world in whatever way we choose.

Moreover, as Bhaskar remarks, this idea goes along with a way of drawing the line between 'private' and 'public' spheres such that strong-willed individuals are free to pursue their own projects of inventive self-fashioning just so long as they don't lay claim to authority in the wider (ethical or socio-political) domain. This may be wise counsel if applied to thinkers – such as Nietzsche or Foucault – whose values or ideas of autonomous selfhood are indeed far removed from any viable conception of the wider public good. However it is a doctrine that leaves little room for the exercise of judgement and moral responsibility in matters of shared concern. Thus it speaks hardly at all to those issues of social, political, and ethical conscience – environmental issues among them – that involve something more than the (notional) freedom to pursue one's idea of the life well lived in accordance with private–individual aims and inclinations. For this is to redefine the concept of 'autonomy' in much the same way – and with much the same drastic narrowing of scope – as affects the concept of 'liberalism' when used by proponents of free-market doctrine or by advocates of reduced welfare provision in the name of private enterprise. Or again – more to the point in this context – it goes along readily with versions of that argument which uphold the full liberty of persons to protest what they regard as bad (antisocial or destructive) techno-scientific developments while treating such protest as strictly a matter of individual conscience and hence as irrelevant to policy decisions arrived at with a view to maximizing profit. In each case there is a severance between private and public spheres which leaves people free to follow their conscience – or engage in the process of creative self-fashioning – just provided they do it, in Rorty's phrase, 'on their own time' and without any claim to moralize or legislate in matters of collective concern.[35] For the rest, such issues are much better dealt with by those – the social, ethical, and political theorists – whose discourse belongs to the public sphere (to the realm of *Wertfrei* adjudicative reason) and should therefore properly find no place for the voice of individual conscience or the expression of personal values.

Of course there is a large current literature on the antinomies of 'liberal' theory, thus construed, and its failure to acknowledge the complex relationship between those various value-spheres that Rorty so blithely puts asunder.[36] However my main concern here is not so much with debates in present-day social and political theory as with their bearing on questions in philosophy of science, and more specifically, the questions that science raises with regard to the scope and limits of human freedom. For on the Rortian (strong-descriptivist) view, the best way to maximize that scope and to minimize those limits is to treat science as just another language-game or cultural life-form, one that is always open to change or revision in keeping with the current self-images and values of the time. Such – he would persuade us – is the benefit to be had by removing science's false prestige as an 'objective', 'constructive', 'progressive', or truth-oriented discourse and henceforth treating its deliverances as strictly on a par with those of the poets, novelists, philosophers, and anyone else with a voice in the ongoing cultural conversation. Moreover, Rorty can call upon a wide range of sources – hermeneutics, narrative pragmatics, postmodernism, poststructuralism, post-Quinean talk of ontological relativity, post-Kuhnian philosophy of science, the 'strong' programme in sociology of knowledge – to support this view of scientific 'truth' as whatever best suits our current descriptive or socio-cultural purposes. For if the world and all its contents are pretty much what we make of them according to this or that preferential language-game or elective 'final vocabulary', then of course there can be no restriction on our freedom to reinvent the world (and ourselves along with it) from one paradigm to the next. Certainly there is nothing 'in the nature of things' – no real-world factual, circumstantial, or causal constraints – that could offer a check to these endless possibilities of creative redescription. To think that there might be is for Rorty just a sign that we have not yet broken with the delusory idea of science as a process of *discovering* those truths about the world that make our statements or theories true or false. Much better, he thinks, to view it as a process of *inventing* new languages – paradigms, images, 'metaphors we can live by' – whereby to provide as many novel perspectives on 'truth' as there may be social or cultural opportunities for changing the current topics of conversation.

Nothing could more clearly illustrate the point that I have been making with regard to the implications of anti-realism in epistemology and philosophy of science. The Heideggerian (depth-hermeneutic) variant is no doubt the most drastic in its claim upon our thinking about issues of truth, knowledge, responsibility, and freedom. But there are also great problems with Rorty's more laid-back neopragmatist version if one asks what sense can possibly be made – in ethical and political as well as in epistemological terms – of a freedom whose limits in the matter of inventive redescription are set only by the limits of our current imagining or our choice among various (more or less novel) metaphors, language-games, etc. Such 'freedom' is entirely nugatory – the merest of wishful fantasies – if it takes no account of the real-world conditions, both restrictive and potentially enabling, which bear upon the human quest for knowledge and truth. In Harry Frankfurt's words, '[t]here must be limits to our freedom if we are to have sufficient personal reality to exercise genuine autonomy at all. What has no boundaries has no shape.'[37] And again, in a passage from his aptly-titled essay 'On Bullshit' which will bear quoting at length:

> '[A]nti-realist' doctrines undermine confidence in the value of disinterested efforts to determine what is true and what is false, and even in the intelligibility of the notion of objective inquiry. One response to this loss of confidence has been a retreat from the discipline required by dedication to the ideal of *correctness* to a quite different sort of discipline, which is imposed by pursuit of an alternative ideal of *sincerity*. . . . Convinced that reality has no inherent nature, which he might hope to identify as the truth about things, he [the anti-realist] devotes himself to being true to his own nature.[38]

However, as Frankfurt remarks, there is something very odd – not to say 'preposterous' – about the notion that a self might be known for what it is (known in its authentic selfhood) more reliably than any knowledge to be had of real-world objects and events. Certainly Kant was under no such illusion, as witness those passages in the first *Critique* that tie the conditions for coherent first-person identity (the 'transcendental unity of apperception') to the conditions obtaining for our knowledge and experience of events in the spatio-temporal domain.[39]

Of course Kant was careful – and indeed went some long and tortuous ways around – to distinguish this order of subjectivity from any notion of the subject empirically or psychologically construed, that is to say, any attempt to derive substantive knowledge of the self from an argument in the purely transcendental (or 'conditions of possibility') mode. Only by maintaining this distinction, he thought, could philosophy be saved from the kinds of dilemma – the failure to connect sensuous or phenomenal cognitions with the concepts and categories of understanding – which had confronted empiricists like Hume on the one hand and rationalists like Descartes and Leibniz on the other. It is debatable whether Kant succeeded in his aim of reconciling transcendental idealism with empirical realism. However, his argument is surely valid to this extent at least: that we can make no sense of an idea of the subject (the knowing, willing, or judging subject) whose 'world' would be entirely a construction out of its own sense-data, language-games, final vocabulary, conceptual scheme, or whatever.

For such a sovereign disposer would encounter no resistance – no check upon its world-creating powers – from anything beyond or outside the domain of its own internal representations. It could therefore achieve no grasp of the distinction between waking and dreaming states, or again, between veridical (undistorted) perceptions and those brought about by various forms of perceptual illusion. Nor could the subject, thus conceived, be in any position to explain – in its own case or that of others – just how (through what kinds of causally explicable process) such illusions typically take rise.

This is indeed the main problem with strong anti-realist or descriptivist theories such as Rorty's: that in counting 'reality' a world well lost for the sake of inventive or imaginative self-creation they effectively dissolve any notion of the self to which that process could refer or apply. This is why, as Frankfurt says, there must be 'limits to our freedom if we are to have sufficient personal reality to exercise genuine autonomy at all'. And this 'personal reality' cannot be achieved without a sufficiently well-developed sense of that other (objective and mind-independent) reality that may always resist our best efforts of creative redescription. For there is otherwise nothing that can halt the drift toward, on the one hand, a wholesale anti-realism devoid of epistemic content, and on the other a kind of transcendental solipsism that views both the subject and its ambient world as just what we make of them according to this or that fictive or imaginary projection.

Notes

1. Michel Foucault, *The Order of Things: An Archaeology of the Human Sciences* (London: Tavistock, 1973); also *The Archaeology of Knowledge*, trans. A. M. Sheridan Smith (London: Tavistock, 1972).
2. W.V.Quine, 'Two Dogmas of Empiricism', in *From a Logical Point of View*, 2nd edn (Cambridge, MA: Harvard University Press, 1961); also *Ontological Relativity and Other Essays* (New York: Columbia University Press, 1969).
3. See Richard Rorty, *Objectivity, Relativism and Truth* (Cambridge University Press, 1991), *Essays on Heidegger and Others* (Cambridge University Press, 1991), and *Consequences of Pragmatism* (Brighton: Harvester, 1982).
4. Joseph Rouse, *Knowledge and Power* (Ithaca, NY: Cornell University Press, 1987) 160.
5. See Alfred Tarski, 'The Concept of Truth in Formalized Languages',

in *Logic, Semantics and Metamathematics*, trans. J. H. Woodger (London: Oxford University Press, 1956) 281–300.
6. Joseph Rouse, *Knowledge and Power*, 161.
7. Ibid., 161.
8. Ibid., 161.
9. See Hans-Georg Gadamer, *Truth and Method*, trans. W. Geln-Doepel, ed. John Cumming and Garrett Barden (London: Sheed & Ward, 1979) and David C. Hoy, *The Critical Circle: Literature and History in Contemporary Hermeneutics* (Berkeley and Los Angeles: University of California Press, 1978).
10. Ibid., 162.
11. Martin Heidegger, *What is a Thing?*, trans. W. B. Barton and V. Deutsch (South Bend: Gateway, 1967).
12. Martin Heidegger, *The Question Concerning Technology and Other Essays*, trans. and with an Introduction by William Lovitt (New York: Harper and Row, 1977) 3–35 (6).
13. Ibid., 25–6.
14. Ibid., 26.
15. Ibid., 15.
16. Ibid., 28.
17. Ibid., 28.
18. See Tom Rockmore, *On Heidegger's Nazism and Philosophy* (London: Harvester-Wheatsheaf, 1992); also Günther Neske and Emil Kettering, eds, *Martin Heidegger and National Socialism: Questions and Answers*, trans. L. Harries and J. Neugroschel (New York: Paragon House, 1990); Alan Rosenberg and Alan Milchman, *Martin Heidegger and the Holocaust* (Atlantic Highlands, NJ: Humanities Press, 1994); Richard Wolin, *The Politics of Being: The Political Thought of Martin Heidegger* (New York: Columbia University Press, 1990); Richard Wolin, ed., *The Heidegger Controversy: A Critical Reader* (Cambridge, MA: MIT Press, 1993).
19. Martin Heidegger, *The Question Concerning Technology*, 324.
20. Ibid., 329.
21. Michel Foucault, *The Order of Things*.
22. Martin Heidegger, *Being and Time*, trans. John Macquarrie and Edward Robinson (Oxford: Blackwell, 1962).
23. See W. V. Quine, *From a Logical Point of View* (op. cit.), *Word and Object* (Cambridge, Mass.: MIT Press, 1960), and *Theories and Things* (New Haven: Harvard University Press, 1981); Ludwig Wittgenstein, *Philosophical Investigations*, trans. G. E. M. Anscombe (Oxford: Basil Blackwell, 1976); and also Hilary Putnam, *Representation and Reality* (Cambridge University Press, 1988) and *Realism with a Human Face* (Cambridge, MA: Harvard University Press, 1990).
24. See Tarski, 'The Concept of Truth in Formalized Languages'; Rudolf Carnap, *The Logical Structure of the World* (London: Routledge and Kegan Paul, 1937); and Carl G. Hempel, *Fundamentals of Concept Formation in Empirical Science* (University of Chicago Press, 1972).
25. Joseph Rouse, *Knowledge and Power* and J. E. Malpas, *Donald Davidson and the Mirror of Meaning* (Cambridge University Press, 1992).

26. Donald Davidson, 'The Structure and Content of Truth', *Journal of Philosophy*, Vol. 87 (1990) 279–328 (284).
27. Quine, 'Two Dogmas of Empiricism' (op. cit.) and Thomas S. Kuhn, 'Postscript – 1969', in *The Structure of Scientific Revolutions*, 2nd edn (University of Chicago Press, 1970).
28. Donald Davidson, 'On the Very Idea of a Conceptual Scheme', in *Inquiries into Truth and Interpretation* (Oxford: Clarendon Press, 1984) 269–70.
29. Malpas, *Donald Davidson and the Mirror of Meaning*, 269–70.
30. See for instance Rudolf Carnap, 'The Elimination of Metaphysics through Logical Analysis of Language', in A. J. Ayer, ed., *Logical Positivism* (New York: Free Press, 1959) 60–81.
31. For a critical survey of the field, see Jerry Fodor and Ernest LePore, *Holism: A Shopper's Guide* (Oxford: Blackwell, 1991).
32. See Jean-François Lyotard, *The Postmodern Condition: A Report on Knowledge*, trans. Geoff Bennington and Brian Massumi (Manchester University Press, 1984); Paul K. Feyerabend, *Against Method* (London: New Left Books, 1975); Richard Rorty, *Essays on Heidegger and Others* (op. cit.); Hubert L. Dreyfus, *Being-in-the-World: A Commentary on Heidegger's Being and Time, Division One* (Cambridge, Mass.: MIT Press, 1991), Stephen Mulhall, *On Being in the World: Wittgenstein and Heidegger on Seeing Aspects* (London: Routledge, 1990), Mark Okrent, *Heidegger's Pragmatism: Understanding, Being and the Critique of Metaphysics* (Ithaca, NY: Cornell University Press, 1988); and see also entries under Note 6 above.
33. See Michael Dummett, *Truth and Other Enigmas* (London: Duckworth, 1978) and Bas van Frassen, *The Scientific Image* (Oxford: Clarendon Press, 1980); also Michael Luntley, *Language, Logic and Experience: The Case for Anti-Realism* (London: Duckworth, 1988) and Crispin Wright, *Realism, Meaning and Truth* (Oxford: Blackwell, 1987).
34. Roy Bhaskar, *Philosophy and the Idea of Freedom* (Oxford: Blackwell, 1991).
35. See Richard Rorty, *Contingency, Irony, and Solidarity* (Cambridge University Press, 1989) and *Objectivity, Relativism, and Truth* (Cambridge University Press, 1991).
36. See for instance Michael J. Sandel, *Liberalism and its Critics* (Oxford: Blackwell, 1984); Michael Walzer, *Liberalism and the Limits of Justice* (Cambridge University Press, 1982) and *Spheres of Justice* (Oxford: Blackwell, 1983).
37. Harry G. Frankfurt, 'On Bullshit', in *The Importance of What We Care About: Philosophical Essays* (Cambridge University Press, 1988) 117–33.
38. Ibid., 133.
39. Immanuel Kant, *Critique of Pure Reason*, trans. N. Kemp Smith (London: Macmillan, 1933).

4

Flaws: James, Nussbaum, Miller, Levinas

Robert Eaglestone

I THREE WAYS OF READING

> The whole conduct of life consists in things done, which do other things in their turn, just so our behaviour and its fruits are essentially one and continuous and persistent and unquenchable, so the act has its way of abiding and showing and testifying, and so, among our innumerable acts are no arbitrary, senseless separations. – Henry James[1]

How are we to read 'ethically'? How, if at all, do literary texts 'show' or 'testify' to ethics, to the 'whole conduct of life'? In the fragmentary text of *The Writing of the Disaster*, Maurice Blanchot describes three different ways of reading:

> There is an active, productive way of reading which produces text and reader and thus transports us. There is a passive kind of reading which betrays the text while appearing to submit to it, by giving the illusion that the text exists objectively, fully, sovereignly: as one whole. Finally, there is the reading that is no longer passive, but is passivity's reading. It is without pleasure, without joy; it escapes both comprehension and desire. It is like the nocturnal vigil, that 'inspiring' insomnia when, all having been said, 'Saying' is heard, and the testimony of the last witness is pronounced.[2]

My exploration of the relationship between ethics and literature can be understood as no more than a gloss on this description of the experience of reading. Even reading the same text, in this case

James's last novel, *The Golden Bowl*, these three different ways of reading result in very different ethical understandings of the literary work. Moreover, it is possible to suggest that the first and second ways of reading that Blanchot outlines are, in fact, dependent on the third: that what we get from literature in relation to ethics is what Blanchot, following Levinas, names the 'Saying', the testimony of the last witness.

II NUSSBAUM: BEING TRANSPORTED BY LITERATURE

> As Aristotle observed, [literature] is deep and conducive to our inquiry about how to live because it does not simply (as history does) record that this or that event happened; it searches for patterns of possibility – of choice and circumstance, and the interaction between choice and circumstance – that turn up in human lives with such a persistence that they must be regarded as *our* possibilities. – Martha Nussbaum[3]

The first, active way of reading, and the ethical understanding of literature it evokes, is perhaps best paradigmatically exemplified by the neo-Aristotelian philosopher Martha Nussbaum. For Nussbaum, literature 'speaks about us'[4] and her way of reading is concerned with transforming the words on the page into a real situation, which transports us to a world of difficult choices and moral dilemmas. Each novel or play offers us an active heuristic working through of ethical issues, a virtual simulation of different moral and ethical problems. Literature, for Nussbaum, is a vital tool to improve the perceptiveness of our ethical inquiry. 'A novel', she writes, 'just because it is not our life, places us in a moral position that is favourable for perception and it shows us what it would be like to take up that position in life.'[5] For Nussbaum, the characters, with whom the readers actively identify, act out difficult and messy problems in moral philosophy in a profounder way than any book of dry philosophical problems ever could.

Nussbaum's readings of *The Golden Bowl* make both the benefits and problems of this approach particularly clear. *The Golden Bowl*, for Nussbaum, shows 'a human being's relation to value in the world to be, fundamentally and of contingent necessity, one of imperfect fidelity and therefore of guilt'.[6] Maggie, who Nussbaum takes to be the central character, aims at harmony and moral perfection. She learns, however, that it is impossible to combine this 'extreme emphasis on flawless living'[7] with the conflicting relationships between her husband, her father and her friend and stepmother Charlotte. Nussbaum argues that Maggie, and we the readers, reach ethical adulthood by her resolution to act, which shatters the harmony of the group and involves difficult moral choices.

There seem to be two sorts of problems with Nussbaum's reading. The first is that, simply, she offers a poor reading of the text. That Maggie is in pursuit of moral purity, for example, Nussbaum takes verbatim from the lips of Fanny Assingham.[8] Fanny Assingham, amongst other things, lies throughout the novel, breaks the symbolic golden bowl to cover up her deceptions,[9] admits that she is no more than a high class pander,[10] and anyway has probably only become involved out of her desire to win a victory in her never-ending war of words with her husband. She is not in any way an objective or neutral observer, and what she says simply cannot be taken at face value. Instead of being in pursuit of moral purity, Maggie can equally well, and on her own admission, be seen as selfish and acquisitive.[11] There are a number of such examples of overdetermination in Nussbaum's analyses. However, this in itself does not discredit her philosophical approach. What does cause problems for it are, however, a number of deep and unquestioned assumptions about the nature and purpose of reading itself.

For literature to work as part of moral inquiry as she sees it, Nussbaum has unproblematically to assume that a text is not a linguistic artifact but a surface behind which there are real situations and real events. This approach means that, for example, although the 'events' of a novel can be interpreted, the representation of the events – in effect the material of the novel itself – cannot. The medium, the words which make up the novel, become invisible. This blinds Nussbaum to anything but a very determinate reading of this indeterminate novel. In addition, in order to achieve the heuristic working through of moral problems, she assumes that there must be a gestalt-type identification with literary characters. 'How would I behave if I was her?' seems to be the key question for Nussbaum. She argues that throughout *The Golden Bowl* we identify fully with Maggie, and see the world through 'her intelligent eyes'.[12] In fact, the novel makes use of a number of shifting viewpoints: even in the second half – Maggie's half of the novel

– the viewpoint is not limited to Maggie. Gore Vidal, in his introduction to the Penguin Edition, writes that he identifies with Amerigo, not Maggie, and finds him the 'most sympathetic' character.[13] Moreover, in his reply to Nussbaum's essay, Richard Wollheim argues that 'specific patterns of changing viewpoints, of shifting identifications are not just contingent but are essential features of novels'.[14] Nussbaum also relies on the idea that a novel evokes only an 'emotional response', contrasting this, perhaps over simplistically, with the 'cold intellectual intelligence' of philosophy. Nussbaum claims not to interpret the novel – the moral adventures of *The Golden Bowl* are simply there, for everyone to see, through the window of the text. Her interpretation is not, for her, an interpretation.

The results of her sort of interpretation are also open to question. In her account, literature nurtures a communal identity: great works 'are moral achievements on behalf of the community',[15] their aims are 'ultimately defined in terms of a "we", of people who wish to live together and share a conception of virtue'.[16] In *The Dialogic Imagination*, Bakhtin discusses Aristotelian poetics, of the sort for which Nussbaum is arguing, and defines it as 'monoglossic', contending that it 'give[s] expression to...centripetal forces in socio-linguistic and ideological life'.[17] That is, it represents an approach to language and literature that aims to create a strong notion of homogenous shared communal identity which overrides individual or cultural differences in the construction of a 'we'. Bakhtin goes on to argue that this monoglossic understanding of language and the novel leads to enslavement and control, and that the novel and a free society are both based on shifting viewpoints expressed by different language uses. In this light, the ethical good of the construction of a 'we', of a communal identity, may be open to question. Many post-colonial thinkers, for example, have echoed Fanon's remarks on the 'European game'[18] which overcodes local shifting identities with a European monolithic universalizing 'we', and brings only suffering and murder. It may be that in a post-modern, post-colonial world, a 'we' may be both actually impossible and ethically undesirable.

In short, Nussbaum has reduced *The Golden Bowl*, and the other texts she examines, into highly complex examples for her active, neo-Aristotelian approach to moral philosophy. She has, in effect, removed the literary from literature.

III MILLER: SUBMITTING TO LITERATURE

> [L]iterature is not a transparent message in which it can be taken for granted that the distinction between the message and the means of communication is clearly established.... [M]ore problematically...the grammatical decoding of a text leaves a residue of indetermination that has to be, but cannot be, resolved by grammatical means, however extensively conceived. – Paul de Man[19]

In contrast to this active sort of reading that 'pushes through the text' is what Blanchot describes as the 'passive kind of reading which betrays the text while appearing to submit to it'. To continue the 'window' analogy, these sort of readers argue, in Derrida's words, that it is necessary to 'take into account the process of vitrification and not discount the "production" of the glass.... The glass must be read as a text.'[20] Indeed, in the paradigmatic case of J. Hillis Miller – much influenced by Paul de Man – this warning or injunction becomes an ethical imperative. In *The Ethics of Reading*, Miller makes it clear that one cannot and should not draw ethical conclusions in the way that Nussbaum does.

Instead, Miller argues that we are forced to respond to the text alone. In relation to *The Golden Bowl*, he writes that 'I want to make James' text my law. I want to follow what he says with entire fidelity and obedience.'[21] Miller wants to submit to the text, to follow it passively. This submission, though, as Blanchot suggests, is really a betrayal. Miller is aware that, however he approaches or reads this text, he will only be able to offer a misreading. The reader must respond – *read* – a text, but at the same time, any reading will betray a text – there can be no 'true' interpretation. By focusing on the act of reading, Miller has taken *The Golden Bowl* away from a discussion of its ethical concerns and into a debate over its meaning. Miller's claim is that, in reading, we respond to 'a linguistic necessity',[22] the necessity to read and thus to misread. We cannot have an 'ontological'[23] ethical response, in the way Nussbaum suggests, because it would never be clear that we were responding to anything but our own misreading of the text. Our response is due to how we have chosen to misunderstand the 'glass', just as each of the characters misunderstands the significance of the golden bowl.

Miller's New Criticism version of the ethics of deconstruction – the ethics of reading as he calls it – is not flawed in itself. Indeed, the claims it makes are so small that a flaw would hardly be possible. Rather, it seems simply to be unsatisfactory in two ways. First, its conception of ethics is so 'thin' as to be almost meaningless. Harpham argues that Miller understands ethics as Kantian ethics:[24] in fact, Miller's position is even more constricted. Miller only understands ethics as a set of textual rules, commandments or laws, and Kant's categorical imperative fits this understanding (suspiciously) well. This understanding of ethics as textual, written rules, means that Miller can deconstruct the ethical just as he might a novel or poem. Moreover, this New Critical deconstruction of the interpretation of a textual commandment frees Miller from any historical or political context in relation to ethics. As Critchley points out, Miller's ethics seem to be limited to the reading of books in the context of a North American university.[25] Miller has sacrificed ethics in the name of what Norris calls a 'highly sophisticated practice of reading, one that obeys the deconstructionist imperative to take nothing on trust and attend always to the letter of the text'.[26]

The second problem is that Miller's reading just does not seem to come to terms with Blanchot's third, uneasy sense of reading. The conclusion to Miller's analysis of *The Golden Bowl* is simply to argue that the 'text gives only itself. It hides its matter as much as it reveals it.'[27] We certainly are made aware of this by James's novel, but the text also leads us somewhere else. The text, for Miller, may be 'objective', 'sovereign' and 'full', but it also opens up and leads us to a world elsewhere. It seems to overflow: it is neither seized nor comprehended, as Nussbaum argues, nor the object of an ever deferred desire, as Miller suggests. Both these approaches are problematic. I want to suggest that the difficulties of understanding how ethics appears in a literary text are best understood through Blanchot's third description of reading: 'that "inspiring" insomnia when, all having been said, "Saying" is heard'.

IV LEVINAS: 'SAYING' IN LITERATURE

> The caress of love, always the same, in the last accounting (for him that thinks in counting) is always different and overflows with exorbitance the songs, poems and admissions in which it is said in so many different ways and through so many themes, in which it is apparently forgotten. – Emmanuel Levinas[28]

'Saying' here is a term Blanchot takes from Levinas's second major work, *Otherwise than Being, or Beyond Essence*. As a result of a complex engagement with Derrida, centrally in Derrida's essay 'Violence and Metaphysics', Levinas reworked his understanding of the fundamental moment of ethical responsibility. In his earlier work, *Totality and Infinity*, this moment occurs when the one acknowledges the other face to face without mediation. However, after Derrida's 'Violence and Metaphysics', which deconstructs Levinas's trust in this unmeditated relation, Levinas revised his understanding. The aim of *Otherwise than Being* is to show 'how the ethical signifies in ontological language'[29] by offering something like an ethical phenomenological analysis of language itself.[30]

Language, Levinas suggests, is made up of the 'Saying' and the 'Said'. The 'Said' is the actual material fact of language: the 'Saying', in contrast, is the impulse which underlies it. The 'Said' is the very ordering of language. Parallel to Derrida's understanding of *Logos*, the 'Said' is a violence that is ineluctably necessary for the beginning of any system. It immobilizes language and, by fixing designation and essence, denies any sort of transcendence. The 'Saying', on the other hand, is a 'subversion of essence, it overflows the theme it states'.[31] The 'Saying' is an uncovering, a 'breaking up of inwardness'.[32] The 'Saying' is the moment of commitment to the other, a moment which exists only through language, only through the 'Said', which thus instantaneously betrays the transcendent 'Saying'. The 'Said' imposes a finitude and limit onto the other, a finitude which the 'Saying' simultaneously interrupts. Levinas's recurring metaphor for this paradox is a piece of thread with knots along its length.[33] The thread – the 'Said' – is interrupted with knots – the 'Saying'. These knots are dependent on the thread and yet are not the thread. The knots are moments of interruption – flaws – that disrupt the 'Said', just as the crack in the bowl disrupts the James novel.

Levinas argues that it is the task of philosophy to 'extract the otherwise than being from the said',[34] to draw awareness to the knots, the ethical 'Saying' entwined with the 'Said'. Philosophy's ethical task is to interrupt and destabilize the closure imposed, of necessity, in the world. It is, to use Derrida's phrase, to state and protect the 'liberty of the question', forever asked in the name of the other.[35]

Blanchot's third experience of reading, when, 'all having been said, "Saying" is heard', can be understood as a response to exactly this. Blanchot makes a divergence – which I have explored elsewhere – from Levinas's thought by broadening out this duty. It is no longer the task of philosophy in particular as Levinas argues, but the task of reading. Just prior to the aphorism with which I began, Blanchot cites a fragment of Levinas: '. . . to save a text from its book misfortune'.[36] The 'Saying' in literature is precisely that uncanny moment of saving a text from being lost in the 'Said' of a book. It is the moment when we are made to feel not at home with the text or in ourselves. We are neither transported to a nether world of virtual life, nor do we simply mouth our misinterpretation of the text. It is in these moments when our sense of our selves and our relation to the Logos is interrupted and put into question that the ethics of literature are at their clearest. These moments of fragmentation are a testimony to the irreducible otherness of the other and to our responsibility.

Levinas writes that the 'Saying' 'overflows with exorbitance the songs, poems and admissions in which it is said in so many different ways and through so many themes'.[37] The difficulty lies, of course, in pointing out these flaws in the 'Said' through critical practice. Each text requires reading in such a way that its 'Saying' can be heard, that the flaws in the 'Said' appear. In terms of *The Golden Bowl*, it is possible to suggest very tentatively that this occurs in at least two interlinked ways. Moreover, these sorts of ways correspond to, but interrupt, Blanchot's first and second responses to reading.

First, *The Golden Bowl* destabilizes the idea that literature 'transports us' into another world. The characters are simply not characters in a recognizable sense. Despite being portrayed as typical 'realist novel' characters – they talk, lean out of windows at crucial moments and so on – they are not. Just when they seem to have become settled, to be *heimlich*, they change. It is not simply a question of 'behaving out of character': the change interrupts the understanding of the character right from the beginning. There are moments when it becomes clear that, for example, Maggie, all the way through the novel, is both totally good and betrayed and at one and the same time totally selfish and manipulative. Unless one is capable of critical doublethink, this radical indeterminacy completely interrupts the novel, leaving any set and ordered interpretation simply impossible. Despite the text's simulated lure into Maggie's mind, the reader is faced with an aporia which flaws not just any one interpretation, but any interpretation. These moments seem to be where Maggie overflows the act of reading. The character remains irreducibly remote and other. Like an insomniac, we can toss and turn and still be unable to get any closer to a resolution.

The second sort of flaw or interruption, linked to this, occurs in those most notorious of Jamesian sentences that make even the most experienced critic ask 'what does it mean by this?'. There are, of course, a number of examples of this. Maggie views her father at one stage, and lists his qualities: these 'placed him in her eyes as no precious work of art probably had ever been placed in his own'.[38] Nussbaum offers a single interpretation of this and passes over the questions it raises: does it mean that no art work had probably been valued so high? Or that she sees him as probably different from any work of art altogether? On the final page the Prince says (or rather 'echoes') 'I see nothing but you'.[39] As happens so often in James, it is not just ambiguous whether this is positive or negative, but radically indeterminate, aporetic. This again flaws any attempt to interpret or to limit the novel. Something, but not something from another world, overflows through the words on the page.

It is these flaws that bring us back, time and time again, to a sense of unease and a sense of questioning, and to a sense of otherness and our experience of otherness. It is this sense of unease, this sense that it can never quite be encapsulated that seems to give literature its most significant appeal to the ethical. It is to this, in some profound way, that readings like Nussbaum's and Miller's respond, yet they try to encapsulate or delimit this unease. This unease is echoed by the bowl of James's title. The flawed bowl means something different to each character. Its meaning lies only in the way it seems to refuse a meaning. Yet, at the same time it cannot be without a meaning. The bowl shatters the fixed arrangement of the characters in *The Golden Bowl*, just as a work of literature, read in this third way, shatters the assumptions and presuppositions of the 'Said'.

Blanchot wrote that 'philosophy, which puts everything into question, is tripped up by poetry, which is the question that eludes it'.[40] This tripping up, however it happens, this putting into question, this ceaseless inspiring insomnia, is the ethical imperative behind any form of criticism.

Notes

1. Henry James, *The Golden Bowl* (Harmondsworth: Penguin, 1985) 36.
2. Maurice Blanchot, *The Writing of the Disaster*, trans. Ann Smock (London: University of Nebraska Press, 1986) 101.
3. Martha Nussbaum, 'Perceptive Equilibrium: Literary Theory and Ethical Theory', in *The Future of Literary Theory*, ed. Ralph Cohen (London: Routledge, 1989) 58–85 (61).
4. Ibid., 61.
5. Martha Nussbaum, 'Finely aware and Richly responsible: Literature and the Moral Imagination', in *Literature and the Question of Philosophy*, ed. Anthony J. Cascardi (London: Johns Hopkins University Press, 1987) 167–91 (187).
6. Martha Nussbaum, 'Flawed Crystals: James's *The Golden Bowl* and Literature as Moral Philosophy', *New Literary History*, 15 (1983) 25–49 (34).
7. Ibid., 32.
8. Henry James, *The Golden Bowl*, 316–17.
9. Ibid., 448.
10. Ibid., 412.
11. Ibid., 506.
12. Martha Nussbaum, 'Flawed Crystals', 47.
13. Henry James, *The Golden Bowl*, 11.
14. Richard Wollheim, 'Flawed Crystals: James's *The Golden Bowl* and the Plausibility of Literature as Moral Philosophy', *New Literary History*, 15 (1983) 185–91 (188).
15. Martha Nussbaum, 'Finely Aware', 190.
16. Martha Nussbaum, *The Fragility of Goodness* (Cambridge University Press, 1986) 14.
17. M. M. Bakhtin, *The Dialogic Imagination: Four Essays*, trans. Caryl Emerson and Michael Holquist, ed. Michael Holquist (Austin: University of Texas Press, 1981) 271.
18. Frantz Fanon, *The Wretched of the Earth* (London: Penguin, 1990) 251.
19. Paul de Man, *The Resistance to Theory* (Minneapolis: University of Minnesota Press, 1986) 15.
20. Jacques Derrida, *Dissemination*, trans. Barbara Johnson (London: Athlone Press, 1981) 233.
21. J. Hillis Miller, *The Ethics of Reading* (New York: Columbia University Press, 1987) 102.
22. Ibid., 127.
23. Ibid., 127.
24. Geoffrey Galt Harpham, 'Language, History and Ethics', *Raritan*, 7 (1987) 128–46 (138).
25. Simon Critchley, *The Ethics of Deconstruction: Derrida and Levinas* (Oxford: Blackwell, 1992) 47.
26. Christopher Norris, *Deconstruction and the Interests of Theory* (London: Pinter, 1988) 165.
27. J. Hillis Miller, *The Ethics of Reading*, 121.
28. Emmanuel Levinas, *Otherwise than Being or Beyond Essence*, trans.

Alphonso Lingis (The Hague: Martinus Nijhoff, 1981) 184.
29. Simon Critchley, *The Ethics of Deconstruction*, 7.
30. Adriaan Peperzak, 'Beyond Being', *Research in Phenomenology*, 8 (1978) 239–61.
31. Emmanuel Levinas, *Otherwise than Being*, 179.
32. Ibid., 48.
33. Ibid., 25, 105, 165–71.
34. Ibid., 7.
35. Jacques Derrida, 'Violence and Metaphysics' in *Writing and Difference*, trans. Alan Bass (London: Routledge and Kegan Paul, 1978) 79–153 (80).
36. Maurice Blanchot, *The Writing of the Disaster*, 101.
37. Emmanuel Levinas, *Otherwise than Being*, 184.
38. Henry James, *The Golden Bowl*, 513.
39. Ibid., 580.
40. Maurice Blanchot, *The Writing of the Disaster*, 63.

5

The Original Traumatism: Levinas and Psychoanalysis

Simon Critchley

> Es gibt gar keine andern als moralische Erlebnisse,
> selbst nicht im Bereich der Sinneswarnehmung.
>
> Nietzsche, *Die Fröhliche Wissenschaft*

Steven Connor is doubtless right in claiming that 'The word "ethics" seems to have replaced "textuality" as the most charged term in contemporary theory.' But what does 'ethics' mean here? What conception of ethics, if any, is implied in this book's title and in the specific linking of ethics to literature? Are we writing about the relative merits of deontological, consequentialist, or virtue-based approaches to ethical theory insofar as they can or cannot be productively applied to literature? Or are we writing about the recent critiques of the very idea of any ethical theory based on rights, consequences or virtues? That is to say, the critique of the legitimacy of the project of ethical theory itself, that has led philosophers like Bernard Williams, Martha Nussbaum and Stanley Cavell towards a privileging of literature insofar as it is able to stimulate the imagination in the consideration of otherwise theoretically intractable ethical problems? This is another way of saying that the book's topic – 'Critical Ethics' – is vast, or, more unkindly, that the word 'ethics' risks producing such inflation in the beach ball of contemporary theoretical debate that the consequence will either be a gradual expansion, a sudden explosion or, more likely, the slow flatulence of deflation. Perhaps this is already happening. Such is the Owl of Minerva problem in editing essays.

In this essay, I want to look into an undeniably influential portion of our book's beach ball that has been a major cause of the contemporary inflation of the word 'ethics', namely the work of Emmanuel Levinas. From relative obscurity, Levinas's work has gained extraordinary prominence in recent years. For example, Vincent Descombes's otherwise excellent history of French philosophy between 1933 and 1978, published in 1979 as *Contemporary French Philosophy*, makes absolutely no mention of Levinas. The writing of such a history without Levinas would be unthinkable now in France or elsewhere for quite determinate cultural reasons that can, in shorthand, be associated with the fallout that followed the Heidegger affair in France in 1987 and the critique of the anti-humanism and perceived ethical indifferentism of *la pensée 68* in the polemics of Luc Ferry and Alain Renaud. In the English-speaking world, Levinas's name has an awesome, almost talismanic, power in contemporary theoretical debate, where readers have turned to his work on the basis of an interest in theorists themselves deeply indebted to Levinas, such as Derrida and Lyotard, and also because of certain perceived ethical blindspots in their work that stand in need of supplementation. For example, this was the reason I wrote *The Ethics of Deconstruction*. In the space of less than ten years, Levinas has become a familiar and perhaps too comfortable part of the theoretical furniture and references to his work abound outside philosophy and literary criticism, in art criticism, cultural theory, international relations theory and contemporary social and political theory. Matters have been brought to a head by Levinas's recent and saddening death, which has led to an extraordinary but not atypical process of canonization in the French press (the same thing happened to Foucault), where a figure such as Jean-Luc Marion has hyperbolically argued that there are only two significant French philosophers in the twentieth century: Bergson and Levinas. It is to say the least unclear whether this canonization will result in expansion, explosion or slow flatulence. That is not my concern here, although flatulence is always to be avoided if possible.

If the contemporary inflation of the notion of ethics can be linked, particularly in theoretical debates in literary and cultural studies, to the name of Levinas, then what is the meaning and force of his conception of ethics? Levinas's work is habitually distilled and banalized into a couple of vague theses: 'ethics is first philosophy', or 'ethics is infinite responsibility to the Other',... blah, blah, blah. To speak in this way, as Lacan reminds us, is to use the other as mouthwash, and whilst this might leave us with fresh breath, and whilst a fresh breath is a fine thing, it provides little else. So, the meaning and force of these theses is usually left unclear in order that Levinasian ethics, so-called, might be easily invoked in a rather indeterminate or even pious way to interpret a text or illuminate a cultural context. Such is what I have called in the past 'Levinasian hermeneutics'. Let us be clear, such an interpretation of Levinas is no crime. I'm happy about it, although not exactly to the point of clapping my hands. But in this essay I would like to push critically a little harder at Levinas's work and look into the conditions of possibility for ethics and specifically the ethical relation to the other. As we will soon see, this will take our beach ball into rather deep, choppy waters, and I apologize for this in advance.

Let me begin by proposing a couple of working hypotheses. A first working hypothesis, then: the condition of possibility for the ethical relation to the other, that is, the condition of possibility for ethical transcendence, communication and beyond that justice, politics and the whole field of the third party with the specific meanings that Levinas gives to these terms, is a conception of the subject.[1] Thus, it is only because there is a *certain disposition towards alterity within the subject, as the structure or pattern of subjectivity*, that there can be an ethical relation. Levinas writes in the 1968 version of 'Substitution', that we will have more than one occasion to come back to:

> It is from subjectivity understood as a self, from the excidence and dispossession of contraction, whereby the Ego does not appear but immolates itself, that the relationship with the other is possible as communication and transcendence.[2]

Or again:

> It is through the condition of being a hostage that there can be pity, compassion, pardon, and proximity in the world – even the little there is, even the simple 'after you sir'. (91)

So, to make my claim crystal clear, Levinas's account of ethics understood as the relation to the other irreducible to comprehension and therefore to ontology finds its condition of possibility in a certain conception of the subject. In Kantian terms, the ethical relation to the other presupposes a rather odd transcendental deduction of the subject. In other terms, it is only because there is a disposition towards alterity within the subject – whatever the origin of this disposition might be, which, as we will see, is the question of trauma – that the subject can be claimed by the other.

Levinas tries to capture this disposition towards alterity within the subject with a series of what he calls 'termes éthiques' (92) or even 'un langage éthique' (92): accusation, persecution, obsession, substitution and hostage. Of course, and this is already a huge issue, this is not what one normally thinks of as an ethical language. A related second working hypothesis announces itself here: namely that the condition of possibility for the ethical relation lies in the deployment or articulation of a certain ethical language. This is already highly curious and would merit separate attention: namely, that Levinas deploys an ethical language that attempts to express what he calls 'the paradox in which phenomenology suddenly finds itself' (92). The *paradox* here is that what this ethical language seeks to thematize is by definition unthematizable, it is a conception of the subject constituted in a relation to alterity that is irreducible to ontology, that is, irreducible to thematization or conceptuality. Levinas's work is a *phenomenology of the unphenomenologizable*, or what he calls the order of the enigma in distinction from that of the phenomenon.

Of course, the claim that Levinas is offering a phenomenology of the unphenomenologizable does not make his work unique, and one thinks both of the late Heidegger's description of his thinking in his final Zähringen seminar in 1973 as the attempt at a 'phenomenology of the inapparent' and the important recent debates that this has given rise to in France about the alleged theological turn within French phenomenology (Janicaud, Marion, Henry). As Wittgenstein might have said, the ethicality of thought is revealed in its persistent attempt to run up or bump up against the limits of language. The ethical might well be nonsense within the bounds of sense demarcated by the *Tractatus*, but it is important or serious nonsense, and it is arguably the animating intention of both Wittgenstein's earlier and later work.

Thus, and here I bring together the two hypotheses, *the disposition towards alterity within the subject that is the condition of possibility for the ethical relation to the other is expressed linguistically or articulated philosophically by recourse to an ethical language that has a paradoxical relation to that which it is attempting to thematize.* As so often in the later Levinas, it is a question of trying to *say* that which cannot be *said*, or *proposing* that which cannot be propositionally *stated*, of *enunciating* that which cannot be *enunciated*, and what has to be said, stated or enunciated is subjectivity itself.

In this essay, I want to discuss just one term in this ethical language, namely *trauma* or 'traumatisme'. Levinas tries to thematize the subject that is, according to me, the condition of possibility for the ethical relation with the notion of trauma. He thinks the subject as trauma – ethics is a trauma-tology.[3] I would like to interpret this word trauma, and its associated ethical language and conception of the subject, in *economic* rather than strictly philosophical terms; that is to say, in relation to the metapsychology of the second Freudian topography first elaborated in *Beyond the Pleasure Principle*. For Freud, it is the evidence of traumatic neurosis, clinically evidenced in war neurosis, that necessitates the introduction of the repetition compulsion. Now, it is the drive-like or pulsional character of repetition that overrides the pleasure principle and suggests a deeper instinctual function than the earlier distinction of the ego and sexual drives. Thus, for Freud, there is a direct link between the analysis of trauma and the introduction of the speculative hypothesis of the death drive, and it is this link that I would like to exploit as I read Levinas.

What is the justification for this economic understanding of Levinas? Well, there is absolutely none really and certainly nothing in Levinas's *intentions* to justify this link. However, as is so often the case with Levinas, his *text* is in a most illuminating conflict with his intentions. It is only by reading *against* Levinas's denials and resistances that we might get some insight into what is going on in his text: its latencies, its possibilities, its radicalities. Although Levinas includes such terms as obsession, persecution and trauma in his ethical language – not to mention his invocation in one place of 'psychosis' (102) and of the ethical subject as 'une conscience devenue folle' – he does this by specifically refusing and even ridiculing the categories of psychoanalysis. For example – and there are other examples – Levinas begins a paper given at a conference with the title 'La psychanalyse est-elle une histoire juive?' with the confession, 'My embarassment comes from the fact that I am absolutely outside the area of psychoanalytic research.'[4] For Levinas, psychoanalysis is simply part and parcel of the anti-humanism of the human sciences, which, in criticizing the sovereignty of 'Man' risks losing sight of the holiness of the human (*la sainteté de l'humain*).[5]

Before giving a more careful reading of Levinas and trying to make good on my initial hypotheses on the subject and ethical language, I would like to illustrate the tension between Levinas's intention and his text in relation to psychoanalysis with an example.

In the original version of 'Substitution', Levinas asks 'Does consciousness exhaust the notion of subjectivity?' (82). That is to say, is the ethical subject a conscious subject? The answer is a resounding 'no'. The whole Levinasian analysis of the subject proceeds from a rigorous distinction between subject and consciousness or between the *le Soi* (the self) and *le Moi* (the ego). Levinas's work, and this is something far too little recognized in much of the rather too edifying or fetishizing secondary literature on Levinas, proceeds from the rigorous distinction between consciousness and subjectivity, where 'c'est une question de ramener le moi à soi', of leading back the ego of ontology to its meta-ontological subjectivity. For Levinas, it is the reduction of subjectivity to consciousness and the order of representation that defines and dominates modern philosophy. It is necessary to reduce this reduction – such is the sense of Husserlian intentional analysis for Levinas, where what counts is the overflowing of objectivistic, naive thought by a forgotton experience from which it lives; that is to say, the pre-conscious experience of the subject interlocuted by the other.[6] Levinas breaks the thread that ties the subject to the order of consciousness, knowledge, representation and presence. Levinas gives the name 'psychism' to this subject that constitutes itself and maintains itself in a relation to that which escapes representation and presence: the subject of the trace, of a past that has never been present, the immemorial, the anarchic, etc. In brief, consciousness is the belated, *nachträglich* effect of the subject as trace, the dissimulating effect of a subjective affect. *Consciousness is the effect of an affect*, and this affect is trauma.

Of course, the Freudian resonances in what I have already said will already be apparent, but any possible rapprochement between the Levinasian analysis of the subject and Freudian psychoanalysis is specifically and violently refused by Levinas in the text we are commenting upon. He writes, once again in the 1968 version of 'Substitution':

> But to speak of the hither side of consciousness is not to turn toward the unconscious. The unconscious in its clandestinity, rehearses the game played out in consciousness, namely the search for meaning and truth as the search for the self. While this opening onto the self is certainly occluded and repressed, psychoanalysis still manages to break through and restore self-consciousness. It follows that our study will not be following the way of the unconscious. (83)

It should hopefully go without saying that this is a pretty lamentable understanding of Freud. But, provisionally, one can note two things: (i) that if Levinas appears to believe that psychoanalysis seeks to restore self-consciousness, then it is interesting to note that he says exactly the opposite – and rightly – in an important text from 1954, 'Le moi et la totalité', where it is claimed that psychoanalysis, 'throws a fundamental suspicion on the most indeniable evidence of self-consciousness'.[7] (ii) Although Freud arguably always harboured the therapeutic ambition of restoring self-consciousness, an ambition expressed in the famous formula, *'Wo Es war soll Ich werden'*, one should note that there are other ways of returning to the meaning of Freud, and other ways of reading that formula, notably that of Lacan, where he interprets the Freudian *Es* as the subject of the unconscious and where the imperative driving psychonalysis is to arrive at the place of the subject beyond the imaginary *méconnaissance* of the conscious ego.[8]

However, the tension that interests me has not yet been established. Returning to the above quote on Levinas's refusal of the psychoanalytic concept of the unconscious, what is fascinating here and typical of the relation between Levinas's intentions and his text, is that Levinas's statement that he will not be following the way of the unconscious is flatly contradicted in a later footnote in the 1968 'Substitution' text, just after a couple of key references to trauma:

> Persecution leads back the ego to the self, to the absolute accusative where the Ego is accused of a fault which it neither willed nor committed, and which disturbs its freedom. Persecution is a traumatism – violence par excellence, without warning, without apriori, without the possibility of apology, without logos. Persecution leads back to a resignation without consent and as a result traverses a night of the unconscious. *This*

> *is the meaning of the unconscious, the night where the ego comes back to the self under the traumatism of persecution [nuit ou se fait le retournement de moi à soi sous le traumatisme de la persécution]* – a passivity more passive than all passivity, on the hither side of identity, becoming the responsibility of substitution. (183, my emphasis)[9]

Here is the paradox (or is it a simple contradiction?): in one breath, Levinas writes that he will not follow the psychoanalytic way of the unconscious because it seeks to restore self-consciousness. But, in the next breath, Levinas gives us the meaning of the unconscious conceived as the night where the ego comes back to the self under the traumatism of persecution. So, the concept of the unconscious, the *pierre angulaire* of psychoanalysis, is strategically denied and then reintroduced with a *méconnaissance* that is perhaps too easily understood within a Freudian logic of *Verneinung*.

My question to Levinas has already been announced but can now be more sharply formulated: *what does it mean to think the meaning of the unconscious in terms of the traumatism of persecution? What does it mean to think the subject – the subject of the unconscious – as trauma?*

In order to approach this question, I would like to return to my first hypothesis and try to show the central place of the subject in Levinas through a brief overview of the main argument of *Otherwise than Being or Beyond Essence*.[10] Levinas begins his exposition by describing the movement from Husserlian intentional consciousness to a level of preconscious, pre-reflective sensing or sentience, a movement enacted in the title of the second chapter of the book, 'De l'intentionalité au sentir'. In a gesture that remains methodologically faithful to Heidegger's undermining of the theoretical comportment to the world (*Vorhandenheit*) and the subject/object distinction that supports epistemology and (on Levinas's early reading in his Doctoral Thesis) Husserlian phenomenology, the movement from intentionality to sensing, or in the language of *Totality and Infinity*, from representation to enjoyment, shows how intentional consciousness is conditioned by *life* (56). But, against Heideggerian *Sorge*, life for Levinas is not a *blosses Leben*, it is sentience, enjoyment and nourishment; it is *jouissance* and *joie de vivre*. Life is love of life and love of what life lives from: the sensible, material world. Levinas's work is a reduction of the conscious intentional ego to the pre-conscious sentient subject of *jouissance*. Now, it is precisely this sentient subject of jouissance that is capable of being called into question by the other. The ethical relation, and this is important, takes place at the level of pre-reflective sensibility and not at the level of reflective consciousness. The ethical subject is a sentient subject not a conscious ego.

So, for Levinas, *the subject is subject*, and the form that this subjection assumes is that of sensibility or sentience. Sensibility is what Levinas often refers to as 'the way' of my subjection, vulnerability and passivity towards the other. The entire argumentative thrust of the exposition in *Otherwise than Being* is to show how subjectivity is founded in *sensibility* (Chapter 2) and to describe sensibility as a *proximity* to the other (Chapter 3), a proximity whose basis is found in *substitution* (Chapter 4), which is the core concept of *Otherwise than Being*. So, if the centre of Levinas's thinking is his conception of the subject, then the central discussion of the subject takes place in the 'Substitution' chapter of *Otherwise than Being*, that Levinas describes as 'la pièce centrale' (ix) or 'le germe du présent ouvrage' (125). However – a final philological qualification – the 'Substitution' chapter was originally presented as the second of two lectures given in Brussels in November 1967. The first was an early draft of 'Language and Proximity', which was published separately in the second edition of *En découvrant l'existence avec Husserl et Heidegger*, elements of which were redrafted in the third chapter of *Otherwise than Being*. The original published version of 'Substitution' appeared in the *Revue Philosophique de Louvain* in October 1968. Although much is missing from the first version of this text, particularly Levinas's qualified endorsement of Kant's ethics, I would say that it is philosophically more concentrated and easier to follow than the 1974 version. So, if the concept of the subject is the key to Levinas's thinking, then the original version of the 'Substitution' chapter might well provide a key to this key.

I would now like to try and analyse this traumatic logic of substitution – a self-lacerating, even masochistic logic – where I am responsible for the persecution that I undergo, and where I am even responsible for my persecutor. No one can substitute themselves for me, but I am ready to substitute myself for the other, and even die in their place.

In the original version of 'Substitution', the first mention of trauma comes after a citation from *Lamentations*, 'Tendre la joue à celui qui frappe et être rassasié de honte' ('To offer the cheek to the one who strikes him and to be filled with shame' – 90). Thus, the subject is the one who suffers at the hands of the other and who is responsible for the suffering that he did not will. I am responsible for the persecution I undergo, for the outrage done to me. It is this situation of the subject being 'absolutely responsible for the persecution I undergo' (90), that Levinas describes with the phrase 'le traumatisme originel'. Thus, the subject is constituted as a subject of persecution, outrage, suffering or whatever, through an original traumatism towards which I am utterly passive. This passage, and the pages from which the quote is taken, is dramatically expanded in the 1974 version of 'Substitution', and Levinas adds:

> A passivity of which the active source is not thematizable. Passivity of traumatism, but of the traumatism that prevents its own representation, the deafening trauma, breaking the thread of consciousness which should have welcomed it in its present: the passivity of persecution. But a passivity that only merits the epithet of complete or absolute if the persecuted is liable to respond to the persecutor. (111)

This 'traumatisme assourdissant', this deafening traumatism (which incidentally recalls the opening lines of Baudelaire's 'A une passante', 'La rue assourdissante', where it refers to the traumatic noisiness of nineteenth-century Paris) is that towards which I relate in a passivity that exceeds representation, i.e. that exceeds the intentional act of consciousness, that cannot be experienced as an object, the noematic correlate of a noesis. Trauma is a 'non-intentional affectivity', it tears into my subjectivity like an explosion, like a bomb that detonates without warning, like a bullet that hits me in the dark, fired from an unseen gun and by an unknown assailant.[11]

Now, it is this absolute passivity towards that which exceeds representation, a non-relating relation of inadequate responsibility towards alterity experienced as persecuting hatred, that is then described in the 1974 version – very suggestively for my concerns – as transference, 'Ce transfert...est la subjectivité même' ('This transference...is subjectivity itself', 111). Thus, *subjectivity would seem to be constituted for Levinas in a transferential relation to an original trauma*, that is to say, the subject is constituted – without its knowledge, prior to cognition and recognition – in a relation that exceeds representation, intentionality, symmetry, correspondence, coincidence, equality and reciprocity, that is to say, any form of ontology, whether phenomenological or dialectical. The ethical relation might be described as the attempt to imagine a non-dialectical concept of transference, where the other is opaque, reflecting nothing of itself back to the subject. In Lacanian terms, it would seem that the subject is articulated through a relation to the real, through the non-intentional affect of *jouissance*, where the original traumatism of the other is the Thing, *das Ding*. It is only by virtue of such a mechanism of trauma that one might speak of ethics.[12]

Thus, the subject is constituted in a hetero-affection that divides the self and refuses all identification at the level of the ego. Such is the work of the work of trauma, *die Trauma-Arbeit*, the event of an inassumable past, a lost time that can never be *retrouvé*, a non-intentional affectivity that takes place as a subjection to the other, a subject subjected to the point of persecution.

It is at this point, and in order to elaborate critically this concept of the subject as trauma, that I would like to make a short detour into Freud.

What is trauma? Trauma is etymologically defined in Larousse as 'blessure', as wounding, as 'violence produite par un agent extérieur agissant mécaniquement'. As such, trauma has both a physiological as well as psychical meaning, denoting a violence effected by an external agency, which can be a blow to the head, or a broken arm as much as the emotional shock of bereavement. For Freud, trauma is an economic concept and refers to a massive cathexis of external stimulus that breaches the protective shield of the perceptual-consciousness system or ego. Trauma is shock and complete surprise. In terms of the Freudian model of the psychical apparatus governed by Fechner's constancy principle, trauma is an excess of excitation that disrupts psychical equilibrium and is consequently experienced as unpleasurable. In Lacanian terms, trauma is the subjective affect of contact with the real. It is the opening up of the ego to an exteriority that shatters its economic unity. Recalling Levinas's allusion to a 'deafening traumatism', trauma is like a bomb going off, like Canary Wharf, producing a sudden and violent pain. With the breach in the ego caused by such a trauma, the pleasure principle is momentarily put out of action. However, the ego responds to the cathexis of stimulus caused by the trauma with an equivalent anti-cathexis, by a defensive strategy that seeks to transform the free or mobile energy of the trauma into bound, quiescent energy. If the defensive strategy succeeds, then the economy of the ego is restored and the pleasure principle resumes its reign.

Whence arises the riddle of traumatic neurosis. Traumatic neurosis is the disorder that arises after the experience of a trauma: a car accident, shell shock or a terrorist bombing. In clinical terms, the neurosis can manifest itself in a number of ways: in a paroxysm, a severe anxiety attack, a state of profound agitation (compulsive twitching) or sheer mental confusion (shell shock). What characterizes the symptoms of traumatic neurosis, like the other neuroses, is both their compulsive character – and compulsion is one of the main traits of the unconscious (*com-pulsare* = the constraint of a *pulsion*, a drive) – and their repetitiveness. In traumatic neurosis the original scene of the trauma, its deafening shock, is compulsively and unconsciously repeated in nightmares, insomnia or obsessive (another Levinasian term in 'Substitution') reflection. The subject endlessly attempts to relive that contact with the real that was the origin of the trauma, to repeat that painful *jouissance*. That is to say, the traumatized subject *wants* to suffer, to relive the jouissance of the real, to repeatedly pick at the scab that irritates it.[13]

Thus, the dream of the traumatic neurotic repeats the origin of the trauma. Freud's huge theoretical problem here is the following: if this is true, that is, if there is a repetition compulsion at work in traumatic neurosis that repeats the origin of trauma, then how can this fact be consistent with the central thesis of his magnum opus, the *Traumdeutung*, where it is claimed that all dreams are wish-fulfilments and are governed by the pleasure principle? *It cannot*, and it is with the evidence of the repetition compulsion exhibited in traumatic neurosis and fate neurosis that the whole sublime architecture of the *Traumdeutung* and the first Freudian topography begins to fall apart. The move from the first to the second topography is that from *Traumdeutung* to *Trauma-Deutung*.

The dreams of traumatic neurotics are not, then, in obedience to the pleasure principle, but to the repetition compulsion. And not only is this true of traumatic neurosis, it is also true of dreams that bring back the traumas of childhood, hence the importance of the Fort/Da game in Freud, where the infant attempts to sublimate the absence of the mother with a game that repeats the trauma of her departure. Thus, the original function of dreams is not the dreamwork *(die Traumarbeit)* that permits the sleeper to sleep on, it is rather the interruption of sleep, *die Trauma-Arbeit*, that is beyond the pleasure principle. Insomnia is the truth of sleep.[14]

In Chapter 5 of *Beyond the Pleasure Principle*, Freud tries to establish the instinctual or 'drive-like' *(Triebhaft)* character of the repetition compulsion and, vice versa, to establish the repetitive character of the drives. Freud's claim is that the representatives or manifestations of the repetition compulsion exhibit a highly *Triebhaft* character, being out of the control of the ego and giving the appearance of a 'daemonic' force at work – such is fate neurosis. Once Freud has established the *Triebhaft* character of the repetition compulsion, he is then in a position to introduce his central speculative hypothesis, namely that a drive is an inner urge or pressure in organic life to restore an earlier condition. That is to say, a drive is the expression of a *Trägheit*, an inertia, sluggishness, or laziness in organic life. It is this speculation about the fundamentally conservative nature of drives – wrapped up in a pseudo-biological phylogenetic myth of origin – that entails the extreme (and extremely Schopenhauerian) conclusion of *Beyond the Pleasure Principle*: namely that 'Das Ziel alles Lebens ist der Tod' ('the aim of all life is death').[15] Thus, death would be the object that would satisfy the aim of the drives.

After this little detour, and by way of conclusion, I want to use the above Freudian insights to throw some light on what seems to be happening in Levinas. As I have, I hope, established, the subject is the key concept in Levinas's work. The subject's affective disposition towards alterity is the condition of possibility for the ethical relation to the other. Ethics does not take place at the level of consciousness or reflection; it rather takes place at the level of sensibility or pre-conscious sentience. The Levinasian ethical subject is a sentient self (*un soi sentant*) before being a thinking ego (*un moi pensant*). The bond with the other is affective.

We have already seen the tension in Levinas's work where – on the one hand – he writes that his analysis of the subject is not going to follow the way of the unconscious because psychoanalysis seeks to restore self-consciousness, but – on the other hand – Levinas gives us the meaning of the unconscious as 'the night where the ego comes back to itself in the traumatism of persecution'. That is to say, Levinas seeks to think the subject at the level of the unconscious in relation to an original traumatism. The subject is constituted through a non-dialectical transference towards an originary traumatism. This is a seemingly strange claim to make, yet my wager is that if it does not go through then the entire Levinasian project is dead in the water.

How does Levinasian ethical subjectivity look from the perspective of the second Freudian topography? In the following way, perhaps: under the effect of the traumatism of persecution, the deafening shock or the violence of trauma, the subject becomes an internally divided or split self, an interiority that is radically non-self-coincidental, a gaping wound that will not heal, a subject lacerated by contact with an original traumatism that produces a scarred interiority inaccessible to consciousness and reflection, a subject that *wants* to repeat compulsively the origin of the trauma, a subject that becomes what Levinas calls a recurrence of the self without identification, a recurrence of trauma that is open to death, or – better – open to the passive movement of dying itself (*le mourir même*), dying as the first opening towards alterity, the impossibility of possibility as the very possibility of the ethical subject.

The Levinasian subject is a traumatized self, a subject that is constituted through a self-relation that is experienced as a lack, where the self is experienced as the inassumable source of what is lacking from the ego – a subject of melancholia, then. But, this is a *good thing*. It is only because the subject is unconsciously constituted through the trauma of contact with the real that we might have the audacity to speak of goodness, transcendence, compassion, etc.; and moreover to speak of these terms in relation to the topology of desire and not simply in terms of some pious, reactionary and ultimately nihilistic wish-fulfilment. Without trauma, there would be no ethics in Levinas's particular sense of the word.

In this connection, one might generalize this structure and go so far as to say (although in a provisional and wholly formal manner) that without a relation to trauma, or at least without a relation to that which claims, calls, summons, interrupts or troubles the subject (whether the good beyond being in Plato, the moral law in Kant, or the relation to *das Ding* in Freud), there would be no ethics, neither an ethics of phenomenology, nor an ethics of psychoanalysis. Without a relation to that which summons and challenges the subject, a summons that is experienced as a relation to a Good in a way that exceeds the pleasure principle and any promise of happiness (any *eudaimonism*), there would be no ethics. And without such a relation to ethical experience – an experience that is strictly inassumable and impossible, but which yet heteronomously defines the autonomy of the ethical subject – one could not imagine a politics that would refuse the category of totality. The passage to justice in Levinas – to the third party, the community and politics – passes through or across the theoretical and historical experience of trauma. No democracy without the death drive. Now, there's a thought.

Notes

1. For an exhaustive and exhausting account of the subject in Levinas, see Gérard Bailhache, *Le sujet chez Emmanuel Levinas* (Paris: PUF, 1994).
2. 'Substitution', trans. Atterton, Noctor and Critchley in *Emmanuel Levinas. Basic Philosophical Writings*, ed. Peperzak, Critchley and Bernasconi (Bloomington: Indiana University Press, 1996) 92. Subsequent page references to this book are given in the body of text.
3. In this regard, see Elisabeth Weber, *Verfolgung und Trauma* (Vienna: Passagen Verlag, 1990); and Michel Haar, 'L'obsession de l'autre. L'éthique comme traumatisme', *Emmanuel Levinas* (Paris: L'Herne, 1991) 444–53.
4. 'Quelques reflexions talmudiques sur le rêve', *La psychanalyse est-elle une histoire juive?* (Paris: Seuil, 1981) 114.
5. On the importance of the notion of *la sainteté* in Levinas, see Derrida's remarks in his stunning recent book, *Adieu à Levinas* (Paris: Galilée, 1997) 15.
6. Emmanuel Levinas, *Totality and Infinity*, trans. A. Lingis (Pittsburgh: Duquesne University Press, 1969) 28.
7. 'Le moi et la totalité', in *Entre Nous: Essais sur le penser-à-l'autre* (Paris: Grasset, 1991) 36–7:

> Ce n'est pas la parole seulement que démolissent ainsi la psychanalyse et l'histoire. Elles aboutissent en réalité à la destruction du je s'identifiant du dedans. La reflexion du cogito ne peut plus surgir pour assurer la certitude de ce que je suis et à peine pour assurer la certitude de mon existence même. Cette existence tributaire de la reconnaissance par autrui, sans laquelle, insignifiante,

> elle se saisit comme réalité sans réalité, devient purement phénoménale. La psychanalyse jette une suspicion foncière sur le témoignage le plus irrécusable de la conscience de soi... Le cogito perd ainsi sa valeur de fondement. On ne peut plus reconstruire la réalité à partir d'éléments qui, indépendents de tout point de vue et indéformables par la conscience, permettent une connaissance philosophique.

8. Lacan, 'La chose freudienne', in *Écrits* (Paris: Seuil, 1966) 416–18.
9. A similar line of thought is expressed in 'La ruine de la représentation', in *En découvrant l'existence avec Husserl et Heidegger* (Paris: Vrin, 1967) 130. Levinas writes:

> Cette découverte de l'implicite qui n'est pas une simple 'deficience' ou 'chute' de l'explicite, apparaît comme monstruosité ou comme merveille dans une histoire des idées où le concept d'actualité coïncidait avec l'état de veille absolue, avec la lucidité de l'intellect. Que cette pensée se trouve tributaire d'une vie anonyme et obscure, de paysages oubliés qu'il faut restituer à l'objet même que la conscience croît pleinement tenir, voilà qui rejoint incontestablement les conceptions modernes de l'inconscient et des profondeurs. Mais, il en resulte non pas nouvelle psychologie seulement. Une nouvelle ontologie commence: l'être se pose non pas seulement comme corrélatif d'une pensée, mais comme fondant déjà la pensée même qui, cependant, le constitue.

10. Emmanuel Levinas, *Otherwise than Being or Beyond Essence*, trans. A. Lingis (The Hague: Nijhoff, 1981). Further page references are given in the body of the text.
11. See Andrew Tallon, 'Nonintentional Affectivity, Affective Intentionality, and the Ethical in Levinas's Philosophy', in *Ethics as First Philosophy*, ed. Adriaan Peperzak (London and New York: Routledge, 1995) 107–21.
12. I have in mind Lacan's formula in his commentary on Sade, '...la jouissance est un mal. Freud là-dessus nous guide par le main – elle est un mal parce qu'elle comporte le mal du prochain.' ('Jouissance is suffering. Freud guides us by the hand on this point – it is suffering because it involves or bears itself towards the suffering of the neighbour'), *L'éthique de la psychanalyse* (Paris: Seuil, 1986) 217.
13. Freud writes in *Beyond the Pleasure Principle*:

> Das Studium des Traumes dürfen wir als den zuverlässigsten Weg zur Erforschung der seelischen Tiefenvorgänge betrachten. Nun zeigt das Traumleben der traumatischen Neurose den Charakter, das es den Kranken immer wieder in die Situation seines Unfalles zurückführt, aus der er mit neuem Schrecken erwacht. Darüber verwundert man sich viel zuwenig. (*Psychologie des Unbewussten, Freud-Studienausgabe*, Band 3 [Frankfurt a. M.: Fischer, 1975] 223)

> The study of dreams may be considered the most trustworthy method of investigating deep mental processes. Now dreams occurring in traumatic neurosis have the characteristic of repeatedly bringing the patient back into the situation of his accident, a situation from which he wakes up in another fright. This astonishes people far too little. (*On Metapsychology*, Penguin Freud Library, Vol.11 [Harmondsworth: Penguin, 1984] 282)

14. Freud writes:

> Aber die obenerwähnten Träume der Unfallsneurotiker lassen sich nicht mehr unter den Gesichtspunkt der Wunscherfüllung bringen, und ebensowenig die in den Psychoanalysen vorfallended Träume, die uns die Erinnerung der psychischen Traumen der Kindheit wiederbringen. Sie gehorchen vielmehr dem Wiederholungszwang, der in der Analyse allerdings durch den von der 'Suggestion' gefördeten Wunsch, das Vergessene und Verdrängte heraufzubeschwören, unterstützt wird. (op. cit. 242)

> But it is impossible to classify as wish-fulfilments the dreams we have been discussing which occur in traumatic neuroses, or the dreams during psychoanalyses which bring to memory the psychical traumas of childhood. They arise, rather, in obedience to the compulsion to repeat, though it is true that in analysis that compulsion is supported by the wish (which is encouraged by 'suggestion') to conjure up what has been forgotten and repressed. (304)

15. Freud, op. cit., 248; trans., 311.

6

Spectres of History: Ethics and Postmodern Fictions of Temporality

Tim Woods

History 'ends' more and more quickly these days, every year bringing in new proclamations of its demise. 'So it goes.' One of the better known recent examples is Francis Fukuyama's *The End of History and the Last Man* (1992). Based on a refraction of Alexander Kojève's Hegelianism, this book initiated a variety of fierce critiques and arguments about what constitutes history and its direction in the postmodern world. Indeed, arguably the invocation of the 'end of history' is a postmodern phenomenon, announcing a general crisis in the representation of temporality. This essay will consider the paradoxical situation of this continuous ending of history. In addressing this issue, numerous allied questions arise: what is an 'end', and can there be positive and negative endings? In considering what is meant by 'end', are we speaking of a 'conclusion', or a 'goal' of history? Depending upon the alternative semantic associations, does the end of history imply that a long-awaited 'happy ending' of history has arrived? Or does it imply that some process of struggle, development, or evolution has concluded? Furthermore, in thinking about temporality, how far can an 'other' time be detected within history? To what degree is human freedom predicated upon what we might call a 'politics of temporality'? Among Kant's, Hegel's and Marx's gigantic achievements in conceiving of history as the substitution of reason for myth, just how successful were they in shaking off the mythical and the mystical, and securing a purely rationalistic history? And finally, and perhaps most significantly, how is justice, or ethical discourse, connected to representations of history? This exploration will occur in particular within a matrix constructed by Derrida's recent consideration of Marx, history and 'spectrology' in *Specters of Marx*, Lutz Niethammer's examination of the 'end of history' debate in *Posthistoire: Has History Come to an End?*, and some postmodern literary explorations of the crisis in representing narrative, history and temporality in the unique blend of science fiction and dystopian fantasy in Kurt Vonnegut's *Slaughterhouse-Five*. It will consider how literary narratives continue to conceptualize and represent the events and temporalities of history in resourceful and innovative structures. The primary focus will be historical 'time as a multidimensional web of plural realities',[1] and it will argue that history, far from having ended, is merely returning, the second time not so much as *farce* as *phantomatic*.

In *Slaughterhouse-Five*, Vonnegut's protagonist Billy Pilgrim is something of a time-traveller. He 'comes unstuck in time' and loses 'control over where he is going next' in his life: 'He has seen his birth and death many times, he says, and pays random visits to all the events in between.'[2] In 1967, he is kidnapped by flying saucer and taken to the planet Tralfamadore. Writing about this experience for his local newspaper, Billy states:

> The most important thing I learned on Tralfamadore was that when a person dies he only *appears* to die. He is still very much alive in the past, so it is very silly for people to cry at his funeral. All moments, past, present, and future, always have existed, always will exist. The Tralfamadorians can look at all the different moments just the way we can look at a stretch of the Rocky Mountains, for instance. They can see how permanent all the moments are, and they can look at any moment that interests them. It is just an illusion we have here on Earth that one moment follows another one, like beads on a string, and that once a moment is gone it is gone forever.
>
> 'When a Tralfamadorian sees a corpse, all he thinks is that the dead person is in a bad condition in that particular moment, but that the same person is just fine in plenty of other moments. Now, when I myself hear that somebody is dead, I simply shrug and say what the Tralfamadorians say about dead people, which is "So it goes"'.[3]

We are talking here about the living-dead, about phantoms and ghosts. Temporality is not treated here in a linear fashion, because the present moment embeds within it protensions and retensions of the past and future. In a striking image of temporality, rather than singular and separate beads on a string, history is better conceived of as the intertwined and parallel strands that are twisted to make up that string: all times are always present and absent. Vonnegut's aim is to allow human actions to be freed from the ideology of linear temporality with its model of the road and life-as-a-straightforward-journey, arranging temporality more as a rhythmic time which abandons the teleology, the transcendence and the putative neutrality of linear time. Rather, temporality is an arrangement in which the other world surrounds us always and is not at the end of some pilgrimage. Yet it need not only be read that way: after all, the Tralfamadorian is *dead*. Time is linear too. So it is not that one can do away with concepts of linear temporality, but one has to recognize that linear temporality is *not the only way* that temporality can be thought: linear concepts need to be supplemented with non-linear concepts. Tralfamadorian time is both linear and non-linear.

Thinking the structures of history, temporality, and spatiality has never been far from Jacques Derrida's consciousness either. However, apart from his teasing responses to Heboudine and Scarpetta's questions in *Positions* about his affiliation to Marxism, any explicit textual and philosophical engagement with Marx and history by Derrida has been eagerly anticipated. Derrida's recent book *Specters of Marx: The State of the Debt, the Work of Mourning, and the New International*, proves to be that long-awaited engagement. Now it is a little known fact that Derrida had thespian aspirations, and that these manifested themselves in a movie with Pascale Ogier called *Ghost Dance* by Ken McMullen in 1982. Although that was some 15 years ago, in recent years, Derrida has been keeping up his regular company with spirits, as evident in his book *De l'Esprit: Heidegger et la question* (1987) and its fascination with *das Geist* and *Doppelgängers*. In his life-long work of demystification and de-idealization embedded in a methodology of permanent linguistic reflexivity, Derrida orients an attack against any form of materialism which evinces a desire for a primary identity of being which acts as a fundamental reassurance for thought. In *Spectres of Marx*, remarking on Marx's belief in the material world, Derrida notices the irony of Marx's preoccupation with ghosts, and the necessity of exorcising spectres. Derrida perceives this to be the metaphysical moment of Marx's philosophical thought – a desire for a purity of presence, the elimination of a heterogeneous account of the present. Refracted through quotations, allusions and references to *Hamlet* – 'Time is out of joint' – and other works by Shakespeare (preserving, incidentally, a methodological critique much adopted by Marx himself), Derrida thus launches a critique of Marx's obsession with ghosts and spectres, hinging on Marx's famous warning at the outset of *The Communist Manifesto*: 'A spectre is haunting Europe – the spectre of Communism. All the powers of old Europe have entered into a holy alliance to exorcise this spectre.'[4] Yet as Derrida argues:

> The spectre that Marx was talking about then, communism, was there without being there. It was not yet there. It will never be there. There is no *Dasein* without the uncanniness, without the strange familiarity (*Unheimlichkeit*) of some spectre. What is a spectre? [...] The spectre, as its name indicates, is the *frequency* of a certain visibility. But the visibility of the invisible. And visibil*ity*, by its essence, is not seen, which is why it remains *epekeina tes ousias*, beyond the phenomenon or beyond being.[5]

The spectre is then, some*thing* which has no *thing*ness: it is the manifestation of the radically other. Derrida's theory of 'spectrality' stresses the manner in which things waver and shimmer in front of us. 'Spectrality' is what shakes our belief in solidity, in the ontological certainty of things, our assurance in the 'real', the solidity of Being itself. 'Spectrality' causes reality to tremble but makes no promises in return. The spectral is uncertain itself. Instead of ontological certainty, one gets what Derrida terms the 'hauntological' uncertainty: hauntology replaces ontology. In other words, Derrida's 'spectrology' is a theory which seeks to remind and privilege the non-identity of the object, the inessential quality of existence, the ghostly absences of presences.

As Jameson argues in his excellent essay 'Marx's Purloined Letter', spectrality is thus critical of any attempt or theory which purports to be an 'unmixed conception of time, some notion of a present that has won itself free of past and future and stands gleaming and self-contained, as a kind of mirage of parousia'.[6] Derrida's whole *oeuvre* is the tracking down and stigmatizing of just such nostalgias for some originary simplicity, of the unmixed in all its forms, in favour of mixed, miscegenated, hybridized and multivalenced forms. Consequently, Derrida's reservations about Marx have to do with Marx's desire to do away with ghosts, his very fear of the ghosts that haunt his work, which suggests a longing for more primary realities, fuller presences, and self-sufficient phenomena cleansed of the extraneous, residual or vestigial:

> Marx does not like ghosts any more than his adversaries do. He does not want to believe in them. But he thinks of nothing else. He believes rather in what is supposed to distinguish them from actual reality, living effectivity. He believes he can oppose them, like life to death, like vain appearances of the simulacrum to real presence. He believes enough in the dividing line of this opposition to want to denounce, chase away or exorcise the specters but by means of critical analysis and not by some counter-magic. But how to distinguish between the analysis that denounces magic and the counter-magic that it still risks being?[7]

Derrida argues that Marx's attempts to *conjure away* ghosts, cannot escape the act of invoking them: *conjuring away* is also a *conjuring up*. Derrida further argues that Marx's anxiety about ghosts and spectres, is really an anxiety about the purity of history, which betrays Marx's own ontological desires for the fullness of Being. Marx harbours a concealed ontological longing lurking in his desire to exorcise ghosts. Yet as Jameson reminds us, 'a world cleansed of spectrality is precisely ontology itself, a world of pure presence, of immediate density, of things without a past: for Derrida, an impossible and noxious nostalgia, and the fundamental target of his whole life's work'.[8] Indeed, our present is traced through with nations dealing with the manifestation of ghosts from the past: America and its Vietnam; the Industrial West and its ecological problems; South Africa and the avatars of *apartheid*; Europe and Bosnia; England and Ireland ... the list goes on. This concept of the 'impure presence' of the present, of the present embedding within it the past and the future, has very specific echoes of Raymond Williams's structural notion of the dominant ideology embedding within it residual and emergent ideologies. As a synchronous development within history, Williams is attempting to stress that ideology is not a pure or simple strand of cultural thought, but a far more heterogeneous and complex concept. This is a striking formulation to which Jameson acknowledges his debt, and it is clearly part of Derrida's understanding of history.

In order to counteract this fascination with the spectacular present, Derrida not only invokes the ghost of Christmas past, but the ghost of Christmas future. For the future holds spectrality within it as well, as it swims blurringly into the present and hints at possible alternative trajectories for the present. It is a form of opening oneself to the impossible and making it possible in its very impossibility. This is the Utopian aspect of spectrality – which Derrida refers to as the messianic – and which Jameson conceives of as 'the form of the most radical politicization... that, far from being locked into the repetitions of neurosis and obsession,... is energetically future-oriented and active'.[9] In this overt appeal to the secular messianism of Walter Benjamin, Derrida means a structure of experience rather than a religion. The messianic ushers in a redemptive possibility in the very heart of political despair (like the 1980s and 1990s), and it does not employ a concept of the linearity of the future: nothing is predictable, nothing can be read in the signs of the times. Whatever may happen cannot be foreseen or imagined. The messianic is spectral (hauntological or beyond being), because it ushers in a radical otherness which cannot be appropriated by a conceptual violence within our existing systemic structures. The messianic above all warns us that the revolutionary event cannot ever be thought; and it is here that one re-engages with Derrida's critique of conventional philosophical thinking in general, as a misguided attempt to think what demands a completely different preparation and approach.

Derrida's critique of Marx's fear of ghosts, this banishment of spectrality, is perceived by Jameson as a thinly disguised attack on postmodernism, 'a present that has already triumphantly exorcized all of its ghosts and believes itself to be without a past and without spectrality, late capitalism itself as ontology, the pure presence of the world-market system freed from all the errors of human history and of previous social formations, including the ghost of Marx himself'.[10] This is a postmodern world which celebrates the present and refuses to mourn the past. Jameson's principal point is that Derrida's appeal to the work of mourning, is engaged in a polemical critique of postmodernism as a state of commodified history which has banished history as a factor in the present. However, it bears with it strong echoes of Jameson's own preoccupation with postmodernism as 'the logic of late capitalism', in which history is rejected in favour of a historicism which nostalgically packages and stylizes the past as a simulacrum and in so doing, dehistoricizes the past. Postmodernism acts as a cultural dominant which stresses 'the fragmentation of time into a series of perpetual presents',[11] in which the exemplary temporal experience is that of the schizophrenic where 'as temporal continuities break down, the experience of the present becomes powerfully, overwhelmingly vivid and "material": the world comes before the schizophrenic with heightened intensity, bearing a mysterious and oppressive charge of affect, glowing with hallucinatory energy'.[12] The materialization of the present is somehow curiously immaterial, ghostly, or hallucinatory. Jameson regards the postmodern age as one dominated by spatiality rather than by temporality, by the synchronic rather than diachronic. At one point in his description of this new cultural environment, he mourns the decline of memory (which he associates with high modernism), and laments postmodernism's rejection of the past which goes hand-in-hand with its rejection of memory as a cultural preoccupation.[13] Yet contrary to the 'charge of affect' above, elsewhere Jameson's sense of the postmodern age is one in which there is a 'waning of affect', which marks the increasing superficiality of aesthetic and cultural production and its association with the shiny surfaces of glittering new commodities, like the reflective windows in the John Portman's Bonaventura Hotel in Los Angeles. Jameson appears to have purloined Derrida's letters; or to put it another way, maybe Jameson the film-critic has seen Derrida's ghost.

For in presenting a Derrida who has shifted away from Heideggerian ontology to a Benjaminian messianic Marxism, Jameson appropriates and resituates Derrida's philosophical process of deconstruction within a Marxist tradition. The sighs of relief are almost audible, as the troublesome practice of deconstruction which has caused so many furious rows and has proved so thorny in acrimonious and vitriolic debates over the past 25 years, is finally welcomed into the open arms of the Left. Derrida is finally one of us! The prophet of deconstruction appears to have ultimately nailed his radical colours to the mast, and unequivocally sharpened his philosophical knives for that sly and subtle enemy, capitalism. As Eagleton caustically observes, '*Specters of Marx* doesn't just want to catch up with Marxism; it wants to outleft it by claiming that deconstruction was all along a radicalized version of the creed'.[14]

Yet is this what is really manifesting itself in Derrida's work? To be sure, Derrida openly lambastes the neo-evangelical language of the apologist who has recently assumed the mantle of the high priest of capitalist justification, Francis Fukuyama. Indeed, the end of history debate is in one sense clearly about the claims that capitalism makes for the inevitable logical supremacy of market forces over other forms of economic practice; and as far as the Left is concerned, it will welcome Derrida's critique. Yet whilst Derrida rightly points to Fukuyama's 'sleight-of-hand trick between history and nature, between historical empiricity and teleological transcendentality',[15] in conflating historical empiricism and transhistoric idealism, his critique does not break any new ground. Nor does Derrida's list of ten plagues which afflict the contemporary international order – including unemployment, political marginalization, foreign debt problems, the arms industry, nuclear weapons proliferation, inter-ethnic wars, drug problems – come as an intellectual revelation to someone who has followed media debates of the past 15 years. So what is Derrida's principal aim with this book? And is it so radical a break with the Derrida of previous years? Perhaps we are not dealing with some ghostly Pauline conversion on the road to Los Angeles, but something that has been lurking in the sinister margins for some years, some spectral trace of Derrida's concerns, which has now materialized.

Derrida's philosophy has always claimed to be a 'strategy without finality' and has always sought to preserve the otherness of the Other, to keep the negative at work, so to speak. The *movement* (I want to refrain from speaking of the concept) of spectrality is precisely to think the otherness of temporality and history. I would remind you of Derrida's description of the spectral quoted earlier: 'The specter, as its name indicates, is the *frequency* of a certain visibility. But the visibility of the invisible. And visibil*ity*, by its essence, is not seen, which is why it remains *epekeina tes ousias*, beyond the phenomenon or beyond being.'[16] And in these last words of resisting the apprehension of alterity by reason, we also find a clue to Derrida's project in *Specters of Marx*: the work of ethics and justice. For *Otherwise Than Being or Beyond Essence* is the title of Emmanuel Levinas's second large treatise dealing with the necessity of ethics as a thinking of the complexities of ontology. And indeed, Derrida's recent philosophy has been engaged with Emmanuel Levinas's work on 'otherwise than being', or that ethical otherness that lies beyond the conceptual framework of consciousness and self-identity. Derrida's sense of urgency in reassessing Marx's oeuvre today, is based upon his sense of the urgent need for an ethical reassessment of the complicit workings of capital and ontology. From within this nexus of Judaic thinkers,[17] Derrida's increasing respect for ethical otherness leads to a conception of history which seeks to open itself to otherness, to embrace the other as an ethical other, and to prevent the erasure of its significant difference. Like Levinas, Derrida opens up the possibility of a fundamental pre-ontological structure of receptivity and donation which has *intrinsic* ethical significance, and which represents an attempt to restore a sense of ethical orientation and political possibility, to defend what he terms an 'emancipatory promise'.[18] Hence, too, his stress on Benjamin's messianic history, and the desire to promote spectrality, with its acknowledgement of protensions and retensions within temporality. For Derrida, *this* is the inheritance of Marxism: it is the Marx that is always already responsive to the human other as absolutely, unconditionally, demanding; a demand which always places one in the position of a responsibility which can never be met, but which can only be abdicated at the risk of refusing a recognizably human *societas*. The *ghost* becomes a *guest*, to whom one owes absolute hospitality. Derrida's Marx is thus a commitment to justice: echoing Molly Bloom's celebratory affirmation, a commitment to:

> absolute hospitality, the 'yes' to the *arrivant(e)*, the 'come' to the future that cannot be anticipated.... Open, waiting for the event as justice, this hospitality is absolute only if it keeps watch over its own universality. The messianic, including its revolutionary forms (and the messianic is always revolutionary, it has to be), would be urgency, imminence, but irreducible paradox, a waiting without horizon of expectation.[19]

Messianism ushers in a Benjaminian Marxism, but it also brings in a Levinasian justice, a preoccupation which Jameson only cursorily acknowledges. Spectrology is thus firmly tied to justice, as a politics of temporality appears to be intricately connected to the ethical and judicial structures of society. Yet this does indicate a shift in Derrida's thought, albeit of a different sort to that envisaged by Jameson; and this is the way in which the signified 'justice' appears to have been accorded transcendental status and exempted from the logic of supplementarity, the perpetually displaced chain of concepts. Otherwise how can justice sit as an unconditional discourse, while at the same time Derrida has long been appealing to the infinite play of the signifier? Derrida appears to have set aside the notion of justice in particular, a notion deeply entwined with the discourse of metaphysics, for preferential treatment, apparently invulnerable to deconstructive procedure, dismantling and undermining.

Walter Benjamin is also the co-ordinate of a matrix which maps French deconstructionist critiques of the 'end of history' debate, onto the German debate concerning 'posthistoire'. Lutz Niethammer's discussion in *Posthistoire: Has History Come to an End?* is concerned to historicize the notion of 'posthistory', demonstrating that the discussion began in the eighteenth century. It traces the chains of association that are the key theses of 'posthistory' to the major traditions that have sought to understand the age, and concludes that '[t]he problematic of posthistory is not the end of the world but the end of meaning'.[20] Niethammer demonstrates that the question of whether history is finished, appears to have long haunted all cultural sciences with the exception of history itself, which seems to be playing a waiting-game to all the other 'post' discussions, waiting to see whether any useful concepts or ideas emerge in such periodizations.

One question that needs answering is: What history has finished? To answer this, Niethammer discerns in the evolution of posthistory an inner freedom for a lost sociality, the construction of an aesthetic myth of private independence. The genealogy of this myth is traced further to Alexander Kojève's post-Cold War espousal of the Japanese Samurai's code of masculine independence as a panacea for what he perceived as modernism's debilitating emasculation of culture.[21] Kojève's version of history as ending in the 1930s with the 'dialectical overcoming' of the master-slave struggle in Stalinism, crumbled as he perceived the increasing hegemony of American materialism in post-War Europe. As Perry Anderson has argued, Kojève's disillusioned argument that the end of history comes with the dance of commodities and capital accumulation, reaches its zenith in Lyotard's proclamation of the end of meta-narratives and Baudrillard's celebration of the simulacrum.[22] Niethammer argues that the posthistory debate (and by extension, postmodernism) is therefore the product of European intellectuals' disillusionment with a 'voluntarist Hegelianism' as a form of desiring Worldspirit; which, coinciding with the failure of national socialism and international communism, goes hand-in-hand with the way in which they generalized their particular failure as a general end of history. Posthistory 'transposes the death of the individual subject to the history of the species, flattens out social conflicts of interest and irregularities, and thus evacuates all movement from history'.[23] The 'end of history' is thus the conflation of the failure of certain particular prophecies and projects with the exhaustion of all historical possibilities, the 'universalisation of the cultural elite's pessimism and disillusionment',[24] or as Niethammer puts it, 'a specific form of projective self-exoneration'.[25] Indeed, one might be more specific and place the responsibility for the 'end of history' argument at the feet of liberals and socialists, owing to their sense of modernity's failure to provide the promise of possible human fulfilment (like Adorno), as they see the possibilities squeezed out by market capitalism. Conservatives have always perceived modernity to be inimical to values in society. So, rather than the plight of the conservatives, it is paradoxically the disillusionment of the leftists like Adorno and Kojève, who saw their old hopes renewed and then dashed at the end of the 1960s, that provides the impetus for this argument of posthistory.

Niethammer finds the solution to this posthistory argument embedded in the secularized utopianism of Walter Benjamin. Benjamin's *oeuvre* is concerned not with the end of meaning, but a testament full of the intention to dig up repressed and buried hopes for the strengthening of those living around him. He is particularly interested in the 'angel of history' image that stands at the centre of Reflection IX of the 'Theses on the Philosophy of History'. Niethammer perceives the angel as an image of 'recalling the hopes of redemption stored in the religious tradition, so as to introduce them as a meaning and yardstick into human contact with history – both in reference to the past and for political action in the present'.[26] This has specific parallels with Derrida's notion of the messianic in *Specters of Marx*, in which the messianic opens up alternative trajectories of history. In Benjamin's 'central concepts of "remembrance", "now-time" ["*jetzseit*"] and "weak messianic power", is contained an appeal for the activation of alternative traditions. By making history contemporary, he seeks to redeem the hopes of those who have been passed over by history: that is, to release them for the freedom of further effectivity, so that their existential tradition-affirming power may be brought to bear in the struggle that must halt the catastrophic storm of history'.[27] Benjamin effectively argues for the use of spectrality, the resuscitation of the past in the present as a form of blasting away the nostalgic promises of a pure present and temporal transparency. He was in agreement with Brecht over the depressing prospect of a 'time without history' (history without class struggle). In this respect, Niethammer argues that historians ought to pay attention to Benjamin's theses, because the 'weak power of redemption and reorientation persists within our memory of the buried and repressed, as a constant challenge to empirical experience. That is neither mysticism nor millenarianism, but an attempt to release, where historically possible, the desires that have been sacrificed to the progress compulsion.'[28]

Walter Benjamin was concerned with arguing how the messianic can 'blast' open history and reveal the particulars, as against the totalizing narratives of historicism, a synthetic historiography which is neither true in the particular nor discussible in general:

> Historicism contents itself with establishing a causal connection between the various moments in history. But no fact that is a cause is for that very reason historical. It became historical posthumously, as it were, through events that may be separated from it by thousands of years. A historian who takes this as his point of departure stops telling the sequence of events like the beads of a rosary. Instead, he grasps the constellation which his own era has formed with a definite earlier one. Thus he establishes a conception of the present as the 'time of the now' which is shot through with chips of Messianic time.[29]

History is an irrepressible *revenant* (to echo Derrida), living-dead which haunts the present, since causes demonstrate a 'posthumous' historicality and materiality, a 'living-on' or survival after the death of the original event, demonstrating a more powerful life in its spiritual presence than in its corporeal absence. Benjamin's messianic theory acknowledges history's 'impurities', history's heterogeneity, that history is if you like, ghost-written. Since history has always been a barbarous document written by the victor, 'good' history (like E. P.Thompson, the Subaltern studies group) is investigations from the 'bottom-up' – rather than the perspective of the victorious intellectual-élite who have generalized disillusionment from the collapse of their own political aspirations, thus making visible the hitherto invisible alternative Messianic and ghostly trajectories. Eagleton describes Benjamin's messianic history as a 'ceaseless detotalization of a triumphalistic ruling-class history; it is in some sense a given, yet is always constructed from the vantage point of the present; it operates as a deconstructive force within hegemonic ideologies of history, yet can be seen as a totalizing movement within which sudden affinities, correspondences and constellations may be fashioned between disparate struggles'.[30] Here is history in which quantum leaps might be made at points of temporal bifurcation to a new state of augmented significance. As orders coalesce out of apparent chaos and disparity, meaning emerges not as a predictable derivative but as an unforeseeable, unprecedented transformation and an aleatorical departure from tradition. Indeed, Benjamin's struggle with what he calls historicism is actually directed against contemporary narratives of linear progress and teleological development. Eagleton regards what he calls 'Benjamin's "revolutionary nostalgia"' as 'the power of active remembrance as a ritual summoning and invocation of the traditions of the oppressed in violent constellation with the political present'.[31]

Benjamin's image of the historian who resists history as a linear narrative like telling the beads of a rosary, brings one back neatly to our starting point with Billy Pilgrim's knowledge gained on Tralfamadore that temporal linearity is an earthly illusion. Vonnegut's powerful pacifist fictional narrative ushers in the political and ethical importance of conceiving history and its othernesses. One can conceive of Tralfamadore as a fictional metaphor equivalent of Benjamin's 'blasting' operation, which metaphorically blasts the meta-narrative of the naturalness of human violence out of homogeneous time, into an historical context which reorientates the actions of military violence in the fire-bombing of Dresden, in order to recuperate the oppressed past, specifically on behalf of children (the novel is subtitled *The Children's Crusade*). Vonnegut's dynamic non-linear narrative dramatizes the moment when the flow of history is arrested by a configuration which shocks the present into releasing the affirmative and emancipatory thinking of the messianic. It is, to quote Derrida, 'inscribing the possibility of the reference to the other, and this radical alterity and heterogeneity, of differ*a*nce, of technicity, and of ideality in the very event of presence, in the presence of the present that it dis-joints *a priori* in order to make it possible . . .'.[32] It is, in other words, a dramatization of Vonnegut's deeply felt need and commitment to justice and ethical responsibility in opening oneself to the other, in recognizing one's indebtedness to the other. The necessary dis-jointure of temporality, the recognition of the heterogeneity of the present, is the de-totalizing condition of justice, which resists reducing the singularity and alterity of the other in some homogenized history. Time being out of joint, or being out of joint with time, indicates a dislocation in Being and in temporality itself. It is this incoercible difference, this interruption of linearity in temporality, which lays the conditions for responsibility and justice.

Despite Jameson's claim that Derrida is attacking postmodernism, it is the case that many so-called postmodern novelists appear to be doing exactly what Derrida is describing – namely an opening up to spectrality. So, perhaps one ought to recognize that there are different ways of conceiving postmodernism. One can perhaps think of postmodernism within a set of dominant/emergent concepts. There is a dominant way of reading postmodernism as 'the end of history'; but there are also emergent ways of reading postmodernism as seeing history everywhere, with all the attendant problems of history as a concept, as narrative, and as representation. Hence, one gets a number of contemporary fictions which *do not deny history*, but rethink and propose alternative ways of thinking history. So the novel becomes a sort of temporal experimentation field: within a linear model of moving from the opening cover of a book to the back cover, one gets a host of different temporal arrangements. One can think, for example, of Jeanette Winterson's *Sexing the Cherry*, or Angela Carter's *The Infernal Desire Machines of Doctor Hoffman*, in which the narratives are much preoccupied with constructing alternative forms of temporality, and considering how conventional linear forms distort or skew one's existential experience.

I have sought to demonstrate several points in this essay. The 'end of history' argument is predicated upon a desire for pure presence, manifested in late capitalism's assertions that pluralistic democracies and free-market capitalistic economies reign supreme. This desire produces a conception of temporality which generalizes the here-and-now as a once-and-for-all, removing all memories of the past and all proleptic anticipations of the future. This 'purified' temporality of a pure presence in the present announces the end of history. This apparent paradox between pluralism and homogeneity in postmodernism seems to be part of its self-mystification. Yet contrary to those who perceive that the recognition of alterity in postmodernism is itself fuelled by the differential mechanism of competition in 'pluralistic' capitalism, and hence potentially divisive, I would suggest that it is *only* through attempts to release the suppressed othernesses into this identity and to confront this temporality with its (invisible) ghosts, the troubling apparitions that return to haunt the ontology of late capitalism, that one is able to renew the course of history. One can think of Paul Auster's story 'Ghosts' in his *New York Trilogy*, in which the main protagonist increasingly recognizes *the impurity of experience*; or Toni Morrison's *Beloved*, in which a child-ghost returns as a reminder of all the racial repressions of slavery: the list could go on. Thus, literature is a site/territory where 'noise' may be fed into the efforts to 'quieten' history. History has the capacity for invention, for departures from traditions, for constructing 'pockets' of illogicality, disruption and imagining 'spaces' of time outside linear narratives of development, progress and purity – all of which amounts to attempts to reintroduce 'spectrality', of confronting history with its ghostly others. And confronting history with its other, is urgent and vital if we are to proceed with a new ethical writing of history which accounts for justice. To quote Derrida one last time (listening for echoes of Vonnegut):

> No justice – let us not say no law and once again we are not speaking here of laws – seems possible or thinkable without the principle of some *responsibility*, beyond all living present, within that which disjoins the living present, before the ghosts of those who are not yet born or who are already dead, be they victims of wars, political or other kinds of violence, nationalistic, racist, colonialist, sexist or other kinds of exterminations, victims of the oppressions of capitalist imperialism or any of the forms of totalitarianism. Without this *non-contemporaneity with itself of the living present*, without that which secretly unhinges it, without this responsibility and this respect for justice concerning those who *are not there*, of those who are no longer or who are not yet *present and living*, what sense would there be to ask the question 'where?', 'where tomorrow?', 'whither?'.[33]

Have we arrived at the end of history? I would say: 'So it goes' – on.

Notes

1. Elizabeth D. Ermarth, *Sequel to History: Postmodernism and Crises of Representational Time* (Princeton University Press, 1992) 67.
2. Kurt Vonnegut, *Slaughterhouse-Five* ([1st edn 1970]; London: Vintage, 1991) 17.
3. Ibid., 19–20.
4. Karl Marx and Friedrich Engels, *The Communist Manifesto* (1848), in *Karl Marx: Selected Writings*, ed. David McLellan (Oxford University Press, 1977) 221.
5. Jacques Derrida, *Specters of Marx: The State of the Debt, the Work of Mourning, and the New International* trans. Peggy Kamuf (London: Routledge, 1994) 100–1.
6. Fredric Jameson, 'Marx's Purloined Letter', *New Left Review*, 209 (1995) 90.
7. Derrida, *Specters of Marx*, 46–7.
8. Jameson, 'Marx's Purloined Letter', 102.
9. Ibid., 104.
10. Ibid., 103.
11. Fredric Jameson, 'Postmodernism and Consumer Society', in Hal Foster, ed., *Postmodern Culture* (London: Pluto Press, 1985) 125.
12. Ibid., 120.
13. Fredric Jameson, 'Postmodernism, or The Cultural Logic of Late Capitalism', *New Left Review*, 146 (1984) 16.
14. Terry Eagleton, 'Marxism Without Marxism', *Radical Philosophy*, 73 (1995) 35–7.
15. Derrida, *Specters of Marx*, 69.
16. Ibid., 100–1.
17. The Judaic context of these thinkers – Levinas, Derrida, Marx, Benjamin – has had considerable discussion in recent years, especially with regard to the implications for a thinking of non-European–Christian concepts of language, temporality, justice and ethics.
18. Derrida, *Specters of Marx*, 85.
19. Ibid., 168.
20. Lutz Niethammer, *Posthistoire: Has History Come to an End?* (London: Verso, 1992) 3.
21. See Shadia Drury, 'The End of History', in *Alexandre Kojève: The Roots of Postmodern Politics* (Basingstoke: Macmillan, 1994) 41–64.
22. Perry Anderson, 'The Ends of History', in *A Zone of Engagement* (London: Verso, 1992) 327.
23. Niethammer, *Posthistoire*, 144.
24. Joseph McCarney, Review of Lutz Niethammer, *Posthistoire – Has History Come to an End?*, *Radical Philosophy*, 80 (1995) 39–41.
25. Niethammer, *Posthistoire*, 143.
26. Ibid., 112.
27. Ibid., 116.
28. Ibid., 120.
29. Walter Benjamin, 'Theses on the Philosophy of History', in

Illuminations, ed. and trans. Harry Zohn (London: Fontana, 1973) 265.
30. Terry Eagleton, 'Capitalism, Modernism and Postmodernism', in *Against the Grain: Essays 1975–1985* (London: Verso, 1986) 136.
31. Ibid., 136.
32. Derrida, *Specters of Marx*, 75.
33. Ibid., xix.

Part III
The Construction of Identity

7

The Ethics of Biography and Autobiography

Larry Lockridge

I shall be arguing that biographers and autobiographers incur different kinds of moral risk, just as they pursue different moral opportunities. To set some contexts, I shall risk an autobiographical account of my work in ethics and literature, begun in the late 1960s.

Those were the days when writers ancient and modern had to be 'relevant'. In an ethical if not political sense, nobody seemed to me more relevant than Coleridge, who coined 'psychosomatic' and 'self-realization', who first used 'existential' in its modern sense, and who was so baffled by moral uncertainty that he sometimes couldn't get out of bed in the morning. He was his own Ancient Mariner, expressing the largest burden of guilt in the nineteenth century.

Coleridge was engrossed in philosophical ethics. In 1969 I wrote a doctoral dissertation on the subject, published in 1977 as *Coleridge the Moralist*. A better title would have been *The Ethics of an Opium-Eater*, for the Sage of Highgate could simultaneously drink laudanum and write ethical screeds. One of these I leaned on heavily – the second volume of his *Opus Maximum* manuscript in Victoria College Library, Toronto. It remains unpublished to this day, yet contains uncanny anticipations of some 20th-century ethical issues, including G. E. Moore's famed 'open question' argument concerning the word 'good'.[1] I made much use of Coleridge's informal autobiographical writings in notebooks and letters, and found anchorage of ethical abstraction in the stories he told of himself, as well as in his poetry. This focus on the ethical helped me construct a Coleridgean personality and *could* underwrite a larger telling of his life.

I pursued the topic more generally and in 1989 published *The*

Ethics of Romanticism – a lengthy multi-writer study in which the biographical element is somewhat less prominent. (This may explain in part why the book has attracted less attention, readers preferring their ethics mired in the stuff of life.) I had thought it advisable to clear ground by confronting Fredric Jameson's animadversions on ethical criticism in his widely read *The Political Unconscious* (1981).[2] Among other counter-arguments, I had in mind that a political education often begins in *moral* outrage. William Wordsworth is moved in 1791 not by political discourse but by outrage at the sight of a hunger-bitten girl leading a heifer. ''Tis against *that* / Which we are fighting', said his revolutionary mentor, Michel Beaupuy (*Prelude* 1805, ix, 518–19). I argued that many critical schools of thought, including Marxist, that have downgraded ethical criticism are crypto-ethical. For instance, many of those books on the 'self' in the 1960s and 1970s were tacitly espousing a self-realizationist ethic, a form of ethical egoism.[3]

The ethical dimension of literature is difficult to evade, in theory and practice. Until recently its very ubiquity has made it feel not very sexy to younger critics in search of a more esoteric way of talking.

My method in both these books was first to recover the relatively neglected ethical writings themselves, many of them from early in the careers of Romantic writers, and then to see how they might intersect literary texts. The latter were themselves permeated with ethical discourse – and, though I was ultimately concerned more with deep implication than with overt statement, it didn't take much insight to see that this particular body of literature was ethically saturated.

I saw an irony in the New Humanist attack on the Romantics earlier in this century. Irving Babbitt thought these writers obliterated moral consciousness through subjectivism, egoism, emotionalism and nympholepsy. But for Coleridge, ethics is first philosophy:

> Without a *Thou* there could be no opposite, and of course no distinct or conscious sense of the term I. . . . From what reasons do I believe in a *continuous* & ever continuable *Consciousness*? From *Conscience*! Not for myself but for my conscience – i.e. my affections & duties toward others, I should have no Self – for Self is Definition; but all Boundary implies Neighbourhood – & is knowable only by Neighbourhood, or Relations.[4]

For this opium-eater, ethics is anterior to epistemology and all other ologies.

Similarly, Shelley argues that the same faculty of imagination that produces and responds to great cultural artefacts is also the source of moral intuitions and acts. Poetry and the moral life are therefore homologous. Since they spring from the same source, to exercise the one is indirectly to exercise the other. It's no contradiction that Shelley can abhor bluntly *didactic* poetry and still have a passion for transforming the world through the ethical power of *visionary* poetry.

I attempted to fill out the philosophical and critical contexts that writers from Blake through De Quincey acknowledged – in works of Hobbes, Shaftesbury, Butler, Kant, Schiller, Fichte, Schelling, Bentham, Godwin, Wollstonecraft and others. I resisted deploying one or another strong interpretive lens of modern critical debate, not undertaking a Marxist or Nietzschean or Freudian or Wittgensteinian or Lacanian or Foucauldian or Levinasian or Bloomean or Derridean or Habermasian or Kristevan reading of Romantic writers. It wasn't that I had no strong allegiance to one or another contemporary critic. Rather, I felt that any such critic would carry along a set of built-in ethical predispositions that could colour or distort my aim of textual retrieval and objective inference. I'm sceptical of a total objectivity, bound as we all are within various interpretive 'horizons'. But I do regard objectivity as a matter of degree, and as possible in some measure.

So I made deliberate use of what I called a 'weak' lens – the descriptive terms and categories of modern philosophical ethics that one finds in the many basic treatments of the subject. With this *relatively* neutral descriptive apparatus as a preliminary tool, and with the supplement of many histories of European ethics, I tried to identify dominant ethical tendencies of Romantic writers in contrast to other ethical possibilities or schools of thought. I hoped to uncover the Romantic 'ought' through critical description, an 'is'.

I concluded that British Romantic writers were doing some crucial philosophical work. They were advancing a kind of ethical thinking that absorbed, resisted, and transformed all other ethical schools of the time – from Hobbesian egoism to sentimentalism to hedonistic utilitarianism to Kantian formalism to common-sense philosophy to Christian ethics. These literary misfits were advancing the work of philosophy, filling in something missing in ethical debate among board-certified philosophers. They sought a rich plurality of values against a backdrop of what they regarded as a diminishment of value, seen in the reductive ethical systems of the day, in the emergent commodification of persons into things, and in the ennui that followed the collapse of the French Revolution. As embattled radical humanists, the Romantics gave strenuous voice to a teleological 'will to value', in what is most accurately termed an '*ideal* utilitarianism', a value pluralism not limited to pleasure or happiness, and embedded in a visionary literature. They well knew the fragility of goodness, the problematics of action and identity, the constraints on freedom. De Quincey, the most 'post-modern' of these writers, sets the tone in his response to Kant, when like Coleridge he pleads for an ethics more congenial to an infirm opium eater. He figures life as a dark forest where proper paths are obscured, and again as a whispering gallery, where our smallest utterances, like our seemingly insignificant gestures or acts, may miscarry and return tenfold to haunt us. The Romantics have a strong intuition of a plenitude of values, but they find it difficult to tell stories that answer to the question, 'What is to be done?'

I was much aware of modern scepticism via deconstruction but had a scholarly and archival bent that survived on the hope that research can still be a discovery procedure, that there is such a thing as stronger or weaker textual evidence, and that not all of literature is rhetorical displacement. But my method in *The Ethics of Romanticism* of declining a strong interpretive lens in favour of a descriptive, relatively value-neutral, 'weak' one has had few takers.

More attention has been given to my recent book, *Shade of the Raintree: The Life and Death of Ross Lockridge, Jr.* (1994), a biography of my father in which I play a bit part, getting born in chapter six.[5] Although I was constructing the story of a person instead of a body of thought, writing this book was not a total shift of gears. Once again I had what seemed a dark Romantic narrative on my hands, again I dealt with difficult ethical issues, and again I was sleuthing for textual evidence in out-of-the-way places. Recovering traces of a writer meant recovering his words, especially his letters, supplemented by the memories and words of others. So I set out on a bizarre paper chase.

As in my study of the ethics of Romanticism, I hoped to avoid what I call 'wishful reading', in which our prior commitments lead us to find what we are looking for. During the 1960s and 1970s, Blake was read as a Maoist by Maoists, a Marxist by Marxists, a Jungian by Jungians, a (flawed) feminist by feminists, an anarchist by anarcho-liberals. I didn't wish to beg the question of *what kind of ethics* I would find in Romantic writers and suggested that a 'relaxation of critical will' might be enabling in the recovery of deep ethical tendencies. Similarly, I didn't wish to turn my father into some version of myself.

I'd propose this as an ethics of interpretation – that we respect the alterity of writers and their words. ('Alterity' is a Coleridgean word.)

Ross Lockridge, Jr had quite a bit going for him. A 33-year-old author from Indiana, he published his first novel *Raintree County* in 1948 to great acclaim. This was an unabashed 1060-page attempt at the Great American Novel. A few reviewers at the time said okay, this is the GAN, and many, stopping short of that, still mentioned Lockridge in the same breath with Dreiser and Sherwood Anderson. One wrote that *Raintree County* was a many-levelled fiction but also a page turner, a readable American *Ulysses*. Lockridge conceived it as a moral fiction in a bleak post-war period – a vital story he thought Americans needed, 'goddam them'.

Publishing a novel was a bigger deal in those days, and the gentleman from Indiana became the season's literary celebrity. Howard Mumford Jones in *The Saturday Review of Literature* said that 'the breath of life sweeps through its voluminous pages, and it may be that *Raintree County* marks at last the end of a long slump in American fiction'. *The New York Times* called it 'an achievement of art and purpose, a cosmically brooding book full of significance and beauty'. The novel was excerpted in *Life* magazine and won the enormous MGM Novel Award, a movie contract billed as the world's largest literary prize. (Years later, the novel was turned into a terrible movie, scripted by the creator of the cartoon character Mr Magoo, starring Montgomery Clift and Elizabeth Taylor.) *Raintree County* was Main Selection of Book-of-the-Month Club, which guaranteed an additional sale minimally of one-third of a million copies in hardcover.

Then, two months after publication, on the evening of 6 March 1948, just as *Raintree County* had reached the number one position on the nation's bestseller lists, Lockridge told his wife that he was going out to mail some letters and would then drive over to his parents' house to listen to the high school basketball regionals. (We were living in a new house back in our hometown of Bloomington, Indiana, having moved from Boston, where the novel was written.) He did mail the letters, but returned to the garage, separate from the house, left on the engine of his new Kaiser, and killed himself.

The New York Times carried the story, front page, as I was myself to understand it for most of my adult life. Ross Lockridge, Jr was found in the front seat of the car, slumped behind the steering wheel, with his legs exiting the car door.

Many of his friends, however, thought Ross the world's least likely suicide and refused to believe it. He was jovial, even-tempered, a family man who sang while he did the dishes, was faithful to his spouse, didn't sexually abuse his four kids, and drank milk instead of booze. Many thought it must have been an accident – Lockridge, who could get absorbed in things, was probably listening to the basketball regionals on the car radio with the engine on and passed out. Or perhaps he *had* yielded to a dark impulse, but then changed his mind, too late fully to exit the car.

In early 1989, shortly after I decided to write a biography of my father, my mother for the first time told me what had happened the night of 6 March 1948. She had found her husband not in the front seat with his legs exiting the car door. Rather, he was in the *back* seat, with the car doors securely shut and a vacuum cleaner hose attached to the exhaust tank and running into the small rear ventilation window, sealed efficiently with a cloth. (Her husband had economized on extras, so there was no car radio, no listening to basketball.) She dragged the body from the car and ran to call the fire department and her in-laws. Her husband's sister arrived a few minutes before the fire department, stuffed the death paraphernalia into a large garbage can behind the garage, and – with the help of Ross Lockridge, Senior – concocted the story that the author had been found in the front seat with legs exiting, as if preparing to leave the garage. They hoped for a verdict of accidental death, to protect the children from the fact of their father's desertion and the larger family from the disgrace of suicide. Working without much of the evidence, the coroner played his hunches and ruled it a suicide anyway.

Hearing this story of a family cover-up four decades after the fact was the most apocalyptic moment for me in writing the biography. I'd never liked the ambiguity surrounding my father's death and was frankly relieved as well as astonished. But more to the point here, the revelation demonstrates in a pointed way what biographers hope to find – an increase in clarity with respect to their subject's life, even to the point of an unnerving revision.

I offer this episode, which differs only in degree from many others, as partial refutation of some recent thinking about biography. Ira Nadel, for instance, writes that:

> the narrativity of biography gives real events the form of a story, imposing meaning and pattern on reality, which does not organise itself into either meaning or truth.... Factual reconstruction can never be the *raison d'être* of biography because it is impossible to achieve. It must be, rather, narrative desire, the urge to tell the story of the subject which in its telling establishes meaning.[6]

The historian Eric Hobsbawm has recently remarked that the verdict in the O. J. Simpson criminal trial stands as a *reductio ad absurdum* of post-modern theories of historical narration.[7] In accordance with 'narrative desire', any exculpatory story could be entertained, even when the odds of the DNA evidence were billions to one in favour of Simpson's guilt.

I feel that to assent to the argument that narrative desire overrides all else in biography would actually lay waste its motive ground in curiosity. There is a great difference between the armchair narratologist imagining a plenitude of possibilities and the practising biographer, who would have little reason to rummage through attics and archives if he or she could simply construct stories from whatever evidentiary traces were already in store. The post-modern argument is, I believe, anchored in false or at least presumptive dichotomizing of fact/value, discovery/creation, reference/language and story/plot.

My experience as biographer has instead reconfirmed for me the potential *mutuality* of narrative desire in the story-teller and expressive agency in the biographical subject. The difference in meaning between the purported front seat and the actual back seat position of the body was, for me, monumental. My father's actual body language in death, revealed by my mother at last, was a function not only of my will to meaning as interpreter but also of his own expressive intentionality as agent and of the total circumstances that led up to and surrounded his final act. All of this announced, unambiguously, 'I really meant to kill myself'. His relatives attempted to change the story, to make available other readings of things, and they succeeded in the eyes of some.

But like any committed biographer, I had to try to *find things out* and I had to choose some stories over others. Choice isn't often so unambiguous as it was in this instance, but biographers are always confronting narrative choices based on their sense of probability. They sensibly do their detective work within this premise of probability, which is a powerful option between a benighted certainty on the one hand and a paralysing (hardly liberating) scepticism on the other. They direct their scepticism more to the weighing of evidence than to the formal (im)possibility of writing a truth-grounded biography in the first place.

How, more precisely, does the ethical enter into this discussion? I'll briefly consider, first, the relationship of biographer to subject during the discovery procedure; then, biographical narrative as written; and finally the relationship of biography to reader.

The biographer is intellectually and morally presumptuous in forging through the debris of somebody else's life. It's an invasion of privacy, with much rummaging through closets and reading of other people's mail. I found a notebook containing my father's shorthand transcriptions of his own dreams, which I paid a court reporter to decode. I felt it was my duty to do so, as a biographer trying to resolve a deep mystery. 'Dare to know' is the biographer's imperative. But, as I was curious as hell, this peering into my father's unconscious was also my inclination.

Surely I imposed on my dead father's right to privacy. The unauthorized biographer's duty routinely conflicts with the subject's rights. This is an irresolvable moral antinomy. To decide it categorically in favour of the subject would be to pre-empt the entire biographical project.

In a sense, the biographer takes possession of another, in the current metaphors colonizing or cannibalizing the life in *finding it out*, and using the subject as a means, especially the personal career advantage of getting a book published. This violates Kant's imperative to treat other human beings not as means but as ends in themselves. Since the subject is defenceless in proportion to the biographer's relentlessness, the biographer incurs the moral jeopardy of a predator.

I am assuming here, but would have to argue it at length, that the biographical subject, dead or alive, is something more and other than a textual construct or trail of traces. Rather, a lingering personhood makes claims on us, even from beyond the grave.

By way of compensation for violation of the subject, the biographer may aspire to certain virtues – of disinterestedness, honesty, accuracy and fairness in a just telling of the life, a life that for one reason or another *ought* to be told, after all. To tell the story of another's life imposes an obligation to be as truthful and fair as possible, whatever one's conception of these words.

Biographers are often said to be story-tellers *on oath*. This is a formula I've pondered and cannot improve on as a rule of thumb. I must say, though, that if biographers had to tell the *whole* truth they'd suffer the predicament of Tristram Shandy; such a story could hardly get started. And as for 'nothing but the truth' – this too is an impossible condition for a biographer, just as it is for a courtroom witness.

But I believe the metaphor is right: publishing a biography inevitably poses the question of the subject's moral worth within the virtual court of a readership, whether or not the biographer encourages such judgement. It is intuitively the case that this person, especially if dead and not ringed around by friends and relatives, is defenceless and entitled to the same fair treatment as any other person, dead or alive. Reflect on our own discomfort when overhearing others speak of us – our indignation when they have it wrong, our despair when they have it right.

Disinterestedness is one of those standards that indict all biographers. I built my interest as son into the narrative upfront, trying to convert a liability into a storyteller's asset. All biographers have an interest of one sort or another, which less pejoratively can be called a perspective. But the standard of disinterestedness remains to help guard against dual errors – the negative idealization of the hatchet job, and the positive of hagiography.

What about the ethics of biographical narrative *per se*? We hear much about how biography, usually regarded as a subset of history, should learn from fiction – and certainly in a formal sense (narrative élan, characterization, setting) I agree. But I'd suggest that *novelization* in biography is a moral error, not just an intellectual. It is a violation of personhood (if hardly the type that sends its perpetrator to hell) – whether it makes the subject look good or bad. By 'novelization' I mean the unacknowledged use of narrative bridges and interior monologue where no direct substantiation exists, or where there is direct counter-evidence. It's a mix of inference and invention that goes unannounced. As such, it differs from honest, outright speculation.

I may have a prejudice here, because an earlier, under-researched biography of my father, the novelist John Leggett's undocumented and best-selling *Ross and Tom* (1974), had an enormous amount of novelization that someone unfamiliar with the life would be unable to detect.[8] I lived uneasily for 20 years with a fictionalized father.

Most biographers narrate within a premise of soft determinism. This is the view that motives and acts of the agent contribute to causal chains in the circumstantial world but do not stand independently of these chains. The biographical subject is assumed to be greatly influenced by parents and siblings, by economic class, by temporal and spatial circumstance – but is also granted some degree of self-motivation and choice. The subjects of biographies tend to be the people we call 'driven' – self-scripting types driven to parental revolt, to unfamiliar roles, to living beyond precedent. We look for continuities, for explanations of later fate in earlier *self*-determination – for we know, as the subject cannot, how it will turn out in the end. Biographers can reverse the arrow of time and have this advantage over autobiographers in being able to narrate the end.

But any sophisticated biographer will also see contingency in the mingled yarn of a life. Random events enter into the causality of the narrated life and take on meaning by virtue of having taken place, losing their contingent character after the fact. My father *just happened* to hear about the MGM Novel Award competition in time to enter it – and winning it, as he later lamented, was his greatest misfortune, his sorry fate.

With respect to my father's suicide, the weight of explanation weighed heavily upon me. One could read the entire life in terms of its ending, or one could say, if only such and such had happened, it could have turned out differently, for perhaps some bad moral luck played a part.

'The answer you seek is in an envelope', read the fortune cookie. But I found matters more complicated.

Three types of narrative explanation implicitly interact in the story I tell in *Shade of the Raintree* – psychological, biological/genetic and sociological/cultural. I won't go into these in any detail here.

But there was evidence that my father suffered from a personality disorder. With the help of three psychologists who independently read a late draft of my manuscript, I diagnosed it as a narcissistic disorder. In him there was a perfectionism and drive to greatness that resulted in his ambitious novel itself. (The theorist Heinz Kohut links narcissism and creativity.) But this same perfectionism led to a grandiosity that fizzled into major depression when the novel was finished. (Here, the more censorious theorist Otto Kernberg could be consulted.) Narcissistic theory tends, alas, to stick it to the mother. My father's mother, a psychologist herself, was implicated in her rather detached pedagogy, her own career as a failed writer, and as someone who looked to her son for a vicarious fulfilment.

But there is also evidence of bipolar illness, more linked to nature than to nurture. It may run in the family. My father's double second cousin, Mary Jane Ward, wrote the 1946 novel *The Snake Pit*, based on her own incarceration in a mental institution. Considerable evidence supports biological and possibly genetic causes of manic-depressive disorder. At one point my father thought there was something wrong with his physical brain, not just his mind, and he may have been right.

Finally, there is the very American story of a Midwestern novelist of modest circumstances who first goes to Paris and then confronts an Eastern literary establishment, winning the big prizes, setting off for Hollywood, getting into a terrible fight with his publisher over splitting up the spoils, and not handling American-style success very well. He got hundreds of rave reviews, but these didn't matter next to the pan that appeared in a prestigious Eastern magazine. He felt like an impostor who'd been found out and ridiculed, especially when, on the day he died, a portion of the *New Yorker* pan was reprinted in his hometown newspaper. My biography has been read as a dark cultural parable of the writer in America.

All three interpretive modes – psychological, biological, cultural – tend to be exculpatory to the extent that they are *explanations*. Moral praise or blame tends to get defused when we see causes deep within or without over which the agent has little control. The moral opprobrium one may find in suicide can be lifted when one considers that for somebody in deep pain – whether from depression or physical agony – suicide may seem the only release. My father died of depression – ending in suicide.

As biographer, I hoped to find a single clear explanation, that answer in an envelope – but perhaps it's part of the ethics of narration that one ought to settle instead for complexity. A human life or personality must retain some mystery in narration, or we've committed a violence by reduction. In my father's case, I decided that it had been a *convergence* of factors – personality, biology, circumstance – that led to major depression. On the basis of my sample group of one, I recently spoke of a convergence theory of suicide to the American Association of Suicidology, noting that in our own field of literary criticism we are going through some nasty theory wars, where a convergence of different types of explanation might be more productive.[9]

What is the ethical role of the reader in the biographical pact? Why read biography? Certainly Wayne Booth's metaphor of 'the company we keep' (or shun) has special bearing on biography, which is both a book and a person, sort of. We might read a biography with a view to its subject as extrapolatable, possibly even companionable.

But I'd propose another critical metaphor here. Readers of biographies are tacitly engaged in a continuous hypothetical *testing* of whether a substitution could be made of their own identity for that of the biographical subject. More than 'playing with' other identities, readers engage in such testing through continuous analogy.

Otherness insists on distance, so I suspect that readers rarely move beyond analogy to identity, to total empathy, or (as Poulet might have it) to wholesale invasion by the biographical subject.

But this is saying something simple. Readers of biographies in effect ask themselves, with fascination when the biography is a good one, whether they are *like* the subject in the choices made, the values pursued. 'Could I conceivably do that? Could I be that?' This creates a reader's appetite of its own. My shift of metaphor from playing to testing suggests that in biography the reader tilts more toward the ethical than toward the aesthetic pole of reading experience.

Turning now to autobiography, more theorized than biography these days, I'd note first that we have an obvious paradox. The very person who has lived the life from the inside out, with first-hand witness of the events narrated, also has the greatest motive to lie.

The first page of Coleridge's *Biographia Literaria* has almost as many lies as sentences. Autobiography is necessarily the least disinterested of all literary forms.

To the extent I was myself a player in the biography of my father – to the extent there was an admixture of autobiography – my text was under suspicion. I escaped it to the extent readers felt I was not trying to upstage my subject. The book was intended to be a biography, not a memoir, not a 'search for the father', and not a suicide survivor's manual. Yet it remains, in part, an autobiography. I begin with the story of what has happened to Ross Lockridge Jr's larger family since 1948. Because I was only five when my father died, I had a child's memories, difficult to sequence and with the feel of a lost dream world.

I tried hard to salvage all direct memories, but what most gave me the impression that I had existed way back then were textual references to me in third person. I wasn't pleased to discover, as recorded in the baby book kept by my mother, that my first combination of uttered words was 'Daddy's book'. I found a letter in which my worried father reports to his mother on my slow mental development. To discover instances of having been textually registered by others was often a mild shock, correcting both somnambulism and solipsism.

The autobiographer's predicament is, of course, to be simultaneously subject and object. In first person narration we need the confirmations of third person as a means of seeing ourselves in the world, of finding ourselves out.

But is the autobiographer 'on oath' in the same way that the biographer is? The simplest answer is, yes – and we could let it go at that. But I believe that there's an asymmetry in their ethical situations.

The argument is rather difficult to make, but I'd draw an analogy with the way we differently regard murder and suicide. We could probably come to some agreement that murder is morally wrong. But we would debate the ethics of suicide all night.

Similarly, we might grant autobiographers a greater latitude and entitlement as to what they can *say about* themselves, just as we grant people greater latitude as to what they can *do to* themselves. Autobiographers are free to hang themselves, as many unintentionally do. The responsibility we bear toward ourselves is real, but we intuit that it is somewhat less than, and perhaps different in kind from, the responsibility we bear toward others. (Autobiography is, of course, written *for* others as well as for the authors themselves, and includes others in its cast of characters – so this issue is not quite like debating the ethics of masturbation.)

The moral jeopardy of the autobiographer is clear enough. Even if we are ethical egoists, who assert that we have both a right and a duty to act in our own interests, we can see a multitude of dark motives behind the autobiographical project: from self-deception to outright lying to self-vindication to revenge to exhibitionism to profiteering to the presumption involved in universalizing a single, local ego. All of this is in addition to the probably dubious life being narrated, for since most autobiographers are already public figures, they are also more likely than the rest of us to be scoundrels. Such a narrative may simply compound the crimes being narrated, as in Nixon's or Kissinger's memoirs.

Given all this, and given that we may find truthfulness in autobiography a desirable if rare event, is there any special indulgence to be extended to autobiographers? In an act of gathering and analysis, the biographer attempts to retrieve somebody else's life as lived (or, with living subjects, lived up to that point). But the autobiographer's act of composition may be regarded as itself *part of* a life still in the making. Writing autobiography is a continuation by other means of the life being narrated, on the edge of the compositional present. Writing an autobiography adds in itself a chapter to the narrated life.

And just as a therapist might encourage patients to tell the story of themselves in different ways in a therapeutic revisionism, so the autobiographer might regard his or her life as an unsettled thing, with a usable past to be salvaged selectively for certain ends. Beyond recording or even discovering the meaning of a life, the autobiographer may be steering the life-in-process in one direction or another, connecting present and projected selves with those elements of the past useful to present and personal *interest*.

The critical emphasis on 'narrative desire' thus makes more sense with autobiography than with biography. As proprietors of our own lives, we are more at liberty to (re)shape them how we will.

Noting that this is in fact what occurs in autobiography, critics have been aligning it more with fiction than with history, or at least have been granting the autobiographer a poetic *licence*. Jerome Bruner's view is representative:

> Any autobiographical reconfiguring of a life . . . is not so much a matter of making new discoveries in the archaeological record of

> our experiences, or of revealing the contents of previously hidden 'memories,' but of rewriting a narrative along different interpretive lines.... I persist in thinking that autobiography is an extension of fiction, rather than the reverse, that the shape of life comes first from imagination rather than from experience.[10]

I regard this as an overstatement but agree that autobiographical truth is something more and other than factuality. If the autobiographer is on oath, it is to construct an identity plausible and public enough for the reader to recognize it, to entertain it. It must be, Bruner says, 'negotiable in the "conversation of lives"'. So considered, a 'self-mythology' may be the autobiographer's truth and a usable public truth as well.

The moral uses of autobiography with respect to readers are many. 'Witness autobiography', for example, brings us face to face with atrocity and genocide, as in slave or immigrant or war narratives. Then too, readers find some of the same ethical engagement with autobiography as biography – a testing of their own identity against the narrator's through continuous analogy. But reading an autobiography is different from reading a biography, because one confronts an additional question: 'Would I be willing and able to *say* this about myself?' Correlative to the autobiographer's egoism is a degree of vulnerability, and many of the major autobiographers from Augustine to Rousseau to De Quincey to Simone de Beauvoir are asking for our indulgence in their cautionary tales, their non-exemplary lives.

Kant was pretty severe on both lying and suicide. Either act, if the maxim upon which it was based were universalized, would contradict the imperative that human beings be treated as rational ends in themselves. But the very impulse toward universalizing is now greeted with moral dubiety in our profession. Kant himself tangled with 'casuistical' exceptions. Even if truth-telling with reference to worlds within and without cannot be absolutely commanded in either biography or autobiography, I think it meritorious whenever and to the degree this happens. Contrariwise, we do acknowledge instances where personal revisionism is a wrong for its endangerment of others – fabricating a medical degree or pilot's licence or using autobiography as a public format in which to lay waste some old enemy. But I think we can usually give autobiographers more rope than biographers in making of their subjects what they will.

Notes

1. Samuel Taylor Coleridge, *Opus Maximum* ms, II ff., 61–2; G. E. Moore, *Principia Ethica* (Cambridge University Press, 1903) 1–21; Laurence S. Lockridge, *Coleridge the Moralist* (Ithaca: Cornell University Press, 1977) 226–7.
2. Fredric Jameson, *The Political Unconscious* (Ithaca: Cornell University Press, 1981) 116 and *passim*.
3. Laurence S. Lockridge, *The Ethics of Romanticism* (Cambridge University Press, 1989) 22–38.
4. Coleridge, *Opus Maximum*, II ff., 143–6; Coleridge, *Notebooks*, ed. Kathleen Coburn (New York: Pantheon, 1957–) II, 3231; Lockridge, *Coleridge the Moralist*, 120–30.
5. Larry Lockridge, *Shade of the Raintree: The Life and Death of Ross Lockridge, Jr.* (New York: Viking Penguin, 1994; Penguin Books, 1995).
6. Ira Nadel, 'Biography and Theory, or, Beckett in the Bath', *Biography and Autobiography*, ed. James Noonan (Ottawa: Carleton University Press, 1993) 11, 14.
7. Eric Hobsbawm, lecture, The New York Institute for the Humanities, 6 October 1995.
8. John Leggett, *Ross and Tom: Two American Tragedies* (New York: Simon & Schuster, 1974). 'Tom' refers to Thomas Heggen, author of *Mister Roberts*. He and Lockridge never met.
9. Larry Lockridge, 'Least Likely Suicide', *Suicide and Life-Threatening Behavior*, 25.4 (1995) 429–36.
10. Jerome Bruner, 'The Autobiographical Process', *The Culture of Autobiography*, ed. Robert Folkenflik (Stanford University Press, 1993) 40, 55.

8

The Ethics of Queer Theory

Colleen Lamos

The study of lesbian and gay literature is based upon the claim to equality: that literary representations of same-sex love deserve the same thoughtful, respectful attention as has been given to those of heterosexual love. This principle of equality is motivated by the seemingly straightforward ethical demand that lesbians and gay men should be free to express their genuine affections. Such a call for liberation, analogous to those of women and of ethnic minorities, is all the more compelling inasmuch as the articulation of same-sex passion has typically been subject to violent suppression. The literary study of lesbian and gay issues is thus driven by the ethical imperative to 'tell the truth' about homosexuality.

Nevertheless, this commitment to fairness and honesty, together with the recognition that same-sex desire has been hidden, distorted, or denied in Western literature encounters a stumbling block if one considers passion – both homosexual and heterosexual – not as the product of an intrinsic orientation but of cultural forces. If homosexuality is constructively intertwined with heterosexuality, there is no unequivocal truth to be revealed about the former, nor a simple equivalence one could assert between the two. As Michel Foucault has argued in *The History of Sexuality*, the often shameful and coerced expressions of so-called perverse sexual desires – what he calls 'the confession of the flesh' – are exercises in the pleasurable production of licit power and the powerful production of illicit pleasure.[1] Hence, the (heterosexual) power that oppresses and the (homosexual) pleasure that conceals or unwillingly admits itself are mutually implicated in complex ways. Rather than simply suffering from oppression and awaiting its release, 'homosexuality', like its conceptual twin, 'heterosexuality', is better understood as an effect of our modern, Western sexual discourse. This theoretical critique of the commonly held belief in the existence of two, essentially different, kinds of passion and persons is compounded by empirical circumstances – namely, the advent of AIDS – that have compromised the notion of sexual liberation for gay men, while women have often viewed the idea of untrammelled sexual pleasure with suspicion.

Sexuality in general, and homosexuality in particular, have consequently become troubling epistemological issues. Instead of merely urging the honest and free expression of same-sex desire, cultural theorists and literary critics are now confronted by the problem of how and what we think we know about sexuality in terms of its textual productions. Concomitantly, the ethical imperative of (homo)sexual liberation has become much more complicated and ambivalent. Responding to this dilemma, queer theory examines and tries to dismantle fundamental Western concepts of sexuality, particularly the binary opposition between homosexuality and heterosexuality. As a result, its project is seemingly 'amoral' insofar as it does not make traditional ethical or juridical claims, yet it also provokes challenging questions to those traditions.

This essay is an exploration of the divergent ethical aims and practices of these two competing theoretical paradigms for the contemporary study of same-sexuality: on the one hand, *lesbian and gay theory*, and, on the other hand, *queer theory*. By juxtaposing them in a way that sharply contrasts their differences, I hope to underscore the tension between these alternatives as a productive conflict. By setting them against each other, we may come to a clearer understanding of the practical and theoretical issues at stake in a consideration of the ethics of sexual theory, whether one calls it 'queer' or 'lesbian and gay' or something else. Finally, these two paradigms have direct and wide-ranging implications for the study and teaching of literary representation of sexuality in general, including but not limited to homosexuality and heterosexuality.

A central dilemma for those engaged in research and pedagogy today concerning sexuality is an ethical one. As I have suggested, for many gay people as well as for their straight allies, the study of same-sex desires is a constructive activity whose purpose is to validate those desires and to create meaningful and positive lesbian and gay identities. In this context, the crucial ethical act is coming out – that is, frankly acknowledging to oneself and to others one's sincere affections. For instance, Ellen Degeneres's highly publicized coming out in the spring of 1997, both *in propria persona* and in her character as 'Ellen' in her prime-time American television programme of that name, appealed directly to the moral injunction to be true to oneself. Similarly, in their introduction to a recent collection of essays on lesbian and gay literary study, *Professions of Desire*, George Haggerty and Bonnie Zimmerman announce that 'this is a field that one does not enter so much as come out in'.[2] By extension, lesbian and gay literary criticism is often aimed at disclosing the significance and value of such affections in literary texts or in the lives of their authors.

Lesbian and gay theory envisions the emancipation of lesbians and gay men by reversing the negative moral valuation of homosexuality within the Judeo-Christian tradition. Urging the ethical parity between same- and other-sex love, many lesbian and gay theorists share the fundamental assumptions common to Western humanism regarding human subjectivity and the intrinsic, incontrovertible nature of sexual desire. By expanding our understanding of 'human nature' to include homosexuality as an equally natural and essential aspect of life, they seek to afford gay people their full humanity in an ethical as well as a political sense. The extension of civil rights to lesbians and gay men is the juridical consequence of the inclusion of same-sex love within traditional axiological and moral concepts. Thus, in his book, *Virtually Normal*, the neo-conservative Andrew Sullivan argues for a 'politics of homosexuality' that would end civic discrimination and extend to homosexuals 'every right and responsibility that heterosexuals enjoy as public citizens'.[3]

The arguments advanced by Sullivan and others for public equality for homosexuals are strengthened by a cursory survey of the systematic and often cruel forms of discrimination directed at them. The shame and degradation commonly experienced by lesbians and gay men, and hence the stratagems of concealment to which they are compelled to resort, are the result of the overt harassment, the covert gestures of contempt, and the physical violence that they frequently suffer. A recent survey cited by Urvashi Vaid in her study of contemporary lesbian and gay politics, *Virtual Equality*, reveals that more than a quarter of gay men in the United States have been beaten up simply because they are gay.[4] Given such empirical facts, it is no surprise that the compelling aims of lesbian and gay literary criticism are to establish the study of lesbian and gay themes and texts as a legitimate field of scholarly inquiry and to expose the homophobia that has deformed or suppressed its literary representation. In so doing, lesbian and gay theory calls upon so-called universal human values and upon historically respected notions of the individual and the social good.

Such a project directly conflicts with the aim of queer theory to deconstruct the ideologies that have produced heterosexuality and homosexuality as categories constitutive of human sexuality and of subjective identity. Instead of normalizing homosexuality, queer theorists reject the normality of heterosexuality. Queer theory is thus unethical in the Nietzschean sense because it belies accepted ethical truths and pursues a negative critique. Like Nietzsche's woman who is a figure for 'the untruth of truth' because she realizes that the supposedly hidden truth of femininity is a lie, 'the homosexual' in queer theory is a figure for the fabricated 'secret' of homosexual desire. That putative secret is an ideological fiction or a monstrous phantasm whose 'truth' is only that there is no essential truth of human sexuality.

The ethical subject of queer theory is thus not defined by an intrinsic sexual orientation – he or she is not naturally gay or straight – but as a collection of various, non-convergent, even conflicting interests.[5] 'Queer', unlike the terms 'homosexual', 'lesbian', or 'gay', does not designate an ontological category or substantive entity. Rather, as Judith Butler has argued in *Bodies that Matter*, it refers to the mobile and relative (indeed, queer) interests that are at work in what is now often termed the performative constitution of subjectivity.[6] As such, 'queer' does not designate a particular direction of sexual desire but describes the heterogeneity and contingencies of the desires at work in the formation of any subjective identity, whether it be heterosexual, homosexual, or otherwise.

An ethics based upon this notion of subjectivity does not appeal to universal human values or to transcendental notions of the good. By contrast, queer theory's ethical claims are pragmatic and relative; 'the good' or 'the right' is what is good or right for certain purposes, under particular conditions, at specific times, for certain groups of people whose understanding of themselves as a group sharing common interests is itself a matter of debate. Hence, the ethical constitution of the collective entity of queer people is as protean and unfixed as that of the queer subject. Instead of envisioning a singular ethical ideal, the ethics of queer theory is a fluctuating process of negotiation, an endless labour that entails debate as much as agreement.[7] In a way, queer theory implies a communitarian notion of justice, but one in which the idea of 'the community' is always and inevitably contested. Far from dissolving into postmodern vagaries, though, queer theory in this larger sense of the term explains the often bizarre confluence of goals among people with divergent interests and the equally strange conflicts among those with apparently convergent interests. Finally, by resisting the impulse toward a prescriptive ethics, queer theory offers a practical ethics based upon the shifting demands of local needs and immediate situations.

A striking example of the difference between lesbian and gay theory and queer theory is the diverse ways in which the 'lesbian and gay community' has been conceived and the ethical conclusions that follow from them. In the wake of the 1969 Stonewall riots, lesbian and gay activists stressed the need for a visible lesbian and gay political collectivity in order to combat the notorious invisibility of homosexuals within straight society. As Eve Kosofsky Sedgwick and D. A. Miller have argued, such invisibility renders same-sex love perpetually deniable and thus effectively non-existent.[8] However, the nature of such a public collectivity has been understood quite differently.

Many lesbian theorists and political activists base their notions of a lesbian community upon a feminist belief in the commonality of interests among women – in short, in a vision of sisterhood. Particularly during the 1970s but still in some quarters today, they have articulated and, in practice, constructed a separate and sometimes avowedly separatist lesbian subculture – what Jill Johnston called a 'lesbian nation' – that is based upon a non-patriarchal ethics of care and co-operation. Following in the footsteps of lesbian feminists for whom a lesbian was a 'woman-identified-woman', Sara Hoagland argues in *Lesbian Ethics* that a lesbian identity and a set of specifically lesbian ethical values spring from a sense of community among lesbian women.[9]

By contrast, queer activists since the early 1990s have envisioned a postmodern, 'queer nationality'. Rather than forming a separate subculture, contemporary queer artists appropriate images from mass culture for subversive ends. In New York, groups of artists like Lesbian Avengers, Fierce Pussy and Dyke Action Machine redeploy advertising imagery and celebrity icons, scandalizing their audiences by placing their parodic imitations of, for instance, Calvin Klein ads in subway stations and other public places.[10] Lauren Berlant and Elizabeth Freeman argue in 'Queer Nationality' that current queer political and cultural productions, such as ACT-UP guerrilla theatre and underground magazines, take up elements of American popular culture in a satiric miming of American national myths.[11] These acts of cultural sabotage, including performances by Sandra Bernhard and other artists, render as a camp charade both Americanness and conventional notions of homosexuality and heterosexuality. In this context, 'queer' refers to the style and political aim of these acts or works of art rather than to the sexual orientation or subjective identity of those who engage in them.

Playing off the idea of the nation as a normative community, 'queer nation' implies a mutable and loose mutuality of interest among changing groups of people. Given the unstable and heterogeneous nature of such a concept, it is unsurprising that it is hotly debated by those who believe that a definite sexual identity is necessary for personal happiness or political work. However, the concept of queer nationality offers a bitingly effective, postmodern version of liberation that is not tied to a teleological script or a utopian ideal.

Furthermore, queer theory suggests what I call a 'proleptic subject'. Such a subject does not possess an authentic, inner self waiting to be set free but is constructed by means of acts that, tentatively and provisionally, presuppose it. Thus, 'we' queers act as if 'we' are what 'we' will only have become by acting now as if 'we' already were queer. Because the *as if* is always a *not yet*, we do not know where we will end up. The ethic implied by this proleptic subjectivity and political strategy does not issue from principles but calls for an examination of how we are constituted as subjects by practices whose effects are relative, multivalent and unpredictable. If we are *always already* shaped by discourses of sexuality and interpolated socially as heterosexual or homosexual, we are also *always not yet* what we are supposed to be; we are never quite what we should be. Nor, in a sense, will we ever be fully 'queer'. For, rather than constructing oneself through performances, as some have argued, the performing and performed subjects never coincide, the difference between them being what one could call the space of ethical interrogation.

These theoretical issues have a direct bearing upon lesbian and gay literary study within the academy. In the United States, a handful of interdisciplinary lesbian and gay studies programmes have recently begun, following a proliferation of intradisciplinary courses on lesbian and gay topics at dozens of colleges and universities. While this voluble affirmation of the love that formerly dared not speak its name is no doubt welcome, it raises significant questions concerning the disciplining of inquiry into same-sex desire. In a word, what does it mean that lesbian and gay studies is becoming a discipline? What are the ethical ramifications of the academic institutionalization of lesbian and gay literary study?

For the study of lesbian and gay issues to gain a place at the academic table entails its conformity to the standards that govern academic fields and requires those who work within it to abide by appropriate disciplinary expectations. Specifically, the effort to establish lesbian and gay literary studies is subject to massive homogenizing pressures, including the demand to demarcate a field of inquiry or a canon and the need to legitimate that field as worthwhile. These institutional pressures have a normalizing and a normativizing effect; in other words, they tend to render lesbian and gay literature a 'normal' sub-field more or less akin to African–American or women's literature, and they bring it in line with the accepted structure of literary canons and the pedagogical practices that sustain them.

Lesbian and gay literary study is currently in a state of flux and sometimes conflict between two forces or tendencies. On the one hand, many scholars are working to consolidate lesbian and gay literature as a unified body of texts expressive of their authors' homosexual orientation, while, on the other hand, others challenge the notion of sexual identity, the distinction between homo- and heterosexuality, and the belief in a self that is grounded in such an identity. The one critical tendency seeks to identify lesbian and gay authors and subject positions, while the other analyses same-sex desires in the writings of authors regardless of their sexual orientation and examines the ways in which such desires intersect with or diverge from a specific sexual identity.

Many American scholars and teachers view lesbian and gay studies as a vehicle for self-understanding. Particularly in discussions of pedagogical practices, a substantial number of teachers of courses in lesbian and gay literature see their job as that of helping their students explore their sexual identities. In teaching as in literary criticism, the 'coming-out story' often dominates the analysis of same-sex desire. Under these terms, the fundamental question becomes, 'Who is and who isn't gay?' These interpretive practices produce a knowledge of homosexuality in keeping with the homophobic belief that homosexuals are fundamentally different from the rest of us, although giving a positive instead of negative valence to that difference.

By contrast, queer theory tries to 'unlearn' the modern notion of homosexuality. Among the ways of disturbing the conceptual coherence of homosexuality as such is to show that same-sex desire inheres in ostensibly heterosexual literary plots or cultural phenomena. Rather than fingering lesbian and gay authors or characters, such critics seek out homoerotic subtexts that preclude any final determination of a work or an author as straight or gay. By thus queering the literary canon, these scholars also question the master-narrative of lesbian and gay studies: the progressivist story of the emergent self-expression of homosexuality. Even more, this strategy disputes the belief in the ontological distinction between homosexuality and heterosexuality. Instead, some queer theorists argue that the homo/hetero binarism is an effect of homophobia, an attempt to neutralize the threat of same-sex desire through a hypocritical gesture of inclusive exclusion, acknowledging yet marginalizing homosexuality as deviant. The epistemological aim of queer theory is not knowledge of homosexuality as such but of the ways in which same-sex desire has been deliberately *not known*, evaded, ignored, or denied.[12]

The ethical ramifications of these two theoretical paradigms for the study of cultural representations of same-sex desire are clear. The easiest route to secure an academic niche for scholars concerned with such issues is to argue on humanistic grounds for the inclusion of lesbian and gay studies as a minority field. Given the bureaucratic structure and institutional constraints of the American university system, it seems probable that lesbian and gay studies will be accommodated in a fashion similar to women's studies and the literatures of ethnic minorities. Such an assimilation of lesbian and gay studies is likely to ghettoize it, thereby confirming instead of calling into question the accepted sexual order. The demand for justice will thus have been evaded even as it appears to have been served.

Nevertheless, if we understand ethical issues as pragmatic, entailing variable interests and relative values, the conflict between these two theoretical paradigms is not a face-off between inert, transcendental ideals but a dynamic process in which divergent interests unwittingly coalesce (and vice versa) for particular ends. In practice, the opposing aims of *constructing* lesbian and gay identities and of *deconstructing* homosexuality and heterosexuality sometimes intersect. This has been the case in the controversy over same-sex marriage now taking place in the United States.

In 1996, the Supreme Court of Hawaii handed down a decision legalizing same-sex marriages in the state. As I write, in the spring of 1997, that decision is under appeal to the US Supreme Court. Proponents of the civic recognition of homosexual marriage claim that, in contemporary Western societies, heterosexual marriage is an intimate, loving bond between consenting adults that is not based upon the possibility or capacity for reproduction. In this light, homosexual marriage is the moral equivalent of heterosexual marriage, for better or for worse. Although advocates of lesbian and gay marriage argue that homosexuality is an affective orientation similar to heterosexuality and is thus, in Sullivan's phrase, 'virtually normal', their humanistic claims have far-reaching yet inadvertent consequences. Positing homosexuality as the moral equivalent of heterosexuality effectively dethrones the latter from its privileged place as the ideal of human love. If homosexuality is virtually normal, then heterosexuality is, *ipso facto,* no longer normative. Despite the efforts of conservative gay commentators to assimilate homosexual relationships to heterosexual marriage, like the efforts of some academic theorists to assimilate lesbian and gay literature to the literary curriculum, gay marriage, like gay literature, relativizes or 'queers' canonical norms of love and literature to an unforeseeable extent – a consequence that has not been lost upon its opponents.

From the perspective of queer theory, the movement to legalize same-sex marriage has a quaint, if not retrograde, air. Rather than a subversive mime, homosexual marriage seems like a pathetic imitation of heterosexual norms. Yet the debate over such marriages offers a useful, if provisional, point of conjunction between queer theory and lesbian and gay studies. Homosexual marriage foregrounds the double-sidedness of imitative gestures – as both confirmation and parody – and perversely certifies yet undermines marital vows as the performative act *par excellence* – the 'I do' – of erotic love. In this sense, gay marriage offers a stunning example of Judith Butler's notion of homosexuality as a parodic repetition of heterosexual norms.[13] Moreover, the critique launched by queer theory on our culture's sexual order, directed against the belief in the intrinsic nature of human desires, intersects in certain, uneven ways with the concern of traditional lesbian and gay scholars in the historical determinants of homosexuality. Rigorous attention to the cultural, economic, and historical forces that have produced the modern concept of homosexuality foregrounds the ways in which both homosexuality and heterosexuality are far from facts of nature. Furthermore, the desire of lesbian and gay theorists to validate lesbian and gay identities has led not only to a more nuanced understanding of gender, class and ethnic differences among those who call themselves gay, but to an unresolved crisis in the concept of identification itself.[14] This theoretical impasse offers a significant site for rethinking the ethical and political matters at stake in competing models of same-sex and other-sex desire.

The ethical questions posed by queer theory have ramifications beyond the specific issues of the aims of lesbian and gay literary study, the responsibilities of academic authorities and of individual scholars, and the rights of sexual minorities. Indeed, questions of sexuality in general have come to assume a central place in many disciplines. Because it bears the ethical burden of seeking justice and combating oppression, yet without appealing to universal or transcendental ethical norms, queer theory is of crucial importance in current debates concerning non-foundationalist ethical values. Broadly speaking, the consuming problem of academic and popular discourse in our day is ethical, as television commentators, newspaper columnists, and academic theorists grapple with the difficult dilemmas posed by postmodern, relativistic criteria of right and wrong. Perhaps paradoxically, the study of a desire that until recently was believed to be contrary to the laws of god, nature, and man may in fact turn out to offer solutions to our compelling ethical dilemmas.

Notes

1. Michel Foucault, *The History of Sexuality*, Vol.1, *An Introduction*, trans. Robert Hurley (New York: Random House, 1978) 60–1.
2. George Haggerty and Bonnie Zimmerman, eds, *Professions of Desire: Lesbian and Gay Studies in Literature* (New York: Modern Language Association, 1995) 2.
3. Andrew Sullivan, *Virtually Normal: An Argument about Homosexuality* (London: Picador, 1995) 171.
4. Urvashi Vaid, *Virtual Equality* (New York: Doubleday, 1995).
5. For an analysis of the subject as constituted by a heterogeneity of interests, see Barbara Herrnstein Smith, *Contingencies of Value* (Cambridge, MA: Harvard University Press, 1987).
6. Judith Butler, *Bodies that Matter: On the Discursive Limits of 'Sex'* (New York: Routledge, 1993).
7. For a discussion of such an idea of justice see Joseph Valente, *Joyce*

and the Problem of Justice: Negotiating Sexual and Colonial Difference (Cambridge University Press, 1995), ch. 1.

8. Eve Kosofsky Sedgwick, *Tendencies* (Durham, NC: Duke University Press, 1993); D. A. Miller, *The Novel and the Police* (Berkeley: University of California Press, 1988).
9. Sara Hoagland, *Lesbian Ethics: Toward New Value* (Palo Alto, CA: Institute of Lesbian Studies, 1988). See also the special issue of *Hypatia*, 7.4 (Autumn 1992), which is devoted to lesbian philosophy.
10. Ann Cvetkovich, 'Activist, Queer, and Transnational Feminisms: State of the Art Visions' (unpublished paper).
11. Lauren Berlant and Elizabeth Freeman, 'Queer Nationality', in *Fear of a Queer Planet: Queer Politics and Social Theory*, ed. Michael Warner (Minneapolis: University of Minnesota Press, 1993) 193–229. Since the publication of Berlant and Freeman's essay, ACT-UP has largely folded and mass-market magazines directed toward lesbians, such as *Girlfriends*, *Curve* and *On Our Backs*, have replaced underground 'zines'. I examine the political and cultural effects of mass-market lesbian pornographic magazines in '*On Our Backs*: The Postmodern Lesbian Position', in *The Lesbian Postmodern*, ed. Laura Doan (New York: Columbia University Press, 1994).
12. See Eve Kosofsky Sedgwick, *The Epistemology of the Closet* (Berkeley: University of California Press, 1990).
13. Judith Butler, 'Imitation and Gender Insubordination', in *Inside/Out: Lesbian Theories, Gay Theories*, ed. Diana Fuss (New York: Routledge, 1991).
14. For new approaches to this issue, see Doan, ed., *The Lesbian Postmodern.*

9

Ethics, Value and the Politics of Recognition

David Parker

The present volume testifies to the claim I have been making for some time that the 1990s have seen a significant turn to ethics in contemporary literary studies.[1] This claim is nowhere more forcefully summarized than in Steven Connor's review of a book of mine, among others, when he says that 'the word "ethics" seems to have replaced "textuality" as the most charged term in the vocabulary of contemporary literary and cultural theory'.[2] I still believe that claim to be true, although I have now come to feel misgivings about some of the things that go by the name of ethics. It would take a further chapter to explain these misgivings fully, but they could be roughly summed up by saying that a range of Deconstructive and political approaches of the 1970s and 1980s recently appear to have found new puff by changing tack slightly and declaring themselves forms of ethics. They have some entitlement to do this as they do offer some view of how a human being should live. The main problem, as I suggest below, is that they tend to place an almost exclusive emphasis on the obligation to respect the 'difference' or 'alterity' of others, which produces a skewed, one-sided and ultimately attenuated ethics that is often silent, and dangerously so, on the whole range of ethical issues not illuminated by their favoured key terms. My argument here is that the mostly favourable early responses to Helen Demidenko's arguably anti-Semitic novel, *The Hand that Signed the Paper* (Sydney: 1994), appeal to, and demonstrate the inadequacy of, an ethics (or a politics) that is skewed in this familiar contemporary way.

In 1995 *The Hand that Signed the Paper* and its young author provoked an unprecedented storm of controversy in Australia, which is so germane to my argument I must begin by sketching in a few significant details. Helen Demidenko, a recent graduate of the University of Queensland, first appeared on the literary scene when her manuscript won the Vogel Prize for the best unpublished novel by an Australian author under 35. It later emerged that the author had First Class Honours in English and a University Medal, and among the courses she did was one on Australian multicultural writing, which made a significant impression on her: there was a special note of thanks to the lecturer who taught it in *The Hand* when it first appeared in 1994.

The novel is framed by the attempts of a young Queensland university student, Fiona Kovalenko, to come to terms with the dark wartime past of her Ukrainian immigrant father, Evheny, and uncle, Vitaly. Fiona has come across old photographs of them in SS uniform showing that they played a none too unwilling part in Nazi atrocities against the Jews. Following moves by the Hawke Labour Government to bring such people to justice, Vitaly, who was a camp guard at Treblinka, is about to be put on trial for war crimes and crimes against humanity. Fiona gets these men, and their sister Kateryna, to talk about the past. From this she gathers that the received picture of the Holocaust is distorted. Jews were not simply innocent victims of the Nazis. Ukrainians hated them because in the 1930s so-called Jewish Bolsheviks had played a central part in the artificial famine in which millions of Ukrainians perished. So when the Nazis arrived in 1941, Ukrainians were not slow to enlist and to assist them in such atrocities as the massacre at Babi Yar. According to the novel, this participation was a payback, part of a continuing cycle of inter-ethnic outrage and revenge of which the Zionist-inspired war-crimes trials were merely the latest manifestation. Fiona's model for the understanding of the Holocaust is Bosnia: both sides have blood on their hands. As she says: 'the Ukrainian famine bled into the Holocaust and one fed the other'.[3] Much of the novel is taken up with narratives by Fiona's relatives and others of the famine and the Holocaust, which flesh out these insights. Fiona comes to identify more strongly with her Ukrainian roots and at the same time manages to get her father to face his past and to feel some sorrow for it. Vitaly dies, robbing the war crimes trials of what Fiona calls 'their victim'.[4] The novel ends with Fiona at the site of Treblinka talking, altogether without rancour, to the descendant of one who died there.

On the back cover of *The Hand* is a comment by Jill Kitson, well-known ABC radio journalist, Vogel judge and one of the novel's greatest promoters, who saw it as a 'searingly truthful account of terrible wartime deeds that is also an imaginative work of extraordinary redemptive power'. By 'searingly truthful' Kitson partly meant that she had read the novel in the way most readers naturally would have at that stage, as a thinly veiled account of events actually revealed to Demidenko by members of her own family. (Indeed, in the original manuscript the autobiographical pact is almost signed: the family name was Demidenko, and was only changed during the editorial process to Kovalenko.) This reading was fostered by the author herself, a forceful and striking six-foot fair-skinned blonde, who appeared at various writers' festivals and literary events in Ukrainian national costume, giving exhibitions of Ukrainian folk dancing, drinking vodka and spicing her speech with Ukrainian phrases. Indeed the relevance of Demidenko's ethnicity to the success of the book is quite clear. In awarding *The Hand* its annual Gold Medal in 1995, the Association for the Study of Australian Literature praised it as 'a text that positions itself within the wider questions posed by multiculturalism'.[5] As we shall see, this view captures something central in the project of the novel.

The high point in the fortunes of Demidenko's novel came in June 1995 when it won Australia's most prestigious literary prize, the Miles Franklin Award. One of the judges, Professor Dame Leonie Kramer, Chancellor of Sydney University, denied that the judges were influenced by what she called 'any fashionable pre-occupation with multiculturalism, as some have alleged', but the judges' citation suggests otherwise. The citation was delivered by Jill Kitson, also a Miles Franklin judge, and some have seen her hand strongly in evidence in its emphases. It says in part:

> [N]ovels about the migrant experience seem to us to be seizing the high ground in contemporary Australian fiction, in contrast to fiction about the more vapid aspects of Australian life. In particular, they are incorporating into the cultural memory first-hand experience of the major historical events of the century, events from which Australia has been largely insulated, but which are a growing component of contemporary Australian life

– even to the extent of requiring of us intricate moral judgments, as the recent debate over the war crimes legislation highlighted.[6]

All I would want to underline there is the view that the novel has significant documentary value, 'incorporating into the cultural memory *first hand experience* of the major historical events of the century'.

It was mainly after the Miles Franklin victory that *The Hand* received searching critical attention. At the same time, those who had had misgivings all along began to express them. Several critics pointed out that the Holocaust could not adequately be understood in the way the Ukrainian characters seem to understand it, as a simple pay-back for what the so-called 'Jewish Bolsheviks' did to them during the famine. For one thing, Ukrainian anti-Semitism stretched back over several hundred years. For another, it is a fantastic distortion to see the brutal policies of the Stalinist period, in the way the Ukrainian characters do, as principally driven and executed by Jews. This, it was forcefully pointed out, was precisely the thrust of Nazi anti-Semitic propaganda calculated to win support in the Ukraine during the German advance into the USSR in 1941. The main critical question, however, was where in the end does the book itself stand in relation to the sometimes virulent anti-Semitic attitudes expressed by its characters and by the omniscient third-person narrator? Where earlier critics had mainly admired the narrative detachment and neutral reportage of the horrors of the Holocaust, some now saw this as a significant lack of moral engagement with them. This is another point I shall return to.

A very heated, many-sided and wide-ranging controversy took place in the media. At one extreme the book was seen as anti-Semitic, 'an apologia for genocide'; and at the other, these very criticisms were portrayed as an assault on free speech, a *fatwa* like that pronounced on Salman Rushdie, and 'a well-funded witch-hunt' against what was, after all, merely a young writer's first novel. Meanwhile the young writer herself joined the fray in print and on television, where she equivocated significantly on the question of her own attitude to the anti-Semitism of her characters and made several quite memorable claims, one of which would come back to haunt her: 'Most of my father's family, including my grandfather, were killed by Jewish Communist Party officials at Vynnytsa.'[7]

In the midst of all this came the startling revelation that Helen

Demidenko was actually Helen Darville, the daughter of immigrant parents from the north of England. There was no Ukrainian family background at all. Her brother described her as a 'smart cookie' (she had by that stage made at least $120 000 out of it all), but I think the evidence suggests that the Demidenko persona was one she had come partly to believe in herself. At any rate, the public retraction, when it came, still hinted that there was a Ukrainian source there somewhere whom she had to protect. There was now embarrassment in some quarters of the literary community. Jill Kitson, the most affected, turned to the defence that *The Hand* was, after all, imaginative literature; the revelations only made her admire the imagination responsible for the book all the more. But there was no avoiding the impression that the tide had turned decisively against Demidenko and her novel, and that those who had heaped honours on it, especially on the grounds that it was based on 'first-hand experience', had some explaining to do. In truth, the embarrassment was so palpable that the novel's former champions could only hope to muddy the water, either by now trying to situate *The Hand* within postmodernist discourse or else by trying to take the moral high ground and arguing that the episode had called into question Australia's claim to be a tolerant society. Some portrayed the book's critics as thought police, intolerant of anything but a politically correct view of history. This muddying process was completed when a cartoon appeared in *The Australian* showing one of its most vehement critics, dressed in Nazi uniform, burning Demidenko at the stake.

That was 1995. In 1996, as well as a score of articles in academic journals, there have been four books on the controversy: a 'kiss and tell' account by the former friend of Demidenko's who sheltered her when she went into hiding following her unmasking; a collected edition of most of the mass media articles, reviews, editorials, interviews and programmes to do with the affair; and two monographs by quite senior and well-known academics, both of Jewish background, one roughly speaking for and the other against. The first is *The Demidenko Debate* by Andrew Riemer, who was one of those early critics to praise *The Hand*. This book of 275 pages argues among other things that the novel is written in a multivocal, postmodernist mode that puts it beyond good and evil. The other book, *The Culture of Forgetting: Helen Demidenko and the Holocaust*, is by Robert Manne, the person who has been most responsible, all along, for drawing attention to *The Hand's* inadequate history, its Nazi ideology and its moral vacuousness. It is a serious and important book, concerned not so much with the dissection of the novel's shortcomings but with the more significant question of what it reveals about Australian culture that such a novel came to be so liberally honoured. He concludes that this came about not because of latent or residual anti-Semitism in Australia but through 'provincial liberal naivety, historical ignorance and sentimental multiculturalism' in a society that had by and large forgotten the radical evil of the Holocaust.

I largely agree with Manne here. I also think he may be right to suggest that *The Hand* is symptomatic of Australia and that the novel probably would not have seen the light of day in Europe or the US. However, I do not think the novel is interesting only for what it reveals about Australia. As I shall be arguing, *The Hand* also points to forms of more profound amnesia that can be found throughout the contemporary Western world.

The important question raised by the Demidenko controversy is not so much how did *The Hand that Signed the Paper* come to be written, but how could such a novel come to be so highly regarded by influential members of the literary community, including members of the literary academy? A significant and arguably representative response here is the one given by the Association for the Study of Australian Literature (ASAL), when it awarded *The Hand* its annual Gold Medal in 1995. The judges, all literary and cultural studies academics, praise it as 'a text that positions itself within the wider questions posed by multiculturalism, [and that] resists monolithic assumptions about culture and identity, assumptions that produced the horrors it so chillingly describes'. The citation goes on to say that the novel's 'dialogue between past and present also forces us to make connections with and reflect upon the instances in the history of human cruelty and abuse of power'.[8] Clearly what the ASAL judges are saying is that *The Hand* should be seen as a politically progressive text in that assumptions of monolithic identity are inevitably bound up, in Stalin's Soviet empire as in pre-multiculturalist Australia, with an oppressive abuse of power. Minorities such as Ukrainians, in other words, are oppressed in both societies because there is no recognition given to their claim to a separate identity – no respect, in short, for their otherness or difference.

The concept of 'recognition' involved here is worth pondering. It is the main focus of Charles Taylor's seminal essay on multiculturalism, 'The Politics of Recognition'.[9] Taylor begins with the premise that our identity as individuals or as groups is constituted dialogically in relation to how we are characteristically seen and portrayed by others. There is a profound connection, in short, between recognition by others and our deepest sense of who we are. If this is so, the absence of recognition, or systematic misrecognition, 'can inflict harm, can be a form of oppression, imprisoning someone in a false, distorted, and reduced mode of being'.[10] This is a familiar feminist argument. Women come to internalize a sense of their own inferiority and therefore believe themselves incapable of taking up new opportunities presented to them. The same is true of many colonized peoples, who take up and come to believe the demeaning images of them projected by their masters, so that in the end 'their own self-depreciation... becomes one of the most potent instruments of their oppression'. As Taylor reminds us, the figure of Caliban in *The Tempest* has come to symbolize this process. On Taylor's account, 'misrecognition shows not just a lack of due respect. It can inflict a grievous wound, saddling its victims with a crippling self-hatred. Due recognition is not just a courtesy we owe people. It is a vital human need.'[11]

When he comes to give the genealogy of the politics of recognition within the development of Western culture, Taylor portrays it as a development of the Romantic-expressivist doctrine of authenticity. Just as on the individual level there is a certain way of being that is my way, so Taylor reminds us that according to Herder a 'particular Volk should be true to itself, that is, its own culture'.[12] Taylor sees in this conception both the roots of modern nationalism as well as one important source of feminism, multiculturalism and queer theory – in short all those movements we call the politics of difference. The late twentieth-century version of Herder's insight is that each gender, sub-culture, colonized people and so on has its own way of being that is distinct from others.

Just how the politics of recognition develops out of this Romantic source is a complex story. What I think is implicit in Taylor's account is that the various forms of the politics of recognition, feminist, multiculturalist and so on, make a *moral*[13] claim on me in the following way: an essential element in understanding the harms of misrecognition is to see that they are of a kind that I would not wish inflicted on myself. In other words, underlying this politics, giving it power, is some form of universalizing conception, such as the golden rule, of treating all others as I would have them treat me. This is the morality of recognizing that others might be other, different, pursuing their own way of being, but they are not altogether discontinuous from myself: there is a commonality between us such that I can begin to understand the harms of misrecognition of the other by putting myself in his or her place.

However, this thought brings us back to the precise reason why the drive for recognition within the politics of difference has the force it has for us. The universalizing act of putting myself in the other's place carries the risk of projecting myself onto the other, of reducing the other to the same. At the root of this politics is the fear that Enlightenment or Judeo-Christian universalism is, as Taylor has termed it, 'a particularism posing as a universal'. Unmasking particularisms that have come to be taken as universals is of course a familiar move in much contemporary theory, and examples abound. The one that first springs to mind is Carol Gilligan's argument that Kohlberg's stages of moral development privilege a fundamentally masculinist concept of moral autonomy over such goods as connectedness, human responsiveness and care. According to Gilligan, the universalizing Kantian discourse enshrines patriarchal non-recognition of another, different, moral 'voice'.

That is one form of misrecognition – the one feminism, multiculturalism and so on mainly focus on: the non-recognition of difference within a universalizing discourse. Let us call that form misrecognition A. Another form occurs when the other is seen as *merely* other and different, altogether discontinuous from myself. Racism and the stigmatizing of outsider groups provide obvious examples. Negative characteristics are selected or invented: blacks are stupid, Jews grasping, which puts those people in a different moral universe from me. The dangers of this form hardly need discussion, but it might be remembered that human groupings have always had such a store of stigmatizing features of other groupings for the eventuality of conflict or war. It is simply easier to kill others if they are *merely* other or different from the sort of person I am. There is an intimate relationship, in fact, between the harm of this form of misrecognition and more grievous harm. This is obvious in an extreme case such as the cartoon rat-like Jews in *Die Sturmer* which were used to legitimate genocide. Let us call this form of misrecognition, where I see the other as *merely* other, misrecognition B.

My reason for making this distinction between A and B is to underline the point that to avoid misrecognition of others I need to attend *both* to their otherness *and* to elements of human continuity between us. An intuition I want to explore here is that the various forms of the politics of difference have been almost exclusively focused on misrecognition A – and have run the risk of either not noticing, or indeed of slipping into, misrecognition B.[14]

To return to *The Hand that Signed the Paper.* The way in which the publishers packaged the novel suggests that they understood that its appeal to readers such as the ASAL judges might be best made in terms of the politics of recognition. The sentence that they extract from the novel to print in bold coloured type on the back cover is this one: 'The brothers Kovalenko ... did not kill Jews just because they were poor and Ukrainian, and did not know any better. They killed Jews because they believed that they themselves were savages.'

And indeed, it is certainly an important emphasis of the novel that the Ukrainians in *The Hand* are victims of misrecognition, by the so-called 'Jewish Bolsheviks', who regard them as cattle, as well as by the Germans. The learned Kommandant of Treblinka, a figure straight out of George Steiner's *Bluebeard's Castle,* is discussing a fine point of the Heideggerian concept of authenticity with a young SS officer, when he discovers that Vitaly Kovalenko is staring in fascination at them. He says, not altogether probably: 'Piss off back to the shooting pits, Ukrainian savage. The mind of Martin Heidegger is far too fine for the likes of you.'[15] On seeing the children the Ukrainians have fathered in the village, his successor observes, with unwitting post-colonialist irony: 'Look ... they have peopled the whole island with Calibans.'[16]

It is also part of the novel's argument that an analogous form of misrecognition has continued into the present and indeed underlies the war crimes trials against Ukrainian migrants to countries such as the US and Australia. The novel clearly conceives of itself as a plea for proper recognition, particularly of the part played by the brutal and shocking Stalinist famine of the 1930s in driving the Ukrainians into Hitler's arms. It should be added, however, that members of the Ukrainian immigrant community in Australia were far from unanimous in seeing this sort of recognition as a favour. Many were offended by what they saw as the stereotyping of them as drunken, anti-Semitic peasants and indeed saw this as perpetuating misrecognition of them. According to a young

Ukrainian–Australian academic, Marko Pavlyshyn, survivors of the famine simply did 'not recognise themselves or their experiences in the novel'.[17] This would have been no surprise to the academic critic, Sneja Gunew, who argues very persuasively that Demidenko herself performed and wrote from a reified conception of Ukrainian identity. These are some of the relatively subtle and benign forms of misrecognition I was referring to earlier. The grosser and less benign sort are there too, as we shall see.

I think the best way to approach the cluster of issues I want to explore is to look at a passage at the beginning of *The Hand*, in which the past Fiona Kovalenko had taken for granted suddenly begins to seem illusory, a construction of Hollywood:

> There is our past, the stuff of gory war films – bad Hollywood, if you will. The nasty ones are in there.... Extras mainly, not people, with helmets low down over their eyes so that you cannot see their faces. They drag Jews out of trains, shove them into gas chambers, line them up and shoot them. They are usually given one line – a barking '*Schnell, schnell, schneller... los, los*' – then they obligingly disappear. It's good that they do... [they] make us uncomfortable, because, if we look too closely, we see sad eyes and tragic fates. They do these things because we believe they are savage people. They keep doing them because such savagery is endemic. They can wear the brutal mask easily. It feels good for the viewer that they seem to believe in their own savageness. At least, then, the two – watched and watching – cannot be confused...[18]

I want to distinguish two distinct implications in this passage. The first is that, if we could look at them more closely than Hollywood allows, these depersonalized movie extras would appear to us as ordinary human beings, more like us than we care to admit. The suggestion seems to be that we are connected with them, which makes us uncomfortable because we prefer the shadow of evil within us to be externalized, projected onto figures, such as Hollywood in fact gives us, who believe in their own evil. In other words, these guards, clearly prefiguring Vitaly Kovalenko and his like, are classic victims of what I have called misrecognition B. We do not see them as part of the human moral continuum to which we belong but as *merely* other. The force of this realization is a moral one: underlying it is the assumption that we share a common humanity with these men whose sad eyes and tragic fates we see as not unlike our own. It is because of that that we can identify with them, put ourselves in their place.

We become aware of the second implication of the passage when we note that it is no accident that it is *Hollywood* which has created this picture of depersonalized savagery. Demidenko apparently believed that with regard to this period of history the Jews have had 'a monopoly on the speaking position'[19] and in fact have constructed the hegemonic narrative of the Holocaust. The film-makers have the power to construct the identities of the guards. This is why it 'feels good [important phrase, as we shall see] for the viewer that [the guards] seem to believe in their own savageness'. It feels good because the viewer is invited to share the film-makers' position of power, the power to create their meaning. 'They do these things *because we believe* they are savage people.' Within the film-makers' master-narrative of the Holocaust, we are the subjects; the camp guards never get to tell their story. We never get to know that they are Ukrainians, many of them, with particular tragic fates shaped by oppression under Bolshevism. To us they are just undifferentiated Nazis, or 'nasty ones'. They are in short victims of misrecognition A, which we, sharing the film-makers' power, inflict on them.

In setting up the issues in this way, the novel is beginning to announce its own main game, which will be to reverse the roles such that the Ukrainian camp guards are given the speaking position. That much may seem merely justice, but we need to note that this is not the justice of the dignity of all human persons but the justice of *vengeance*. In *The Hand*, the Jews become either 'the nasty ones' or the depersonalized extras; it is now their turn to have misrecognition inflicted on them. At the level of the novel's own explicit discourse, we are in the world of Bosnia, with two ethnic groups, Jews and Ukrainians, caught up in a cycle of outrage and revenge, of which the war crimes trials and the novel itself are the latest manifestations. But more importantly, at another level the novel is part of what Taylor calls the tendency of neo-Nietzschean theories to turn all issues into those of 'power and counter-power'.[20] My contention would be that this is the master-discourse of the novel, in which the key operative terms are the neo-Nietzschean ones of power and desire. The main characters are not moral subjects in that they deliberate and choose actions. There are countless places in which the novel explains how they were not responsible. Universalizing morality is not simply absent from the novel, as some critics imply; there are signs here and there that it is actually under attack. This is where the novel's neo-Nietzschean politics of difference merges into the much more sinister uses made of Nietzsche by the Nazis.

Let me attempt to make good these claims with some examples from the novel. As I have suggested, the film-makers' power is supposedly continuous with the power of the 'Jewish Bolsheviks' over their Ukrainian victims. Kateryna tells the story of how, at the height of the famine, her mother goes seeking milk for her dying child to the kommissar's house:

> The kommissar was not at home, but his wife – a Jewish doctor – was. She sent out a guard, then came herself. She said it would be good if a few more of us died, there were so many. We bred like yard dogs. My mother begged for some medicine. Anatoly was so sick now he had to have medicine. Mrs Kommissar refused. 'I am a physician, not a vetinarian', she said softly, enunciating her words with a kind of feral sharpness. 'Get away.'[21]

This much-discussed scene can only have seemed credible on the premise that it was first-hand oral history. Its purpose nonetheless is clear: not only does it show why the Ukrainians hated 'Jewish Bolshevik' oppressors such as 'Mrs Kommissar', it is calculated to draw readers into sympathy with that feeling. In these early scenes, such inhumanity is associated with Jewishness (and Bolshevism) with a consistency that makes it hard to see where the novel can be dissociating itself from the bitter anti-Jewish feelings of the peasants. Its strategy seems to be that readers will be enticed, against themselves so to speak, to identify imaginatively with anti-Semitic hatred.

So when the Nazis arrive in 1941, the sense of Ukrainian liberation and empowerment in relation to their oppressors is at very least understandable. Vanya, the drunken Kommissar (a Ukrainian and not so bad as his wife), is caught by the 19-year-old Vitaly and pleads for his life with reminders of things he did for the Kovalenkos. 'I don't hate you, Vitaly. Don't punish me. Please.' The third person narrator continues: 'Wheedle. Bargain. Smile. The boy's face was marked with angry splendour.' Vanya goes on pleading but 'Vitaly did not listen. He had nothing else to say. He didn't really hate the kommissar, but it felt good all the same. He looked over the gunsight....'[22] Vitaly is clearly having a great time with the kommissar; the power to take revenge, the power to kill enemies, feels really good. There is something perhaps fresh in the frankness with which the good feeling of revenge is dramatized in a 19 year old. But the scene is also set up so that the reader, drawn into sympathy with Ukrainian hatred of their oppressors, is invited to enjoy something of the good feeling too. The wheedling, pleading coward who was so impotent during the famine hardly seems to deserve a life; and the look of 'angry splendour' is precisely the right one to have when you are about to take such a life away.

The boy's 'angry splendour' in fact reflects the atmosphere of the German thrust into the USSR. Bolshevik control in the Ukraine ends with vengeful massacres and rapes that are described as 'terrible, terrible'[23] and yet the instruments of death have a terrible beauty too, such as the Stukas that fly 'beneath northern lights, screaming'.[24] Throughout all the killing, there is a strong undercurrent of the carnivalesque, the overturning of repressive order and a powerful release of desire. The German and Ukrainian killers, always seen from the same female point of view, despite the supposed variety of narrative voices, are mostly seen as strong, masterful, blond and tall. The Ukrainian women are fascinated by the fair, pink skin of the soldiers from the Reich and 'satisfied themselves' with these men 'with great energy upstairs in the kommissar's house'.[25] But nothing seems as sexy to these narrators as the killing itself. The Polish girl, Magda, falls for Vitaly: 'She has seen him before, shooting a Jew in the street. She liked him then.'[26] The point has been repeatedly and rightly made that the Jews are reduced to cyphers and that nothing is felt for them as they die. But what *is* felt is sexual desire for the killers. Kateryna Kovalenko watches as the SS, aided by Ukrainian recruits, shoot a group of NKVD they have captured. Her eye fastens on 'a tall fair-skinned man in black' who is directing operations, shouting to his Ukrainians: '"Not like that, like this. Shoot here. Then you don't waste bullets".' Finally, the job done efficiently, one of 'the tall German's underlings passed him a megaphone, and he stood on top of the pile of bodies that his troops had made'[27] to make a speech. This is the man who sweeps Kateryna off her feet.

He, Wilhelm Hasse, directs operations at Babi Yar, in which

35 000 Jews are machine-gunned into a pit in two days. The important thing about him is that he feels nothing either during or after the killings – like most of the Ukrainians, in fact, though they are supposedly drunk with vodka. The key question is how this insensibility is valued or disvalued by the novel. A fairly clear answer is supplied by looking at the man who is set against him by way of contrast, Hasse's immediate subordinate, Erich Kretschmann. He is firstly a sexual loser, we realize, as he glumly watches his boss and Kateryna enter the officers' mess 'fresh and lively, not at all like people who had been screwing for the last forty-eight hours solid'. Kretschmann by contrast goes off alone to recall awaking from a dream the night before:

> He looked out onto the street. The synagogue across the road was burning fiercely. He was afraid now. He remembered the painting that his mother had suspended above his bed when he was a small child. It showed a giant, unblinking human eye within a triangular border, and bore on the blank space beneath the eye an inscription: 'Thou God Seest Me'. Thou God seest me. He pulled the sodden sheets up under his chin, and prayed.[28]

The point about Kretschmann is that he aspires to be a detached Nazi overman like Hasse, but cannot. As we see here, the burning synagogue and the all-seeing Judeo-Christian God of his childhood haunt him. These symbolize the morality of 'thou shalt not kill' and 'thou shalt love they neighbour as thyself', the morality, in short of common humanity, which must at least obliquely remind him that those Jews he is killing are human beings like himself. As we have seen, something like this thought, in relation to Ukrainians, flickers across the novel itself. But here it is associated with weakness: the sheets are 'sodden'; Kretschmann is at heart a cry-baby, victim of child-morality, slave-morality, the other-regarding morality of the weak.

We see this during Babi-Yar, when he cannot machine-gun Jewish families without feeling ill and vomiting. 'Kretschmann is sick again. There is conversation above. He hears Hasse laugh. "Don't some people give you the shits? Yes, it's such a shame. Such a shame".'[29] Another thing that has affected Kretschmann at Babi-Yar is seeing Voronikov, a big Ukrainian, who is being eyed off by a pretty German girl, as he lustily beats Jews senseless with an iron bar. In later years, we are told, Kretschmann joins the Peace Corps, but as he dies 'the last image he will see is that of the big curly-headed corn-fed boy with the strong, white teeth, with just a hint of murder in his sloe green eyes'.[30] Unlike Hasse and the murderous Ukrainians, Kretschmann is a wet, with a lack of manly self-respect eating his heart out. When he becomes a guard at Treblinka, Vitaly epitomizes the manly ideal. 'It is in this state of lordly power', we are told, 'rich, handsome and free – that he meets Magda Juskowiak'.[31] We know *Ubermensch* lords of life when we see them because they are irresistible to women.

Thus we see the side of Nietzsche taken up by the Nazis used here to bury the universalist moral claims of shared humanity. An extreme doctrine of racial 'difference' must at all costs hold out deeply rooted European religious and moral traditions that insist on fundamental commonalities and continuities between all human persons. By the same sort of manoeuvre, that whole Judeo-Christian-Kantian discourse is so to speak pushed into the unconscious of this text. Like Hasse and the murderous Ukrainians, the novel itself is insensible of the humanity of Jews and the meaning of their terror and deaths is never realized.

At one point we come across the following sentences describing the day-to-day activities of the Ukrainian guards at Treblinka: 'Sometimes Ivan M is one of these guards. He is a corporal, and he has Vitaly throw infants in the air so that he may attempt to catch them on his bayonet. Full stop – end of story with regard to infants.' There are many ways of talking about what is wrong with this much-discussed passage, but I am inclined to say that the third-person narrating consciousness is simply inhumane in not registering, by some inflection or other, the horror of this atrocity.[32] It is a classic case of misrecognition B – the Jewish infants simply are not part of the same human continuum as the narrating consciousness or indeed as Vitaly's own infant, who is lovingly suckled and cooed over by his wife Magda.

In an age of 'grunge' fiction, this lack of moral sensibility in a young novelist may not be so exceptional, but it is another matter for the critics who praised and honoured the novel not to have registered concern. My hypothesis is that even the relatively conservative Miles Franklin judges, as much as their ASAL counterparts, were snared by the novel's supposed multicultural resistances to 'monolithic assumptions about culture and identity, assumptions that produced the horrors it so chillingly describes'. To return to those words a moment. It is not hard to see how 'monolithic assumptions about culture and identity' might apply to Stalinist atrocities in the Ukraine, but what about the Nazi atrocities – based on highly differential assumptions about culture and identity?

My conclusion is that, within contemporary literary/cultural studies, conventional ethical thinking is so skewed by the dominant language of difference that it tends to lack a moral vocabulary with which to register Nazi and other highly particularist forms of violence.[33] So while I would like to share Steven Connor's confidence that 'the word "ethics" seems to have replaced "textuality" as the most charged term in the vocabulary of contemporary literary and cultural theory', I would want to add that such ethics will lack credibility unless it also embraces what, in the ordinary other-regarding sense, we tend to call 'morality'.

Notes

1. See, for example, 'Evaluative Discourse: the Return of the Repressed', *The Critical Review*, 31 (1991) 3–14; 'The Turn to Ethics in the 1990s', *The Critical Review*, 33 (1993), 3–16, a revised version of which appears in *The Ethics of Literary Theory*, co-edited with Jane Adamson and Richard Freadman (Cambridge: Cambridge University Press, forthcoming); *Ethics, Theory and the Novel* (Cambridge University Press, 1994).
2. *TLS*, 5 January 1996, 24–6.
3. Helen Demidenko, *The Hand that Signed the Paper* (Sydney: Allen and Unwin, 1994) 3.
4. Ibid., 85.
5. *The Demidenko File*, ed. John Jost, Gianna Totaro and Christine Tyshing (Ringwood, Victoria: Penguin, 1996) 79.
6. Ibid., 26.
7. Ibid., 66.
8. Ibid., 79.
9. Charles Taylor, *Multiculturalism: Examining the Politics of Recognition*, ed. Amy Gutman (Princeton University Press: 1994) 25–73.
10. Ibid., 25.
11. Ibid., 26.
12. Ibid., 30.
13. As will become clear, I am reserving the word 'moral' for that side of ethics concerned with the universalizing demand that I treat all others as continuous with myself and deserving of equivalent respect. In other words, my use of the term is somewhat like that of Bernard Williams in *Ethics and the Limits of Philosophy*, except that I do not follow him in giving morality short shrift.

14. The basis for this argument, namely the need to attend to both the otherness of others as well as to elements of human commonality, is elaborated at length in *Ethics, Theory and the Novel*. I see that Christopher Norris, who is also represented in the present volume, develops a related argument in *Truth and the Ethics of Criticism* (Manchester University Press: 1994).
15. Helen Demidenko, *The Hand that Signed the Paper*, 99.
16. Ibid., 146.
17. Ibid., 280.
18. Ibid., 7.
19. See Robert Manne, *The Culture of Forgetting: Helen Demidenko and the Holocaust* (Melbourne: Text Publishing, 1996) 20 and ff.
20. Charles Taylor, *Multiculturalism: Examining the Politics of Recognition*, 70.
21. Helen Demidenko, *The Hand that Signed the Paper*, 15.
22. Ibid., 44.
23. Ibid., 48.
24. Ibid., 43.
25. Ibid., 46.
26. Ibid., 107.
27. Ibid., 50.
28. Ibid., 61.
29. Ibid., 67.
30. Ibid., 68.
31. Ibid., 104.
32. It makes no sense to argue that the evil of such deeds 'speaks for itself', as if it wasn't possible for an author to take (say) a cruel, subtly voyeuristic pleasure in them. The text must in some way signal its responses and valuations.
33. Once again, though he comes to it from a very different direction, Christopher Norris comes to much the same conclusion in *Truth and the Ethics of Criticism*.

10

Moral Synonymy: John Stuart Mill and the Ethics of Style

Dan Burnstone

I

'A common language in which values may be expressed': this is a phrase John Stuart Mill might well have used to describe utility – the common denominator of different ethical values in utilitarian moral reckoning. In fact, this is Mill's phrase describing money as a circulating medium.[1] In utilitarianism, utility is the ubiquitous form of moral currency; like money in the capitalist economy, it functions as the 'universal equivalent' in the moral economy.[2] It is therefore unsurprising that economic idioms abound in discussions of utilitarianism, with their talk of trade-offs, calculation, and costs. But it is not the parallel with economic exchange that I want to focus on in this essay. Mill's reference to 'a common *language*' points succinctly to a different connection which will be the centre of attention, and that is between forms of ethical and linguistic equivalence.

It is this conjunction that the term 'moral synonymy' is intended to capture. By moral synonymy I want to indicate a particular conjunction of perspectives on ethics and language, or more precisely, style – a conjunction which, I shall argue, Mill's work can help us both to see and to see *through*. A bare and schematic anticipation of my approach would be to say that what a belief in *commensurability* is to the realm of ethics, a belief in *synonymy* is to the realm of language. This article will explore the interrelationship of these two ideas. In the end I shall suggest that the collaboration between ethics and style denoted by moral synonymy imposes severe limitations on thinking about ethics and literature, and that an examination of moral synonymy and its implications should be part of the currently revived attempts to work out the relationship between ethics and literature.

Synonymy is the idea that identical meaning can be expressed in different linguistic forms. Style – as linguistic form of expression – can be varied or discarded without altering the body of sense it clothes.[3] To believe in moral commensurability is to believe that there is some common value by means of which different values can be measured against each other, and conflicts between them rationally decided. One leading candidate for the role of common value is, of course, utility, and utilitarianism will be taken here as typical of a commensurabilist approach. So, to outline the parallel between ethics and style that we will focus on: just as the believer in synonymy thinks that distinct linguistic styles may be shown to be so many different vehicles for expressing common meanings, so the utilitarian thinks that distinct values turn out ultimately to be so many forms for conveying the common value of utility. Utilitarians, as commensurabilists, happily commit the ethical variety of the 'heresy of paraphrase'. They are happy to reduce different values merely to *styles* of utility. This is why I want to call utilitarianism a kind of moral synonymy.

II

We can understand ethical commensurability more clearly by turning briefly to Mill's work. Mill relies on utility as the single criterion for settling ethical conflicts. In *Utilitarianism* he proposes happiness not as one among the ends or criteria of morality, but as the *only* one. He argues that 'to desire anything except in proportion as the idea of it is pleasant, is a physical and metaphysical impossibility' (X, 238). Such assertions are the source of familiar difficulties for Mill's moral theory, for there would seem to be ends other than happiness under the title of which people desire things. Moreover, some of these ends are arguably not only irreducible but also prone to come into conflict with utility (autonomy is a good example of one such value). So it is improbable that happiness is the unique categorial end.[4] There is in fact a tension – vital to Mill and to this article – between Mill's formal philosophical adherence to utility and his practical recognition of the diversity of values; but nevertheless, he always professes ultimate allegiance to the idea that utility can be considered as the 'common umpire' in ethical disputes (X, 226).

We can see here that utility allows commensurability. It is the common consideration in terms of which two or more possibly conflicting values can be measured and so compared. The reductive implications of this strategy for resolving moral conflicts have been explored recently by, among others, Bernard Williams and Steven Lukes. Lukes has challenged the ambition to devise what he calls 'a homogenous descriptive magnitude' which could be used to subject diverse moral goods to 'a complete and transitive ordering'. He points to the role of certain 'reductionist meta-ethical assumptions or prejudices' in generating these elements of moral theory.[5] Williams has also drawn particular attention to the effects of a reductive view of ethical rationality which he has branded 'the rationalistic conception of rationality'. This 'rests on an assumption about rationality to the effect that two considerations cannot be rationally weighed against each other unless there is a common consideration in terms of which they can be compared'.[6] Williams has been among the most persuasive critics of the attempt to divest practical reasoning of its radically first-person character and to confer upon it the impartial standpoint of factual or theoretical deliberation about the truth.[7] He is like Weber in insisting that the drive to rationalize moral thought comes not from purely rational demands but, as he puts it, 'from social features of the modern world, which impose on personal deliberation and on the idea of practical reason itself a model drawn from a particular understanding of public rationality'.[8]

A feature of Williams's critique is the suggestion that comparison between moral goods can be made, and made rationally, *without* adopting a rationalistic conception of rationality. Even more fundamental is the contention that certain conflicts – notably those involving a collision between an individual's deepest personal attachments and impartial moral rules – ought not to be subjected to an impartial principle of adjudication at all. I cannot pursue these criticisms further here, but we can see how for John Stuart Mill certain assumptions or prejudices about language run parallel with and sustain a belief in commensurability. Mill is, however, a complicated case. As we shall also see, his outlook on language actually tends to conceal his own scepticism about commensurability, a scepticism indicated by the fact that *On Liberty* is frequently taken to advocate a liberal belief in the irreducible diversity of separate values. Isaiah Berlin has done much to advance this interpretation, arguing that it is when Mill is urging this diversity that 'his voice is most his own'.[9]

We will return to this tension. First we need to look at some of the passages in Mill's work which show leanings towards synonymy. One such is Mill's review of the lectures of the French historian Guizot in which he speculates on the advantages of developing what he calls a 'European style'. In what sounds like an early plea for a Common European Currency, he suggested that the interests of European civilization would be served by a 'general assimilation of tone and manner between languages'. The translator 'has a constant opportunity to gain over the *national* ear by means of the *universal* understanding' ('Guizot's Lectures on European Civilization', XX, 372–3). Mill thinks that misunderstanding in translation is mostly caused by metaphorical and other linguistic foibles that are peculiar to individual languages. He sounds confident that by stripping away what he calls 'combinations, figures, forms of thought', ideas can be freed from their quirky and confusing national dress and appear in a universal guise. An enlightenment faith in the capacity of rational discourse to overcome parochial barriers of language and reach the 'universal understanding' appears undimmed.

Elsewhere, Mill appeared to give unequivocal assent to synonymy by defining philosophical uses of language precisely by reference to their capacity to detect and pin down common meaning. Philosophical intelligence presupposes 'the faculty of recognising identity of thought notwithstanding diversity of language,...with the converse power of detecting difference of meaning under identity of expression' (XX, 93). The source of this assertion is one of Mill's translations-cum-summaries-cum-commentaries on Plato's dialogues, and it is apt that in general these translations treat the literary form and linguistic peculiarities of the dialogues precisely as a 'diversity of language' that may be ignored. The dialogues are culled for philosophical content, which is read through the lens of nineteenth-century logic and empiricism. The possibility that linguistic form might make a philosophically interesting contribution to meaning seems to pass unrecognized.

Yet the prospects for synonymy and translation in Mill's work do not always look as good as these moments suggest, especially when further light is cast by two important influences on Mill: Bentham and Wordsworth. Confidence in synonymy can, for example, be imperilled at the very point of expression. In another of his few general statements about language and philosophy, Mill wrote, 'language is as it were the atmosphere of philosophical investigation, which must be made transparent before anything can be seen through it in the true figure and position' ('Nature', X, 378). But we might ask: how transparent is the atmosphere of this statement itself? A metaphor is needed before it becomes possible to say that the linguistic climate should be clear of exactly such metaphorical disturbances.

Mill's assertion inherits a recognition made explicit by Bentham, whose theory of language makes inescapable the conclusion that what Mill calls 'the true figure' beyond language is itself a function of figurativeness.[10] Bentham's project of language reform centred around the effort to expose and eradicate 'fictions' or 'fictitious entities' – those meanings or concepts which, according to Bentham, possess no more than a linguistic or metaphysical reality. Bentham included predicates or qualities such as 'motion', 'power' and 'relation' among these fictions; he was even more determined to demystify those fictions that play a role in political or moral thinking – terms such as 'obligation', 'right' or 'property'. But Bentham's attempt to confine figurative language in its proper place was doomed inexorably to emphasize its indispensability and ubiquity. Certain fictions and figures were, he was eventually forced to concede, 'absolutely necessary' to thought and communication.[11] His project simply couldn't avoid the paradox that we can only reform language and its fictions from a position *within* language and its fictions.[12] And if that's so, then the bid for linguistic transparency appears question-begging.

Bentham's general dilemma casts light on Mill, as does another detail in his theory. Bentham made much of a distinction between 'solitary' and 'social' uses of language, which he glossed with a further distinction between 'intransitive' and 'transitive' functions. Bentham thought that in intransitive uses language was employed self-reflexively for the purpose of self-understanding. When used this way, Bentham said, language 'amalgamates itself with thought'. By contrast, in its transitive functions, language is 'the medium of communication between one mind and another, or others'. The transitive function includes addressing the will as well as the understanding and therefore involves 'excitation' alongside 'simple communication'.[13] There is a striking homology between Bentham and Mill at this point.

Mill thought of poetry as a kind of intransitivity that escaped the corruptions of worldly rhetoric. Famously, he defined poetry as 'of the nature of soliloquy' and distinguished it sharply from eloquence: 'eloquence is *heard*; poetry is *over*heard' ('Thoughts on Poetry and Its Varieties', I, 348–9). Poetry scrupulously avoids contact with the 'outward and every-day world'; it is 'the natural fruit of solitude and meditation', whereas eloquence arises from 'intercourse with the world' (I, 349).[14] Poetry, in short, is sealed off from the transitive realities of society and politics.

Mill's literary theory was formed in the period of his greatest devotion to Wordsworth, and there is a close alliance between his view of poetry and Wordsworth's ideas about poetic language. In particular, Mill assimilated Wordsworth's reaction against what was perceived as the artificial style and diction of the eighteenth century. Eighteenth-century writers were deemed to have made words a mere clothing and not an 'incarnation of the thought'. What they had neglected, according to Wordsworth, were 'those expressions which are not what the garb is to the body but what the body is to the soul, themselves a constituent part and power or function in the thought'.[15] Against the translatability and algebraic rationality associated with eighteenth-century writing, is set a notion of the *indivisibility* of thought and expression. Indivisibility included the idea, derived from Rousseau, that in undistorted conditions thoughts and feelings inescapably give rise to particular linguistic correlates. Mill gives us a more uncompromising and idealized version of Wordsworth's 'Preface', when he argues that poetry performs this natural embodiment: at its most simple, it is nothing but 'the thoughts and words in which emotion spontaneously embodies itself' (I, 356).[16] To conscious stylistic choice, Mill concedes only that when 'intellectual culture' affords a choice between different modes of expressing the same emotion, 'the stronger the feeling is, the more naturally and certainly will it prefer the language which is most peculiarly appropriated to itself' (I, 362).

We saw earlier that Mill appeared to endorse synonymy. But a belief in synonymy seems incompatible with the Wordsworthian view of the *natural* relation between meaning and expression. How can unique relations between ideas and their expression coexist with the interchangeability of linguistic form implied by synonymy? We seem here to have come across a deep divide in Mill's thinking. On the one hand, literary uses of language forge unique and indissoluble stylistic unions; on the other, philosophical uses presuppose that any such union can be prised open and its constituent parts set in new (and no less 'natural') conjunctions.

III

Mill's work does not resolve this contradiction, but it does find a way of transposing the incarnational view of language into the ethical key. To get to the heart of this transposition: what Mill does is effectively to identify stylistic indivisibility with *invisibility*, and to create an ideal of action in which acts have the same transparency with respect to motives and character that style has with respect to thought or emotion.

The clearest expression of this connection in Mill's thought is in an essay on the French political journalist Armand Carrel, revered by Mill for his courageous conduct during the 1830s, as editor of the *National*. The *National* was called 'a personification of Armand Carrel'.[17] As this suggests, Carrel's writing exemplified a particularly intimate bond between personality and the written word. Carrel, according to Mill, never separated himself from his newspaper; what was said in and about the *National* could correctly be assumed to be said by and to Carrel himself. But despite the fact that the utterances of a political writer and activist would appear to be prime examples of transitive language, Mill does not treat Carrel's writing as a discredited manifestation of eloquence – as an exhortation to action or a courting of public favour. It is instead a report of action or even a 'mode of action' in itself, displaying an incorruptible fusion of word and deed (XX, 194). Carrel's practice is granted the same transparency that Mill had previously only attributed to the Romantic lyric poet. Mill writes that Carrel, 'casts in one and the same mould the style and the thought' (XX, 196). Carrel was said to have written as if with the point of a sword, and appropriately he died fighting a duel to protect his political reputation. There would be a perfect figurative unity to Mill's account of Carrel's life and actions if it were not for the inconvenient fact that Carrel was shot.

Writing about Carrel prompts Mill to speculate on the qualities that make a great writer, and these bring to the fore a connection between style as a feature of language and action as a feature of character. Mill argues that writers' qualities are built on their 'qualities as human beings', and for these to show through, style cannot be made an end in itself: 'if a writer who assumes a stile for the sake of stile ever acquires a place in literature, it is in so far as he assumes the stile of those whose stile is not assumed; of those to whom language is but the utterance of their feelings, or the means to their practical ends' (XX, 171).

What is striking here is the inclusion of 'practical ends' alongside the non-instrumental 'utterance of... feelings'. This blurs the distinction between transitive and intransitive, social and solitary, which had sustained Mill's earlier reflections on literature. Improbably, Mill assimilates what are 'means' to an end to the standard of innocence from ulterior motive that he had previously reserved for lyric poetry. He also lets through without questioning the convenient but problematic equation of the mere absence of self-advertising stylishness with the presence of unmediated natural feeling.

What Mill appears to give us is a view of the ethics of style in which style is only above suspicion when you can see right through it. It must be the self-effacing and spontaneous form in which meaning is embodied. For moral agency too, actions – as styles of expressing motives – should similarly be see-through. Aesthetic delight in moral agency – in the display of excellent qualities of character – can be said to depend on such perspicuity. What would detract from such delight is the awareness of a histrionic *intent* to display the motive in the act; it should be perceived as an unintentional performance or side-effect.[18]

In this way, literary considerations of style leave an ethical residue in Mill's work in the form of a concern for the expression of moral character in action. This is all very well, but of course cases of transparent agency like Carrel's are rare – they are the exemplary instances which most will fall short of. More familiar in Mill is the opacity of action as a medium revealing character, or its infidelities. And of course one trumpeted advantage of the utilitarian standard is precisely that it avoids the problem of opacity: all it requires is access to the consequences of actions; it does not need to know anything about the agent behind or within them. Utilitarian ethics in fact often *demands* what its critics complain of – an asymmetry between the appraisal of people and of actions, of motives and of consequences.[19] Mill's response to this disjunction was to say that judgements of *morality* strictly speaking are one thing; other types of appreciation are something else, and he set aside the categories of the 'aesthetic' and 'sympathetic' for the judgement of aspects of action relating to the 'beauty' and 'loveableness' that agents manifest when performing them ('Bentham', X, 98). The crucial point, though, is that judgements of these two – of aesthetic and sympathetic qualities – can vary independently of judgements of morality.

Mill's thought is always more than its systematic exposition, however, and to conclude that there is simply a stand-off between an aesthetic concern for moral character and a utilitarian attention to the results of action would be unjustifiably downbeat. A final attention to style helps us see why.

IV

One theorist calls style 'the exemplary mark of subjective agency',[20] and if that is right then the complicity between synonymy and commensurability that I have been looking at would help to obscure and underplay these marks of agency. The point can be put by saying that the distinctiveness of style may be an index of the distinctness of individuals, their viewpoints and values. So, giving substance to style would be to resist the tendency to reduce values to a single measure, with the *loss of value* which that can entail. Giving style its due would also be to do justice to the reality of conflict. Paraphrasing the individual text's style without significant loss models the difficulty and the reward of recasting one kind of value in a form that will be adequate to it.

Charles Altieri, whose definition began the previous paragraph, does not make self-consciousness a necessary condition in his theory of stylistic agency, but he does say that 'the concept of style has its greatest resonance when we come to appreciate the rendering of intentionality as a deliberate communicative act'.[21] I have suggested that the *innocent* performance of qualities of character is a prerequisite for the appreciation of moral excellence, and this would seem to count against Altieri's preference for deliberateness. Furthermore, in some contexts, it may not be best to think of agency as something that expresses a prior subjective disposition or set of intentions. As Altieri himself has noted, when thinking about writers 'who treat styles more like states people enter than attitudes subjects hold', style in language can figure as a way of discovering or exploring intentions that do not exist in advance of the conditions created by the style.[22]

Style and ethics converge on the recognition that interpretation (of texts and of people) requires attention to the surplus meaning that literary and non-literary acts unwittingly convey. What is indirectly revealed in and by a text's style may be more significant than what is self-consciously proclaimed by its author. Informed readings of individuals will take stylistic body language as a symptomatic indicator of character. This necessity of interpretation was abundantly recognized in Mill's time. Nineteenth-century critical discourse, inspired by the expansion and innovation in first-person literary forms, particularly autobiography and dramatic monologue, homed in on the expressive riches of just these textual elements. An emblem of what is a large body of criticism is T. H. Wright's argument in favour of 'that theory of style... which identifies it with character – with unconscious revelations of the hidden self'.[23] Mill's work contains many echoes of this discourse, as in the remark in his diary which protests against the common error of supposing that actions are the only true test of a person's character. Mill concludes that actions may be the fittest test 'for the world at large', but not for intimate friends. To those 'who care about what [someone] is and not merely about what he does, the involuntary indications of feeling and disposition are a much surer criterion... than voluntary acts'.[24] Similar thoughts are prominently at work in Mill's praise of his friend John Sterling for his 'indirect and unconscious influence', an influence rated by Mill as higher than that 'which we calculate upon & to which we can attach our name'.[25]

Involuntary indications of character bypass the histrionic potential of voluntary acts. They are a transitive form of the intransitive and authentic activity which carries no designs. Stylistic *activity* might here be contradistinguished from deliberate stylistic acts, as the unselfconscious mode of being 'in character'.

We have here one direction in which the ethical relevance of indirection can lead. There is another. One of the paradoxes of simple hedonism which Mill stumbled on was that happiness was not best pursued by direct striving after it. Make it your 'principal object' and you will not attain it; 'those only are happy', Mill wrote in his *Autobiography*, 'who have their minds fixed on some object other than their own happiness.... Aiming thus at something else, they find happiness by the way' (I, 146–7). Style, as I have read it in conjunction with Mill's ethical concerns, enacts the necessary relegation of instrumental thinking as a direct means of achieving some prized ethical values. It provides a model for the way that ethically desirable states or traits can only be achieved 'by the way'. To act with their attainment in view is self-defeating. The capacity, for example, for spontaneity – a quality Mill admired in proportion to the degree he felt he lacked it – is not one that can be directly willed by an individual or commanded by someone else. Tell someone: 'Be spontaneous!' and they are sure to fail: such states are essentially by-products.[26]

We can extend this argument to a more centrally prized ethical trait: autonomy. In doing what *On Liberty* calls 'pursuing our own good in our own way' (XVIII, 226), autonomy is the by-product of the successful realization by people of their own values and commitments. It is not that the possession of autonomy is prior to and the cause of the embodiment of these values and commitments in a life; rather, it is the embodiment which achieves or manifests autonomy. In this sense its presence or absence in a life is perceived retrospectively. As with the meanings which are read from style, autonomous behaviour cannot fully be contained in a prior intention.

So, a notion of style as the mark of individuality and uniqueness, especially when shorn of any limiting insistence on intentionality, does say something valuable about moral agency. It clearly marries with Mill's liberal insistence, in *On Liberty,* on idiosyncrasy, experiment, and difference. That argument might indeed be read as a fervent defence of personal style. A person's own 'mode of laying out his existence is the best', Mill claims, 'not because it is the best in itself, but because it is his own mode' (XVIII, 270). The alignment between style (or mode) and personal value provides a necessary resistance to the reductive conceptions of rationality with which we began. Yet we should not conclude from this that Mill endorses a Nietzschean or postmodern creation of the self through style.[27] Indeed, there is something ascetic about his view that style should strive for unselfconsciousness and lack of artfulness. Mill puts plainness before playfulness, self-loss before self-invention. In his admiration for Armand Carrel, he makes style *exemplary* rather than narrowly personal so that it manifests a public virtue – of political integrity – and not simply a personal peculiarity. Style in this sense is the proper way something should be done, not the unique way that someone has of doing it. Mill entertains a classical view of personal style as 'public tenet' as well as a liberal-Romantic view of style as an expression of personality.[28]

V

'I do not for a moment imagine that any part of what I have to relate, can be interesting to the public as a narrative or as being connected with myself': so Mill begins his *Autobiography*, with what must be one of the most vain and least honoured attempts to ward off readerly curiosity ever made (I, 5). It is with a brief attention to the *Autobiography* that I will end, because that work puts the apparently stable dichotomies of individuality and representativeness which we have just encountered through some necessary convolutions and complications. In doing so, it has implications not only for the reading of style but also for that of ethical comparability.

Mill pretends to be without a style of his own. He claims in his *Autobiography* to be of no interest as an individual, of use only as an example – of a kind of education, and an intellectual progress. Mill's self-effacement is one of the things that leads Richard Rorty to include him among those who are now 'honored in the abstract but forgotten in the particular' – the fate of writers whose work is socially useful but which does not produce what Nabokov called 'aesthetic bliss'.[29] Mill appears on this count to fall short of the status of 'strong poet'. It is certainly true that he consistently tries to persuade his readers that as a thinker he is merely subordinate or intermediary – a synthesizer rather than an originator of intellectual currents, not himself one of the 'original thinkers' but an 'interpreter . . . and mediator between them and the public' (I, 251). Despite the insistence in *On Liberty* that individuals should not allow others to write the script of their life for them, it does seem that Mill fails to make his story his own.

But this is not quite right. Mill's *Autobiography does* make his story his own, but only by representing it as not his own story. In the end there is something utterly distinctive about Mill's determination to be without distinction. At this level, his work confounds inherited notions of individuality (shared by Rorty, I would argue) which can only think of it as Romantic individuality. This work refuses to define itself either by opposition or conformity with first- or third-person standpoints. The relationship between these perspectives is more complex and dynamic than is allowed by the univocal alignment of style with personal uniqueness. This alignment, though useful, carries reductive limitations of its own if it promotes a static antithesis between public and private, between the morally synonymous and the morally unparaphrasable.

In ethics Mill helps us to see the force of the commensurabilist position and of its denial; simultaneously, his philosophy suggests that to accept that these are the only available choices is to submit to one of the reductive assumptions that need to be overcome. On the one hand he reminds us that people can be squeamish or self-indulgent in the face of real problems, that fine and fastidious moral sensibility can be a selfish luxury, and that there are times when you have to make tough decisions and this will involve getting your hands dirty. Reading his work shows us how the aesthete's fear of perpetrating the heresy of paraphrase might be the moral connoisseur's reluctance to contaminate a particular good by comparing it with another. Mill was very clear that one form of moral squeamishness turns out to be a way of protecting those who, literally, can afford to have clean hands and fine feelings.[30] The force of such criticism of anti-commensurabilist positions cannot be underestimated, particularly when it exposes the political agenda which such positions often serve.

But on the other hand Mill's work can also suggest that we cannot do away with the objections to full-strength commensurability. If anything, it is commensurability which underplays the real difficulty of moral conflicts for individuals by assuming that there is always a single right answer, and by pretending that the sacrifice and regret involved in alleviating or resolving conflict can somehow be made to disappear.

Clearly, some of us some of the time act as if synonymy were possible, otherwise how could I, for example, successfully recapitulate any part of what I've been saying without saying it in just the same form again. Clearly also, some paraphrases are better than others, or than none at all, even though not everything worth saying can be reductively paraphrased. By the same token, the fact that moral values may be irreducible does not always imply that they cannot be compared.[31] In the end the relevant question is not the abstract one of whether synonymy or commensurability are possible according to strict criteria; instead, it is one of deciding in practice where their possibility should be entertained, and what force that should have. Perhaps deliberation about a moral dilemma will be better – will constitute a better re-description of all the features we need to know about – if it is accepted that something is probably going to get lost in the translation. As with paraphrase, one should strive to make the loss as small as possible, but too confident a belief that everything worth keeping can be kept is likely to go against that effort. This was something which Mill, who was himself occasionally a translator, and fluent in Latin, French, and Greek, would have known.

Notes

I am very grateful to Stefan Collini, Fiona Green and, especially, to Jonathan Rée for criticism of earlier drafts of this essay.

1. Mill, *Principles of Political Economy*, in *The Collected Works of John Stuart Mill*, general editor John M. Robson, 33 vols (University of Toronto Press, 1963–91) III, 502. All quotations are from this edition and are identified in the text by volume and page number; the only exceptions are references to Mill's letters, which, because of their length, are given in notes below.
2. Marx, *Grundrisse*, trans. Martin Nicolaus (London: Allen Lane, 1973) 142.
3. See E. D. Hirsch, 'Stylistics and Synonymy', *Critical Inquiry*, 1 (1975) 559–79. This definition of synonymy is intended as a generally or pre-critically serviceable one (and one that applies to Mill). The complexity of the philosophical problem of synonymy cannot be captured in this essay. It has received extensive discussion within analytic philosophy, much of it generated by the work of Quine. See, for instance, his *Word and Object* (Cambridge, MA: MIT Press, 1960).
4. This is argued by John Skorupski, *John Stuart Mill* (London: Routledge, 1989) 300–7.
5. Steven Lukes, *Moral Conflict and Politics* (Oxford: Clarendon, 1991) 45.
6. Bernard Williams, *Ethics and the Limits of Philosophy* (London: Fontana, 1985) 17–18.
7. Ibid., 66–9. See also 'Conflicts of Values', in *Moral Luck: Philosophical Papers 1973–1980* (Cambridge University Press, 1981).
8. Williams, *Ethics and the Limits of Philosophy*, 18. On this theme in Weber, see Rogers Brubaker, *The Limits of Rationality: An Essay on the Social and Moral Thought of Max Weber* (London: George Allen & Unwin, 1984); for Weber's analysis of the historical process by which reason came to be embodied in eventually self-sustaining institutional forms, see *The Protestant Ethic and the Spirit of Capitalism*, trans. Talcott Parsons (London: Routledge, 1992), first pub. 1930.
9. Isaiah Berlin, 'John Stuart Mill and the Ends of Life', in *Four Essays on Liberty* (Oxford: Oxford University Press, 1969) 178.
10. The sources for Bentham's thought on language are: *The Fragment on Ontology*, the *Essay on Logic* and the *Essay on Language*, all in vol. VIII of *The Works of Jeremy Bentham*, ed. John Bowring, 11 vols (Edinburgh: Simkin, Marshall, 1843). For this point, see *Essay on Language*, 331.
11. Ibid., 331.

12. On Bentham's linguistic reform see Jonathan Rée, *Philosophical Tales* (London: Methuen, 1987) 97–106, and C. K. Ogden, *Bentham's Theory of Fictions* (London: Kegan Paul, 1932).
13. Bentham, *Works*, VIII, 301.
14. The manifold problems with Mill's definition of poetry – in particular its tendency to consider all poetry in terms of the purely lyrical – cannot be fully spelled out here.
15. Wordsworth, 'Essays on Epitaphs, III', *The Prose Works of William Wordsworth,* ed. W. J. B. Owen and J. W. Smyser, 3 vols (Oxford: Clarendon, 1974) II, 84–5.
16. Wordsworth of course said that 'all good poetry is the spontaneous overflow of powerful feelings', but he went on immediately to add that for it to have value, the poet must also have 'thought long and deeply' ('Preface' to *Lyrical Ballads*, in *Prose Works*, I, 126). Mill ignores the caveat.
17. This was the judgement of Emile Littré, quoted by Mill in his essay, 'Armand Carrel', XX, 197. As editor of the *London and Westminster Review,* Mill clearly thought to model himself on Carrel.
18. For a fine discussion of 'the display of excellent character as an unintended side-effect of actions with other aims', see Flint Schier, 'Hume and the Aesthetics of Agency', *Proceedings of the Aristotelian Society*, 87 (1986–87) 121–35, esp. 123.
19. See in particular, *Utilitarianism*, X, 219 and 220 n.
20. Charles Altieri, 'Personal Style as Articulate Intentionality', in *The Question of Style in Literature and the Arts*, ed. Caroline van Eck, James McAllister and Renée van de Vall (Cambridge University Press, 1995) 201.
21. Ibid., 201–2.
22. Charles Altieri, 'Style *as* the Man', in *Analytic Aesthetics*, ed. Richard Shusterman (Oxford: Blackwell, 1989) 64.
23. T. H. Wright, 'Style', *Macmillan's Magazine*, 37 (1877) 78–84 (83).
24. Mill, *Diary*, 2 March 1854, XXVII, 658.
25. Letter to Sterling, 29 May 1844, XIII, 629. Compare also Mill's judgement of his father's influence on his own character – that it depended not only 'on what he said or did with that direct object, but also, and still more, on what manner of man he was' (*Autobiography*, I, 49).
26. On the self-defeating rationality involved in 'states that are essentially by-products', see Jon Elster, *Sour Grapes: Studies in the Subversion of Rationality* (Cambridge University Press, 1983), Chapter 2.
27. The textualized and Romantic self in Richard Rorty's work, for example, adopts style as the means of self-transformation and perfection in private moral life. Rorty acknowledges his debt to Nietzsche, and to Alexander Nehamas's reading of Nietzsche's style. See *Contingency, Irony and Solidarity* (Cambridge University Press, 1987) 27.
28. For the idea of personal style as public tenet, see E. L. Epstein, *Language and Style* (London: Methuen, 1978) 23.
29. Rorty, *Contingency, Irony and Solidarity*, 152.

30. See, for example, Mill's early attack on the *Edinburgh Review* for its effete preference for individual sensibility over social improvement ('Periodical Literature: *Edinburgh Review*', I, 322–3).
31. Williams implies this in 'Conflicts of Values', see pp. 77–80; for a fuller argument in favour of limited comparability, see Walter Sinnott-Armstrong, 'Moral Dilemmas and Incomparability', *American Philosophical Quarterly*, 22 (1985) 321–8.

Part IV
Ethics and the State of the Humanities

11

The Benefit of Doubt: The Ethics of Reading

Lori Branch West

> iter, again, probably comes from itara, other in Sanskrit, and everything that follows can be read as the working out of the logic that ties repetition to alterity
>
> Derrida, 'Signature Event Context'

'Repetition', Kierkegaard writes, 'comes again everywhere'[1] and this seems especially true of contemporary literary discussions. As primitive ritual or unenlightened superstition, subtle panoptic control or intentional brainwashing, mindless habit or neurotic compulsion, and for all its uncanny 'coming again', repetition suffers a certain notoriety as being somehow opposed to knowledge. However varied the schools of thought frequently lumped together as 'postmodern', many of them have sought to demystify the foundations of enlightenment as constructs of repetition, curiously displaying a bias against repetition that is itself deeply rooted in enlightenment, while never quite escaping repetition's ghostly reappearance.[2]

In this essay, I attempt to configure literary ethics and a value for reading outside the economic–epistemological configuration of 'getting something out of the text', in which 'knowledge' is extracted from a text and 'meaning' is the exchange value of that knowledge. Repetition, in the form of rereading, allows us to speak of the value of reading in terms of *giving the Other the benefit of the doubt*, for in an epistemologically uncertain universe, ethical reading of the Other's words is never a matter of the perfect exchange of knowledge nor of one-time occurrence. Ethics and ethical relation can be imagined as the benefit of doubt – the benefit of unknowing – which we give to the Other (and which returns to us) when we reread her texts in an attempt to acknowledge the insufficiency of any one reading to the Other's being. Thus I begin this essay by correlating works by Jean-François Lyotard and Jacques Derrida with an eye toward their interlacing of ethics, epistemological uncertainty, and repetition, and I then move to a more unusual but no less stimulating topos for exploring ethics and repetition, namely liturgical practice considered as an ethical approach to the Other based in rereading and epistemological uncertainty. Because language is not a vehicle for law-like knowledge and because of its potential for being reread in giving the Other the benefit of the doubt, language presents intentionality and ethics together as possibilities; in other words, as Kierkegaard more tersely has it, perhaps 'Repetition is a task for freedom.'[3] In the concluding section, I sketch a brief prospectus for literary study reimagined as liturgical, ethical relation to the Other. By approaching literature and ethics 'liturgically', I aim not only to reconfigure the work we do in departments of literature, but also to critique the commonplace association of deliberate, repetitive practice with intellectual or ethical bad faith and to recover notions of practice and resistance that are more than merely transgressive.

DOUBT AND ETHICS

In *The Differend*, Lyotard's semiotic and epistemological starting point is that 'differends' are possible: 'phrases', he writes, are constructed according to the rules of various phrase regimens, and 'genres of discourse' provide rules for linking together various heterogeneous phrases;[4] a 'differend' occurs as a 'conflict, between at least two parties, that cannot be equitably resolved for lack of a rule of judgment applicable to both arguments' since 'a universal rule of judgment between heterogeneous genres is lacking in general'.[5] Because there is no universal discourse to determine the validity of every possible phrase, each time an addressor links one phrase to another, she is acting in non-knowledge, in uncertainty as to how she ought to link: 'It is necessary to link', writes Lyotard, 'but the mode of linkage is never necessary.'[6] In his view, the work of the philosopher is not to arbitrate between differends according to a rule or self-legitimating narrative but to articulate particular differends, attempting to do justice to the unknowable Other who is ever 'but the addressor of a current phrase'.[7] Listening to the words of the Other at this moment and asking '*Arrive-t-il?*' ('Is this happening?') is the ethical task; the Now, the occurrence, the *Arrive-t-il?* is the ethical moment. Ethical relation takes place in and as a differend – the phrase being uttered in the Now – between the past and future.[8]

Lyotard's 'philosophical reader', then, cannot simply cite the phrase of the Other in an ethical writing-off but participates in a ritual of sorts, rereading and reflecting. Discussing Plato's *Phaedrus*, Lyotard writes, 'Simulacrum is deceitful as idol (*eidolon*); but, taken as *eikos* (verisimilar), it is a signpost on the path to the true, to the "proper".'[9] The phrase of the Other is all one 'has' of the Other, so to speak, and even all the Other has of the Other, so his phrase cannot be made into a 'fact' or idol to possess, but it must be taken as his sacred icon, an image to be given all the benefit of unknowing and lavished with endless reexamination. Knowledge's perpetual incompleteness and a phrase's perpetual inadequacy to the reality of all possible phrases carry what Lyotard calls the 'authority of the infinite' and the 'call of language':[10] the call, we might say, to infinite rereading, rehearing, reflecting. The rereading to which Lyotard calls us has a ritual, but one whose 'rule' is not prescribed by the authority of the past or by a hierarchy of genres but by the Now, by the phrase of the Other which calls us to reflect and to witness differends in what we might call the ritual of the Now. This ritual of re-asking oneself *Arrive-t-il?* Lyotard calls 'the ultimate resistance that the event can oppose to the accountable or countable use of time'.[11] The structure of *The Differend* is itself an object lesson in this sort of rereading; each of the book's 264 sections contains multiple notes referring the reader to other sections of the book, and the final note in section 264 refers the reader back to 'No.1*ff*.' If one were to read this book as it asks to be read, one could not 'save time' but would read it literally again and again.

In essays such as 'Force of Law', 'Limited Inc abc', and 'Eating Well', Derrida's epistemological starting place is that 'knowledge' is limited to the realms of calculation and law and that calculation and law are not ethics. Ethical choice operates in the realm of non-knowledge, for if a decision were made with perfect, complete 'factual' knowledge, it would be only a calculation and fall short of the free will (however limited) upon which any idea of ethics is predicated. In 'Force of Law', Derrida writes:

Law is not justice. Law is the element of calculation, and it is just

> that there be law, but justice is incalculable, it requires us to calculate with the incalculable; and aporetic experiences are the experiences, as improbable as they are necessary, of justice, that is to say of moments in which the decision between just and unjust is never insured by a rule.[12]

Justice is a matter of neither economics nor algorithm; thus the moment of decision can be 'free' and therefore potentially just because it is undecidable:

> The instant of the just decision...must rend time and defy dialectics. It is a madness. Even if time and prudence, the patience of knowledge and the mastery of conditions were hypothetically unlimited, the decision would be structurally finite, however late it came, [a] decision of urgency and precipitation, acting in the night of non-knowledge and non-rule.[13]

Undecidability, this 'acting in the night of non-knowledge and non-rule', lends acts the excessiveness which allows them to supersede law and calculation and to approach the infinite limit of justice. In 'Eating Well', he remarks:

> The surplus of responsibility of which I was just speaking will never authorize any silence [regarding violence against the Other]. I repeat: responsibility is excessive or it is not a responsibility. A limited, calculable, rationally distributed responsibility is already the becoming right of morality; it is at times also, in the best hypothesis, the dream of every good conscience, [and] in the worst hypothesis, of the small or grand inquisitors.[14]

Recalling Dostoevsky's *The Brothers Karamazov* ('I am responsible to all and for all') and Levinas's *Totality and Infinity*, the Other's alterity and one's having always been in relation to the Other evoke a limitless responsibility, and Derrida uses 'eating well' as a metonymy for this obligation:

> 'One must eat well' does not mean above all taking in and grasping in itself, but learning and giving to eat, learning-to-give-to-the-other-to-eat. One never eats entirely on one's own: this constitutes the rule underlying the statement, 'One must eat well.' It is a rule offering infinite hospitality.[15]

This 'infinite hospitality' entails a recursiveness related both to Lyotard's (re)witnessing of the differend and to Derridean iterability. In 'Signature Event Context', Derrida argues that iterability, structurally inherent to writing, is 'a force that breaks with its context, that is, with the collectivity of presences organizing the moment of its inscription', and yet that by virtue of this force, no context can entirely enclose a phrase, and that even if the author and her intentions are irrevocably lost to the reader, writing can still be readable.[16] Drawing together Derrida's and Lyotard's ideas, we might say that in rupturing every text from the context of its inscription or utterance, the structure of iterability constitutes the phrase as a differend between its addresser and addressee, as that which marks both the impossibility of the addresser ever being fully present to the addressee in a phrase and the obligation of the addressee to read the phrase again. In Lyotard's terms, though an addressee is unable to 'know' the addresser of any given phrase, an addressee can (and ought to) reread the phrase in the ethical effort to testify to the differend which the phrase signifies, suffers, and causes its addresser and addressee to suffer by its multifaceted inadequacy.

Just as for Lyotard reading outside the realm of the knowable obligates the reader to reread and reflect without regard to 'saving time', so for Derrida an honest reader is not 'hasty'[17] and recognizes iterability as both the possibility and the impossibility of writing and reading: '"Ritual" is not a possible occurrence, but rather, as iterability, a structural characteristic of every mark.'[18] A sort of 'ritual reading', then, is in many senses the reading to which Derridean iterability and ethics lead us. Iterability 'implies both identity and difference',[19] and as such it authorizes us neither, in Lyotard's words, to give up on language, for some trace of identity is iterable in a text, nor to read only once, for difference as a trait of each iteration precludes the possibility that one reading could claim total 'authority'; like psychoanalysis, rereading is interminable.[20] Iterability lends to the text an always double-edged 'perhaps', writes Derrida, which places it outside the authority of law-like, ontological discourse[21] or, as Lyotard might say, outside the realm of necessary modes of linking.

The question of ethics and the question of the possibility of textual 'meaning' outside knowledge-communication, then, are like the two sides of a coin, or better, of a Möbius strip. It is because language does not communicate law-like knowledge that it presents ethics – justice or the opportunity to exceed calculation – and what we might call 'meaning' as possibility. Because iterability implies both identity and alterity, and because iteration is an uncanny sort of re-occurrence involving neither perfect repetition nor complete newness and neither the perfect presence nor the utter absence of the Other, language makes possible in rereading an intentionality of practice impossible in calculation or in the overwhelming presence of knowledge *qua* communicable essence. From the standpoint of reading, we might say that ethics consists in giving the Other's phrases the benefit of the doubt and that ethical relation with the Other is the potentially excessive benefit of doubt. Thus the potential to reread, to bring the Other's phrase back into occurrence in the midst of non-knowledge, to attempt to do justice to one who is never but the addresser of a phrase, constitutes a paradigm for potential ethical relation to the Other viable within certain postmodern critiques of Enlightenment epistemology. In rereading we may speak of a dialogic ethics and an ethics of dialogue: not knowledge-extraction from words but the on-going, in-folding, recursive attempt to do justice to the Other in words. Of course, we can never know the sincerity, or to use Derrida's term, the 'seriousness' of any utterance (whether it is meant to facilitate dialogue or to manipulate us), and even the very existence of the Other is always a matter of not-knowing, of doubt and of belief. But precisely because of this non-knowledge and non-coincidence of discourse and being, we find ourselves perpetually called to rereading; like Derrida at the beginning of 'Force of Law', we are always having to try to speak to the Other in the language of the Other.[22] If justice is excessive, if responsibility to the Other is limitless, and if Others relate in good measure by 'reading' each other's phrases, then ethics is in one sense the obligation to an endlessly iterative, recursive reading of the words of the Other. In what is hopefully, then, a not-too-arcane manoeuvre, I now turn to liturgy – liturgy *qua* ethical rereading – to further an imagination of literary rereading in ethical terms.

LITURGY AND THE BENEFIT OF DOUBT: ETHICS AS REREADING

It is not too simplistic to say that the academic study of Christian liturgy is the child of Reformation and Counter-Reformation attempts to legitimate church authority in juridical, contractual terms; for both Roman Catholics and early Protestants, the search for liturgical origins in apostolic authority amounted to the search for the charter of their legal and sacramental being.[23] As such, the suggestion that the study of liturgy might prove useful in imagining postmodern literary ethics indeed seems strange. 'Liturgical theology', however, comes to us primarily from the diaspora of Russian Orthodox intellectuals and theologians just before and after the Bolshevik Revolution. Eastern and Western Christendom having been largely out of communication since the Great Schism of 1054, the relocation of many Russians in the West and especially in Paris prompted the articulation of their religious and philosophical tradition in the discourse of (post)Enlightenment epistemology and reading.

Liturgical theology as a genre eschews any reflex dismissal of all religious thought as 'onto-theological discourse', for as opposed to the dominant Western genres of dogmatic and systematic theology, liturgical theology is predicated on relation to God as the attempt to learn to speak to Him in His own language and so to do justice to His phrase in Christ as both person and divine Word. For Alexander Schmemann, for instance, the liturgical rereading of the Divine Word is 'a sacramental act par excellence because it is a transforming act',[24] transforming the person who at once speaks and hears the words of the Other, vivifying the phrase of the Other in the Now. In liturgical practice, it is as though the intention of the Other, which animated the text at its writing but which is cut off from it via iterability, is re-infused into the text as the benefit of the doubt: the benefit of believing in the existence and alterity of the Other in the realm of non-knowledge. The reader is always at risk of being duped by giving the benefit of the doubt, and it may very well be that the liturgical reader in any religion is being duped by a malicious or non-existent 'big Other'. But liturgical theology is predicated on this very possibility, just as the possibility of ethical relation is afforded by non-knowledge.

The primary texts explored by theologians like Schmemann, those associated with the Eastern Orthodox liturgy and monastic hours, are fascinating for their simultaneous simplicity and ornate intertextuality as well as for the manner in which they are reread. Among Orthodoxy's many liturgies, the one most often celebrated, *The Liturgy of St. John Chrysostom*, dates to the fourth or fifth century and contains over 200 verses of Scripture in addition to readings from the Gospels and Epistles. Together with the appointed hymns and texts which change daily, nineteen books are necessary to contain the yearly cycle. No official attempt has been made to reduce that corpus, which itself seems to signify a sort of infinitude of rereading in the attempt to do justice to the Other. Parish celebration of some of the monastic hours is common, and individuals pray and recite psalms usually twice a day. Corporately or in private, reader and hearers stand, and before and after the reading all simply chant the *Doxa*: 'Glory to You, O Lord, Glory to You' – to the you in whom the words had their unrecoverable origins and to the you who is allowed to speak again through the act of the addressee's repeated readings. Likewise every liturgy begins by chanting the Great Doxology, which climaxes by saying three times, 'Blessed are you, O Lord; teach me your precepts', or, teach me your words.

Alexander Schmemann's liturgical theology holds that liturgical relation is something human beings are called to do, in the words of *The Liturgy of St. Basil*, 'for the life of the world', since without this sort of reading and giving the world cannot live. Describing the relation of the communicant to the Other and to God in the Eucharist, Schmemann conceives of liturgy, *leitourgia,* as literally 'the work of the people' in hearing the call 'to bear testimony to [Christ]', to the divine Word,[25] with all of life becoming part of this liturgy, this listening and thanksgiving to God. For Schmemann, the power of liturgy comes from wilfully entering into the realm of non-knowledge and relation to the Other; he calls this witnessing 'the very calling of the Church, the sacrament by which it "becomes what it is"'.[26] Elaborating on this non-violent approach to the Other, he writes:

> It is within this peace – 'which passeth all understanding' – that now begins the liturgy of the Word. Western Christians are so accustomed to distinguish the Word from the sacrament that it may be difficult for them to understand that in the Orthodox perspective the liturgy of the Word is...sacramental....The sacrament is a manifestation of the Word. And unless the false dichotomy between Word and sacrament is overcome, the true meaning of both Word and sacrament, and especially the true meaning of Christian 'sacramentalism' cannot be grasped in all their wonderful implications....In the liturgy the proclamation of the Gospel is preceded by 'Alleluia', the singing of this

> mysterious '*theoforous*' (God-bearing) word which is the joyful greeting of those who see the coming Lord, who *know* His presence, and who express their joy at this glorious 'parousia'. 'Here He is!' might be an almost adequate translation of this untranslatable word.[27]

In this complex text, Schmemann implies that in configuring word and sacrament as distinct from one another, Western theology has made word nothing by making it only the vehicle of something else. For Schmemann, word and world can be embraced as sacrament, and eucharistic life consists in the caring, liturgical, endless exploration of the word as iterable 'begotten' of the unseen Other. Emphasis falls not upon the one proclaiming the word but on the fact that it is being proclaimed in the Other's stead, paradoxically both by us and to us, on the Other's behalf. Embracing this reading on the Other's behalf transforms *Arrive-t-il?* into *Il arrive*; the impersonal 'Is it happening?' is transfigured by reading's volitional embrace into 'He is coming! She arrives! Here he is!' The object pronoun becomes person. Moreover, Schmemann's insistent play on 'see' and 'know' emphasize that in this central 'act of faith' believers do not see or know but rather only give the Other the benefit of the doubt and so 'see' the coming – the 'parousia' – of the Other, 'only' in word.

Schmemann's discourse is far from valuing liturgy only in terms of ontology and presence, his subjunctives (''Here he is' ... *might* be an *almost* adequate translation ...') nicely reflecting the complexity of his position. The issue of presence and absence in liturgical theology is largely transmuted into a question of one's ability or inability to listen to the Other, to allow the Other to speak, highlighting a desire for coincidence between speaking and listening while always marvelling at and seeking to do justice to the Other without presuming to contain her. Schmemann's writings stress not immediate presence but immediate practice and the urgency of becoming one to whom the Other can speak if the Other so desires.[28]

> This is why the reading ... of the Gospel in ... the Church is a liturgical act, an integral and essential part of the sacrament. It is heard as the Word of God, and it is received in the Spirit – that is, in the Church, which is the life of the Word and its 'growth' in the world.[29]

In his view, the church gives the Other's word the benefit of the doubt – they hear it 'as' the Word of God – and in so doing they give it and the world life, that speaking life without which, in Derrida's words, 'we' are silent victims and iterability is only the inscription of death.[30]

For Schmemann, in giving the Other the incalculable gift of the benefit of the doubt, one eats well, in the evocative Derridean sense and in the sense of what occurs in the Eucharist as a mystical meal. What was 'just' bread and wine, only 'word', has in this giving been changed but not obliterated; it is now bread and wine and Word as life, as the impossible mystery of communion in the realm of word with the Other whom our act of believing allows to speak. In remembering the Other, the believer is also remembered, in the multiple senses of that word, as sung during communion: 'Receive me today as partaker of your mystical supper . . . I will not speak of your mystery as your enemies do. . . . Remember me, O Lord.' The Eucharist becomes an act of readings from which no one is excluded but he who will not leave off speaking of the Other in totalizing terms of knowledge. Being becomes something given one by the Other, by the Other's memory of one's words. And as there is no singular, perfect reading, the Eucharist is not apocalyptic but part of what Schmemann calls the endless sanctification of time in the present; as with Lyotard and Derrida, there are only particular readings which together in iteration may approach the infinite limit of justice. To Lyotard's question of whether there can be any honour in thinking or reading in the absence of a rule to arbitrate authoritatively among the genres, liturgical theology answers yes, because this radical gift of believing in the alterity and existence of the unknown Other can never be accused of doing violence to the Other *via* a reading which would presume to know her. This giving engenders an existential excess of intentionality in the liturgical reader which can only be called beautiful when it is used, in Lyotard's terms, not in the 'intellectual' mode of furthering one's political advantage or of relying on the emotions borne of sacrifice, but in the volitional quest to acknowledge rightly and justly the excessive alterity of the Other and to embrace in non-knowledge the benefit of doubt, to 'bless' the name of the Other and to call her good. To graft together phrases from Lyotard, Derrida, and Schmemann: the ethicality or 'sacramentality' of reading comes not from the sacred or ethical 'value' 'in' the text but rather in the liturgical enactment of the text as occurrence in the benefit of doubt.

The 'value' of reading is never calculable as in a configuration of the sacred-text-as-contract but consists in its iterability, its incalculable potential for that eerie sort of repetition called occurrence.

LITURGICAL RELATION: REREADING AS ETHICS

What, then, would be the implications of reimagining the reading we do in literature departments as liturgical, ethical relation? This is, I contend, what contemporary ethical discussions urge us to do: to question the value of knowledge and to see if we might conceive of the value of reading in terms other than the discovery, acquisition, and trading of knowledge as commodity – in other words, to imagine the benefit of doubt. Literary study seems eminently suited for such a reimagination. When we take up a poetic text, for instance, read it again and again, pause, reflect on it, read it again a day, a week, a year or years later in a different course or context, when we try to imagine the situation to which it once could have been true, when we formulate understandings of such a discourse and put them into dialogue with others' understandings, what we do is – or at best can be – very much like liturgical relation to the Other in religious practice, entailing the same non-closure, numinosity, and vulnerability before the Other, the same sort of performativity, and the same ghostly (non)presence of the Other to the self and of one to oneself. The literary reader operates within the same non-knowledge that the liturgical believer does: in non-knowledge of the addressor's context, intentions, benevolence or maliciousness, and even of his existence. Most crucially, the professional reader of literature comes to this task facing the same potentials borne of non-knowledge: the potential for the most ethical, non-violent of relations, as well as the potential for a violent fundamentalism that would categorically silence utterances outside a given genre.

Re-envisioning literary practice in terms of ethical, liturgical relation could prompt any number of changes of practice in literature departments, but space permits sketching only a few here. First, this configuration would allow us to speak of the author – the addressor of a text – again and anew, outside ontology and a conception of law-like intention, putting us in relation to her just as we are in relation to anyone – in words, with a sober sense of humility and even awe before her non-appropriable alterity. It would also allow us to conceive of the value of reading and teaching literature not as the production of knowledge but as ethical praxis. In *The Practice of Everyday Life*, Michel de Certeau describes repeated, day-to-day practices as embodying the 'ways of believing and making people believe' even long after active subscription to a set of narratives has dissipated.[31] The deliberate practice of liturgical rereading, ethically conceived, can be a tool in displacing the disguised litanies of consumerist culture rather than merely transgressing them.[32] Additionally, this configuration of the value of reading could prompt a substantial reimagination of the academic paper and perhaps even an hierarchical reversal between publication and the work of rereading in the classroom, assigning much more value to the recursive attempt to do justice to a text in class than to the extraction of academic currency from it.

Not least of all, the recursive reading practices of the classroom embody a potential to do justice not only to particular texts and authors but to the experience of reading that has drawn many of us into this profession. This reading experience asks to be called by its right name: not 'knowledge', nor even 'meaning' rather capitalistically constructed as 'getting something out of the text'. In *Social Values and Poetic Acts*, Jerome McGann refers to the 'literary form of knowledge' which functions by deploying the 'abstractness of proverbs or the illusions of ideology...[and] dispel[ling] these ghostly shapes by transforming them into recognizable human forms: by incarnating them into worlds that are detailed, specific, and circumstantial'.[33] This 'incarnation', in much the way that Schmemann's sacramental acceptance of the Other's word begets an incarnation, is the 'miracle' of reading (as so often it is called by parents and grade school teachers) which many of us have experienced in loving the work of a particular author, lavishing her texts with countless rereadings, and marvelling at her mind, absent yet somehow uncannily (re)present(ed) to us in her text. This experience of reading, figured as the acceptance of the verbal incarnation of a real Other whom we can never know or prove, would suggest that giving the benefit of doubt, as I have tried to figure it – believing from a state of non-knowledge that she exists, that her words are 'worth' countless reconsiderations in the Now – is a better and non-economizable name for our pursuit. Only by calling our endeavour by its right name, by admitting it to be comprised of incremental, repeated acts of belief in an ever-inadequate liturgy of rereading, can we begin to account for our belief investments as volitional acts, as the words of the Other challenge us to do.

Finally, and only partly tangentially, such a reimagination would also release me of the compulsion I have felt throughout this essay to apologize for reflecting on ethics in the vein of theology. The only reason to apologize for reflecting on ethics in this vein is that it has been delegitimated as non-knowledge by the dominant mode of discourse; the only reasons to apologize for writing in a genre of non-knowledge are reasons that still cling to the transport *via* words of meaning-*qua*-knowledge as the basis for (economic) self-legitimization. I, the I that exists only to you as either the addresser or addressee instance of a phrase, exists in the realm of non-knowledge inhabited by liturgical theology, a theology which by the logic of liturgy, in Derrida's words, 'ties repetition to alterity'. While certainly I must always apologize to you for being an inadequate reader and hearer of you in the addressor instance, it is (happily) not necessary that I apologize for speaking to you in religious-sounding language. For in some sense to read is to be religious: it is to situate oneself in a realm of language which is always already a matter of ethics and of non-knowledge, of doubt and of belief. To acknowledge the imperfection of knowledge and to imagine that there are benefits to this imperfection is to begin the ethical, deconstructive work of claiming the benefit of doubt, and it is this work of ethics and literature that can begin to reconstruct our culture's institutions of knowledge from within.

Notes

1. Søren Kierkegaard, *Journals and Papers* (1843) 326. This and the following quotation from Kierkegaard (also from *Journals and Papers*) are quoted in the editors' supplement to Søren Kierkegaard, *Fear and Trembling and Repetition*, ed., trans., intro. and notes by Howard V. Hong and Edna H. Hong, *Kierkegaard's Writings* VI (Princeton University Press, 1983). I owe a great debt of gratitude to Diane Elam of the University of Wales at Cardiff, for whose fascinating doctoral seminar in 'The Literature of Ethics' a longer version of this paper was originally written. I also thank Gayle Margherita and Kevin West of Indiana University for their generous feedback and encouragement in later revisions of this paper.
2. For the concept of ghostly, uncanny repetition, see for instance J.

Hillis Miller, *Fiction and Repetition: Seven English Novels* (Cambridge: Harvard University Press, 1982).

3. Kierkegaard, *Journals and Papers*, 323.
4. Jean-François Lyotard, *The Differend: Phrases in Dispute*, trans. Georges Van Den Abbeele, *Theory and History of Literature*, no. 46 (Minneapolis: University of Minnesota Press, 1988) xii.
5. Ibid., xi. I disagree with Christopher Norris's assessment of Lyotard as 'anti-realist'. Lyotard's conception of the real in *The Differend* seems to be that valid articulations of it may be contradictory and that the work of ethics is carefully to articulate the paradoxes of truth so that a party speaking in one discourse will not be forever silenced under a hegemonic discourse. Throughout *The Differend*, Lyotard returns to two examples of this silencing, that of the Holocaust victim (who, if able to testify to the Holocaust, 'disproves' the Holocaust by still being alive) and that of the philosopher subjugated to institutional economic imperatives for efficiency and 'saving time'. Lyotard asserts that the work of the philosopher is opposed to this injunction for efficiency, for if differends exist, the 'efficient' solution to them – delegitimating a claim from one genre in terms of a politically hegemonic genre – is a violence to reality.
6. Lyotard, *The Differend*, 29.
7. Ibid., 11.
8. Here I enact a shift in the use of the term 'differend'. Temporally, a phrase-being-uttered exists as an irresolvable moment of tension between the one who addresses it and is always past to it and the one to whom it is addressed and is always future to it, especially in that it puts an ethical charge on the latter to do something in the future: namely, to read the phrase reflectively again and again, to give it occurrence. Put differently, two of the most important 'genres' producing differends are the genre of discourse relating to past events and the genre relating to future events. The utterance in the Now appears as the differend between these two temporalities and between the being of the addressor and the addressee, even if the utterance is intended to efface that differend.
9. Lyotard, *The Differend*, 22.
10. Ibid., 31.
11. Ibid., xvi.
12. Jacques Derrida, 'Force of Law: The "Mystical Foundation of Authority"', trans. Mary Quaintance, *Cardozo Law Review*, 11 (1990) 919–1045 (947).
13. Ibid., 967.
14. Jacques Derrida, '"Eating Well", or the Calculation of the Subject: An Interview with Jacques Derrida', trans. Peter Connor and Avital Ronell, *Who Comes After the Subject?* eds Eduardo Cadava, Peter Connor and Jean-Luc Nancy (New York: Routledge, 1991) 96–119 (118).
15. Ibid., 118.
16. Jacques Derrida, 'Signature Event Context', in Gerald Graff, ed. and intro., *Limited Inc.* (Evanston IL: Northwestern University Press, 1988) 1–23 (9).

17. Jacques Derrida, Afterword, 'Toward An Ethic of Discussion', in Gerald Graff, ed. and intro., *Limited Inc.* (Evanston IL: Northwestern University Press, 1988) 111–60 (125).
18. Derrida, 'Signature Event Context', 15.
19. Derrida, *Limited Inc.*, 53.
20. Ibid., 39.
21. Ibid., 83.
22. Derrida, 'Force of Law: The "Mystical Foundation of Authority"', 921.
23. For a history of liturgical study, see Paul F. Bradshaw, *The Search for the Origins of Christian Worship: Sources and Methods for the Study of Liturgy* (New York: Oxford University Press, 1992) and *The Study of Liturgy*, ed. Cheslyn Jones, Geoffrey Wainwright and Edward Yarnold (London: SPCK, 1978). As an alternate approach to liturgical study, the evolving field of ritual studies has generally failed to conceive of liturgy outside the denigration of ritual and repetition as superstition or compulsion. For example, Catherine Bell's influential *Ritual Theory, Ritual Practice* (New York: Oxford University Press, 1992) consistently portrays ritual as panoptic control or ideological crutch. Despite occasional deft handlings of writers such as Derrida, Bell fails to consider ritual *qua* iterability as inherent in the structure of language itself.
24. Alexander Schmemann, *For the Life of the World: Sacraments and Orthodoxy*, 2nd rev. edn (Crestwood, NY: St. Vladimir's Seminary Press, 1973) 33. This book was published in Britain as *World As Sacrament*.
25. Ibid., 25.
26. Ibid., 26.
27. Ibid., 33.
28. For instance, in the works of fourteenth-century Byzantine theologian St. Gregory Palamas, the ascetic, meditative practices of the hesychast are not causally related to the mystical vision of God's energies (i.e. they cannot in any way be said to induce this vision) but only calm his passions and intellectual illusions so that he is able to hear or see should God choose to address him; liturgical praying and rereading of the words of the Other are essential to becoming able to listen to those words. The unique relation one has to one's own words, deeds, and intentions, coupled with one's non-knowledge of the Other's intentions (and thus of the ethicality of her actions), places the onus of ethics on self-examination; agency is properly directed toward interrogating one's own actions, and responsibility is conceived of rather performatively, as in 'taking responsibility' for an act in confession.
29. Schmemann, *For the Life of the World*, 33.
30. Derrida, 'Signature Event Context', 8.
31. Michel de Certeau, *The Practice of Everyday Life*, trans. Steven Rendall (Berkeley: University of California Press, 1984) 177–89.
32. I here have in mind theorists who seem unable to theorize resistance to hegemonic systems in terms other than transgression. Judith Butler, for instance, in *Gender Trouble: Feminism and the Subversion of*

Identity (New York: Routledge, 1990), figures resistance only as parody, satire, and transgression, failing to imagine a subversive lifestyle that does not depend on the system it transgresses for its being.

33. Jerome J. McGann, *Social Values and Poetic Acts: A Historical Judgment of Literary Work* (Cambridge, MA: Harvard University Press, 1988) 107.

12

Care of the Self or Care of the Other? Towards a Poststructuralist Ethics of Pedagogy

Margaret Toye

The term 'ethical turn', usually within quotation marks, is often used to describe the increased interest in ethics proclaimed to have been occurring within Anglo-American literary theory and criticism for approximately the last decade. This 'turn' has taken many different forms, ranging from texts by and about poststructuralist ethics, to work on present and past ethical philosophy, from a reusing of older forms of ethical and evaluative criticism to a refashioning of these concepts – indeed, a number of very different discourses fall under this vast umbrella, and it sometimes seems that the question should be raised as to whether any two people writing under this designation are actually referring to the same thing. A mark of the discourse at present includes a difficulty in determining what exactly ethics *is* – as well as a resistance to others' employment of it, and for some, a resistance to the term itself. Often defined negatively – it is *not* morals but connected to morals; it is *not* politics but important to this sphere – 'ethics' is not usually examined in isolation, but always seems to be connected to a large range of issues. These issues include politics, aesthetics, language, the subject, agency, desire, pleasure, truth, eros and freedom. Thus encompassing a great deal, ethics also has what Geoffrey Galt Harpham refers to as a 'tar-baby character' which 'permits it to absorb its enemies'.[1] Harpham writes that: '[t]he attempt to go beyond, beneath, or outside ethics by proposing an alternative ethical theory happens with sufficient regularity to prompt the reflection that these pseudo-disputes recur not *between* ethics and some other perspective or discourse but *within* ethics'.[2] Harpham suggests considering ethics as a 'matrix', 'hub', or 'conceptual base', 'from which the various discourses and disciplines fan out and at which they meet'.[3] One interesting aspect of this unique discourse is the manner in which the ethical tradition is continually mapped out in terms of varying series of binary oppositions. The field is constantly being split into two distinct camps on a range of levels: there is masculine v. feminine ethics, Jewish v. Greek ethics, an ethics of idealism v. an ethics of utilitarianism, and an ethics of goodness v. an ethics of value (see appendix for further examples). This binary model also seems to be an integral defining feature of the field itself: ethics is often presented as pertaining to the ongoing choice between two things: 'good v. bad', 'good *for* v. good *as*', 'either/or', etc. In this essay, I want to concentrate on one binary opposition that seems to me to underlie many of the divisions in the tradition, namely, ethics as a focus on the 'self ' versus ethics as a focus on the 'other'. The importance of this division in the field seems evident once it is stated but no one seems to have traced the importance of this opposition as such in any extensive way.[4] I will briefly situate the self/other opposition historically, examine a few contemporary approaches to ethics, and then open up these issues to the field of pedagogy.[5]

It is difficult to quickly summarize how the self/other opposition works throughout the history of ethics. David Parker, in *Ethics, Theory and the Novel*, provides a possible sketch of the tradition, which he summarizes through three different threads, while Steven Connor indicates that the first two categories actually shade into each other (Kant being the connector between the two). First, there is 'an other-regarding Kantian-moral one that derives ultimately from the Judeo-Christian religious tradition' which emphasizes 'the value of disinterested duty';[6] second is one that comes from the Enlightenment and its privileging of 'disengaged rationality, autonomy, freedom, human equality, and universality'; and third, there is a Romantic–Nietzschean emphasis on 'self-fulfillment and expressive integrity'.[7] Ethics therefore can be viewed as shifting back and forth from an exterior locus in the other to an interior locus in the self, and this shift can in turn be mapped onto the Enlightenment v. Romanticism opposition, which is often represented by the figures Kant and Nietzsche. There is a potential other opposition in Parker's divisions with Judeo-Christianity occupying the pole of the 'other'; however, he does not name a tradition for the opposite pole of the 'self'. Indeed, Parker's divisions suggest that a focus on 'the self' does not come to us until as late as the Romantics, and for that matter, he suggests the category of reason does not arrive until the Enlightenment. Yet, if we turn to Charles Taylor's *Sources of the Self* – the text on which Parker declares that he has based his divisions – we find a much wider range of historical positions, including a focus on both reason and the self in Ancient Greek philosophy. I want to emphasize that when I indicate a self/other opposition within ethical discourses, I recognize that 'self' and 'other' have meant very different things at different times. Taylor points out that the Greek focus on self-mastery is very different from the Augustinian shift to radical interiority, which is different from the Cartesian disengaged subject, which is different from the contemporary subject. As John Rajchman argues, an important aspect of the modern subject is that which comes to us through Freud – a subject which has an unconscious. In fact, the terms 'self' and 'other', while seemingly mutually opposed on either side of a dialectic, sometimes become quite intertwined, and part of my interest is in establishing the relation between them and the status of each within different discourses: there is the other opposed to the self, the other within the self, the other as self, the self as other, absolute alterity and absolute interiority, and symmetricality and asymmetricality between self and other.[8]

I CARE OF THE SELF

In the collection of essays entitled *Ethos: New Essays in Rhetorical and Critical Theory*, the editors James and Tita French Baumlin describe a very different approach to ethics from the contemporary tendency to categorize ethics as an interest in the Other. Their work is based in the rhetorical tradition where the classical term *ethos* is understood to refer to the role that character plays in oral discourse.[9] This conception comes from Lysias's *ethopoiia*, which focuses on the way in which character is conveyed through language, and stresses the important role that a speaker's character can play in the art of persuasion.[10] Ethics becomes a question of how one presents oneself as 'a good person' through language. Just as there are contemporary debates as to the relation of the subject to language, so too can this problem be found within the history of this discourse. Plato operates under the assumption that the speaker-agent and speech-act are inseparable,[11] whereas Socrates emphasizes the disjunctive relation that occurs between a speaker and a 'ghostwritten' text – a speaker '*speaks* the words' but does not 'appear *in* them'.[12] Two distinct positions – the Isocratian and the Aristotelian – arise within this tradition. The former considers that moral health can be measured not only by one's discourse, but by one's way of life, and therefore emphasizes the need of the speaker to *be* good, whereas, in contrast, Aristotle considers rhetoric to be amoral, yet he notes how appearances can play a role in the art of persuasion, and the way in which discourse actively constructs character, and therefore asserts that it is sufficient to *seem* good.[13] Western culture has largely followed the Platonic and Isocratian tradition through Augustine, Aquinas, Descartes and Kant, while the sophists Gorgias and Protagoras, the Renaissance sceptics Machiavelli and Montaigne, Nietzsche and several modern theorists belong to the Aristotelian tradition.[14]

This rhetorical focus on the self, while often elided as part of ethical discourse, brings to the ethical 'matrix' a great deal of contemporary theory which addresses the problem of the subject and its connection with language, its construction v. its essence, and issues of identity politics. While most poststructuralists concentrate on 'the other' as their ethical focus, traces of this emphasis on the self can also be located within the work of a number of theorists. One example is Julia Kristeva's 'The Ethics of Linguistics', where she argues for the importance of putting the subject back into the study of linguistics. She criticizes the discipline's privileging of 'the aura of *systematics*', and 'rules' and for its dissociation of 'the problem of *truth* . . . from any notion of the *speaking subject*'.[15] A new ethics of linguistics, she argues, would follow 'the resurgence of an "I" coming back to rebuild an ephemeral structure in which the constituting struggle of language and society would be spelled out'.[16] Such an ethics would entail a privileging of what she elsewhere calls 'a subject in process', a subject of poetic discourse, of rhythm, heterogeneity, and negativity which thus has otherness at its very core. Gayatri Chakravorty Spivak similarly addresses the problem of the ethical subject of discourse but within a postcolonial and feminist context. In 'Can the Subaltern Speak?' she concludes that '[t]here is no space from which the sexed subaltern subject can speak'.[17] She brings into question the *ethos* of First World, Third World and gendered subjects, and foregrounds the issue of who speaks for whom and from what subject positions.[18] Her self-reflexive performance of her positionality is an element which also continues within this tradition of the ethical focus on the self, as does her interest in a 'non-ideal' ethical theory based on a Marxian subject foregrounding a theory of value rather than of goodness.

But it is Michel Foucault's work on ethics which I want to emphasize: his ethics is distinct because of its extensive theorizing of ethics as a focus on the self.[19] While his method of genealogy and his style itself have been analysed as part of his ethics, it is his later explicitly ethical work, in the *History of Sexuality* series and in interviews, which most often provides material for this topic. Foucault divides 'morality' into three categories: (1) the first category considers morality as a *moral code*. Of interest here are the stated prescriptions and rules of conduct;[20] (2) the second category addresses the *morality of behaviours* – acts rather than prescriptions. The actual behaviour and conduct of individuals can be measured in relation to the stated rules and values;[21] (3) the third category deals with Foucault's main interest: *morality as ethics*. For Foucault, ethics deals with the relation one has to oneself, that is, the way in which one ought to form oneself as an ethical subject, which one does by acting in reference to the prescriptive elements of the code. This third element is broken down into four sub-categories:[22] (a) *the ethical substance*: the way the individual constitutes a part of him/herself as the material of moral conduct[23] (examples of materials include 'flesh' and 'sexuality');[24] (b) the *mode of subjection*: the way the individual establishes his or her relation to the rules and recognizes him or herself as obliged to put the rules into practice'[25] (for example, one acknowledges oneself as member of a group for which it is a rule: 'because I am the king', or 'because I am a rational being');[26] (c) this category has a number of names, including: *the forms of elaboration* or *ethical work*[27] and *the self-forming activity* or *asceticism*,[28] and addresses the ways in which one performs practices on oneself, to bring one's conduct into compliance with a given rule, and to attempt to transform oneself into the ethical subject of one's behaviour (examples of practices include learning and memorization);[29] (d) the last category deals with the *telos* of the ethical subject: the ethical action is not just moral unto itself, but it also aims beyond itself, which commits the subject not just to other actions, but to a certain mode of being characteristic of this ethical subject (for example, the aim toward a state of purity which will give salvation after death).[30] Foucault indicates that his interest lies not in the codes, which he states actually do not change very much through time or place in the West, but instead, in 'the way the individual is summoned to recognize himself as an ethical subject'.[31] He continually repeats his interest not in morals but in ethics: 'not in the code' but 'in what I call the "ethics", which is the relation to oneself'.[32]

The specific phrase '*care* of the self' comes from the third century B.C. concept of *epimeleia heautou*, meaning 'taking care of one's self'.[33] Foucault notes that this focus on the self does not just mean being interested in oneself, or having 'a certain tendency to self-attachment or self-fascination'.[34] Instead, it refers to 'a sort of work, an activity; it implies attention, knowledge, technique', and has to do with 'making one's life into an object for a sort of knowledge, for a *techne* – for an art'.[35] While Foucault emphasizes that he is not trying to discover, in the past, solutions to present problems, he sometimes uses this phrase 'care of the self' when referring to contemporary society and indicates possible affinities between the two societies. He indicates that the Greeks were interested in what was known as 'an aesthetics of existence' focused on the question of 'how to live', and suggests that in response to the contemporary notion that 'the idea of the self is not given to us', we similarly could engage an aesthetics of existence in which 'we have to create ourselves as a work of art'.[36] He also discusses writing as 'an exercise of oneself in the activity of thought'.[37] As John Rajchman argues, Foucault's thoughts on ethics are intimately bound up with those on aesthetics, style, and ethos as a way of being, including his own. When Foucault turned to the subject of ethics, he abandoned his earlier style of writing and had to rethink 'what *his* style in philosophy, was'.[38] Foucault's care of the self offers a critique of ethics located in an external public law, as well as one located in a psychoanalytic emphasis on a subject focused on internalizations and a duty to its inner desire. Instead, he points towards the emergence of a new subject, and therefore of a new ethics, which would be based in new forms of community and co-existence.

II CARE OF THE OTHER

The other focus – on ethics as care of the other – is the more prominent one in poststructuralist work. While this emphasis often occurs in the ethical tradition through the position of 'duty' arrived at through 'reason', in poststructuralism it usually appears as a response to Emmanuel Levinas's reformulation of ethics as care for the Other, rooted in an affective relation – against thought and reason.

Levinas's revolution in ethics – his 'ethics of ethics' or 'metaethics' – places ethics as first philosophy, over ontology and epistemology, in a critique of the philosophical tradition, but especially of Heidegger. His ethical focus is on the Other; that is, the relation one has with the Other, the responsibility one is called to by the 'face' of the Other, and the demand that is placed on the self by this 'face'. Not only does this encounter demand a care for and a responsibility for the Other, but it also recalls the self's responsibility and it puts the ego, the knowing subject, self-consciousness, spontaneity, the Same, into question, calling the self to justify him/herself. In a sense, there is a double focus in this ethics, or rather, since this ethics emphasizes a *relation*, what Levinas describes as the 'apperceiving in discourse [of] a non-allergic relation with alterity',[39] there is an implication as to the importance of both self and other on either side of this relation – a refashioning of self, other, and their relation to each other.

The status of the other is intriguing in Levinas. 'Face' is the term used to describe the way in which the other is presented to the self – the way in which the self and other are able to enter into a relation. It is not visual, it does not take place within thought, but in an immediate relation, in which the Other in this encounter exceeds '*the idea of the other in me*'.[40] This non-identity and non-similarity of the other with the self is an important feature in Levinas's thought. Also, there are various 'others' in his work – there is the Other as a point of exteriority, outside of the economy of the Same; then there is the singular Other, the '*autrui*' – the other human being; and there is also the Other as a deity, which for Levinas is based on a Jewish God.

It is this exteriority, this infinity, this absolute alterity that is unique but problematic in Levinas. As a critique of the economy of the same, the other is 'Other with an alterity that does not limit the same, for in limiting the same the other would not be rigorously other'.[41] The Other does not share a 'common frontier'. As such, he places the Other in the realm of what he calls the 'infinite' rather than of totality – totality being that which pertains to the economy of the same, and the infinite indicating a realm outside – a realm of the 'perfect' containing 'a height and a nobility, a transascendence'.[42] This alterity is absolute. Levinas writes: 'The other metaphysically desired is not "other" like the bread I eat, the land in which I dwell, the landscape I contemplate, like, sometimes, myself for myself, this "I", that "other".... The metaphysical desire tends toward *something else entirely*, toward the *absolutely other*.'[43] Of the other human being, he argues: 'The Other as other is not only an alter ego: the Other is what I myself am not... it can be said that intersubjective space is not symmetrical.'[44] It is on the points of absolute exteriority and the asymmetry between two human beings that many critics find themselves parting company with Levinas, especially the way in which Levinas treats sexual difference and the asymmetry between Man and Woman.

III A COLLAPSING OF BOUNDARIES: THE OTHER AS THE SELF; THE OTHER WITHIN THE SELF

While Derrida, Julia Kristeva and Luce Irigaray have all worked within Levinas's privileging of ethics as the care of the other, they have all offered criticisms of his work as well. Derrida's ethical work also includes his responses to speech-act theory but I shall here only address part of his work on Levinas. Derrida's relationship to Levinas is complex. While he has always engaged deconstructively with Levinas's writing, working within but moving to aporia in the work, Simon Critchley and Robert Bernasconi have suggested that through time, his writing has become closer to Levinas, as both he and Levinas respond to each other in their work. In 1986, Derrida remarks, '[f]aced with a thinking like that of Levinas, I never have an objection. I am ready to subscribe to everything that he says'.[45]

But Drucilla Cornell and Christopher Norris, drawing on Derrida's earlier work, take pains to point out his criticism of Levinas's radical alterity in terms of the asymmetry between the self and Other. Cornell writes:

Derrida explicitly reminds us of the Hegelian lesson that the

> hypostatization of difference – alterity is absolute – reinstates absolute identity. As Hegel tells us again and again, difference from the Other is an internal relation to the other.... The other is an other who can open herself to me precisely because she is an other 'in my economy'. Without this strange symmetry, or the introduction of a positive notion of infinity in which the encounter with the infinite Other is an encounter with God, Levinas's insistence on the *phenomenological* as well as the ethical asymmetry of the Other would degenerate into the worst sort of violence.[46]

She argues that 'ethical asymmetry, if it is to be ethical, now defined as respectful of the otherness of the Other, must be based on phenomenological symmetry'.[47] Without this 'moment of universality' she states, 'the otherness of the Other can be only too easily reduced to mythical projection'.[48] Cornell bases her critique on the work of Simone de Beauvoir, Irigaray and Derrida to criticize Levinas's portrayal of the relationship between Man and Woman as asymmetrical, in which Woman's otherness is not recognized and rather than a relation of mystery, this asymmetrical figure actually leads to a relationship of domination.

Christopher Norris similarly argues that 'one can have no access to the "other" – to modes of knowledge or experience that exist (so it seems) at the furthest remove from our own – except by way of a language that presupposes at least some measure of shared conceptual ground'.[49] He states that 'any ethics of "absolute alterity" – in so far as such an ethics is thinkable at all – has the untoward consequence of transforming the other into a non-subject, an empty locus or passive receptacle for whatever construction the philosopher may place upon it'.[50] He points to the passage in 'Violence and Metaphysics' where Derrida argues for the notion of the 'other' as 'alter ego': 'the alter ego signifies the other as other, irreducible to *my* ego, precisely because it is an ego, because it has the form of an ego. The egoity of the other permits him to say 'ego' as I do; and this is why he is Other, and not a stone, or a being without speech in my *real economy*'.[51]

These criticisms of Levinas are similar to those which Derrida directs towards Foucault's *Madness and Civilization*, where Derrida perceives Foucault attempting to mount a critique of Reason from a space outside – Derrida's point being that one has to criticize from a space within due to the differential nature of signs. But it is interesting that in the case of Levinas, Derrida phrases this critique in terms of an 'alter ego' – an other self: 'the other is absolutely other only if he is an ego, that is, in a certain way, if he is the same as I'.[52] This notion of the Other as a parallel self offers us an interesting figure, which I want to suggest is similar to a kind of doppleganger: the other as an exterior uncanny double.

In contrast, Kristeva, in *Strangers to Ourselves*, offers a model of the Other based on Freud's conception of 'the uncanny', of 'the other *within* the self'. She writes:

> Strangely, the foreigner lives within us: he is the hidden face of our identity, the space that wrecks our abode, the time in which understanding and affinity founder. By recognizing him within ourselves, we are spared detesting him in himself.... The foreigner comes in when the consciousness of my difference arises, and he disappears when we all acknowledge ourselves as foreigners, unamenable to bonds and communities.[53]

For Kristeva, the healing of xenophobia occurs when internal otherness is recognized. She writes: '[b]y recognizing *our* uncanny strangeness we shall neither suffer from it nor enjoy it from the outside. The foreigner is within me, hence we are all foreigners. If I am a foreigner, there are no foreigners.'[54] Kristeva here performs an interesting move by collapsing the difference between exteriority and interiority – she seems to suggest that both alterities share the same status – but she ends up privileging the inner, in the sense that she suggests that consciousness of the inner can cause the exterior other to disappear such that the name 'foreigner' could in this situation become obsolete.

In a connected manner, Slavoj Žižek calls for the recognition of the collapse of a kind of Althusserian 'big O' 'Other' of power through the realization that fear of the Other is based on fear of something within ourselves, i.e. pleasure. He writes: '[w]e always impute to the "other" an excessive enjoyment: he wants to steal our enjoyment (by ruining our way of life) and/or he has access to some secret, perverse enjoyment'.[55] Thus he claims *'[t]he hatred of the Other is the hatred of our own excess of enjoyment'*.[56] Both Kristeva and Žižek seem to argue for the recognition of a similar structure and offer a personal solution to cultural problems – a healing of social ills towards the external Other by a recognition, perhaps a 'caring for the Other', within.

However, I worry about the collapse of such distinctions. *Is* the status of the Other *within* the same as the status of the Other *without*? Is there no difference between interiority and exteriority? If there is not a psychological or phenomenological difference, is there not at least an important material difference between them? For that matter, what about the differences among the Other as a deity, the Other as external to the economy of the Same, and the Other as a human being? Almost all (except Levinas and Irigaray) ignore the Other as deity; most seem to focus on the Other as human being, and some deal with the philosophical problems of positing an absolute alterity in a philosophical mode. It is this last point which is intriguing to me – the possibility of positing a realm external to thought, to the economy of the Same, while avoiding both the violence and the reinstatement of absolute identity which Cornell indicates would occur in this move to a 'beyond'. While this move is problematic, it seems necessary for perspectives such as feminism and postcolonialism – in order to move past economies rooted in patriarchy and colonialism, there has to be the creation of an elsewhere. The only option open seems to be the strategy that many theorists have employed of positing another realm which is not absolutely exterior, but connected to the economy of the Same, of the Symbolic, etc., but which is not contained by it – because it is another *economy* it does not become identical to this one, yet it offers the possibility of an 'elsewhere'. Possible 'elsewheres' include: Kant's 'sublime', Georges Bataille's 'general economy', Roman Jakobson's 'poetic language', Žižek's and Judith Butler's 'foreclosure', Showalter's 'wild zone', Teresa de Lauretis's 'space-off', Hélène Cixous's 'écriture féminine', Irigaray's 'mimicry', and Kristeva's 'semiotic'.

IV PEDAGOGY

In the pedagogical situation in the literary academy, one is constantly making choices in the teaching of literature: between the claims of the texts and those of the students; among one's own ethics, and those of a variety of others. There are various interpretive positions to negotiate, and many issues of value, including those within canonical debates. But more specific to this essay is the issue of how the ethics of self v. the ethics of the other relates to this field.

The self/other binary underlies many pedagogical models, including those of poststructuralism – the pedagogical relation is most often figured as taking place between two people: between a teacher, who is often also figured as master, and a student (for example, as in both the Socratic and the psychoanalytic models), or even in other binary relations which can be subsumed under pedagogy, for instance, between a text and a reader or a text and a writer. There is some interesting work being done in an attempt to collapse this self/other opposition. Shoshana Felman and others use the Lacanian psychoanalytic model of transference as a pedagogical paradigm. Lacan's ethics of psychoanalysis encourages the analysand to recognize its misrecognition – of the authority it places on the other (the analyst), and instead, to locate the Other within themselves, in their unconscious rather than externally in the other person. This suggestion is of course similar to Kristeva's and Žižek's social models, as discussed previously. Within critical pedagogy, in the work of Paulo Freire, Henry Giroux, Peter McLaren and others, there are also attempts to de-privilege the teacher's authority, and thus the strict binary between teacher and student, the one who knows versus the one who learns, but in this case through the notion of 'empowerment'. Starting with the lived experience of students, the teacher tries to 'empower' students to become politically active and critical of the power relations in which they find themselves. However, as many feminist critics have recently pointed out, some of these formulations actually threaten to reinstate that which they criticize. Carmen Luke, Jennifer Gore and others question the subject position and the kind of power relations critical pedagogy implies, and their arguments indicate that it is potentially male teachers and male students which these theories privilege. It is the teacher who bestows a power conceived of as 'property',[57] and who decides what kinds of activities count as 'political'. In this light, the Lacanian model could be similarly criticized – the focus on the Other within ignores the power the analyst wields and the potentially unethical relations which fall outside of this theory's stated goal.

But rather than merely focusing on ways in which this self/other binary can be deconstructed or reconstructed, I would argue that there is a problem with the constant repetition of this underlying figure within pedagogical theory. It shares with communications models the problem of always representing communication as occurring in a private intercourse between two people, whereas pedagogy almost always involves more levels than just this one. Instead, pedagogical models should be conceived as rooted in a complex matrix of relations, which include relations between and among teachers, students, teaching assistants, texts, administrators, staff, departments, and other institutions. To ignore whole levels neglects important parts of this phenomenon and therefore relevant ethical issues could be disregarded. This matrix model, especially when it reaches the institutional level, becomes very connected to political issues on all levels. Perhaps this is a function of the underlying figures in 'ethics' and 'politics' – ethics often figured as occurring between two, and politics the realm of the social – of the more than two. (As a brief example, there is Simon Critchley's analysis of Levinas, where ethics is understood as a relation between a self and an Other, and politics is 'conceived of as a relation to the third party'.)[58] I raise the question: can ethics be conceived beyond this model of two without necessarily becoming politics?

Most work on poststructuralist pedagogy has taken place from the position of *one* perspective – most often the psychoanalytic, derived from Lacan (Felman, Jane Gallop, Gregory Jay, and others) and the post-Marxist (Pierre Bourdieu and Jean-Claude Passeron and many others who focus their analysis on the institution of literary studies), but there is also some important writing on this topic from within deconstruction (Gregory Ulmer), as well as Foucauldian work (Jennifer Gore). However, in my own work, I believe it is important to use a variety of perspectives, and to allow them to call one another into question, to address various levels of the matrix.

I will therefore conclude by suggesting how this analysis of an ethics of self and an ethics of the other can relate to the field of pedagogy. The issues which I raise here, and which for now I shall leave at the level of the question, touch on various levels of the matrix, because of their grounding in a variety of perspectives. A focus on the student as an ethical other can include questions as to the status of the other – 'does one treat the student as an alter ego?', 'how are one's relations to students mediated by this other within the self?', 'what kinds of projections and transferences are involved in the teaching situation?', and 'is there an ethical relation with each student, or are they an anonymous mass onto which one projects one's own desires?' We can ask not just what kinds of characters or people we believe we are trying to produce in the students, but what kinds of 'characters' or 'roles' do teachers perform? What kinds of identities do we inhabit or project, or as Gallop would say, 'impersonate'? What is the role of the intellectual and what are the relations between and among our duties within and outside of the academy? Further, what kinds of practices of the self and disciplinary mechanisms do we ourselves engage in and encourage in the classroom? What pedagogical telos are we operating towards? Especially now, at a time when it seems the humanities are at a point of crisis, do we tell ourselves that we are trying to create 'better citizens', 'inheritors of a cultural tradition', 'critics of the status quo'? What reasons do we give for these practices: 'because I was taught this way'? 'nothing else works'? 'it's for their own good'? What are our pedagogical transcendental signifiers: 'excellence'? 'back to the basics'? 'critical thinking'? What kinds of self-stylizations are we forced to engage in – requirements of dress, the presentation of ourselves as professionals? In the realm of textual studies, what is the status of the other in the texts we teach? Is it an absolute other? Or an alter ego? Are characters in texts the only possible focus on the 'other', or do we engage language itself as an 'othering' effect? What kinds of symbolic violence do we perform in the teaching situation? Is it possible to escape merely repeating the ethic of the dominant power which Bourdieu indicates is perpetuated through pedagogic action? Does our pedagogic model privilege a repetition of the Same, emanating from the mouth of a subject-who-knows? Do we allow ourselves to be confronted with otherness? Do we acknowledge a realm about which we do not know? What is the relation between our content and form of teaching? What ethics and theories do we propose and which do we enact? What is it to be a good teacher? A good student? What is an ethical pedagogy?

Appendix

Selected binary oppositions into which the field is often divided:

Ethical traditions: moral/ethic; ancient/modern; Epicurean/Stoic; Jewish/Greek; Jewish/Christian; masculine/feminine; conservative/radical; normative/descriptive; imperative/declarative; absolutist/relativistic; substantive/analytical; idealist/utilitarian.

Ethics as: good/bad; good/evil; good *for*/good *as*; ought/is; either/or.

Ethics which stress: ideals/practices; reason/emotion; universal principles/communal consensus; Enlightenment/Romanticism; abstract problems/practical problems; theory/pragmatism; reason/leap of faith; code/ascesis (subjectivizations); motives/actions; natural/theological virtues; law/sympathy; space/time; solids/fluids; law/love; strong/weak; consciousness/unconscious; superego/law of desire; justice/care; goodness/value; use value/exchange value; exchange value/surplus value; reflection/action; narrative/poetry; grammar/poetic language; symbolic/semiotic; law of the father/body of the mother.

Notes

1. Geoffrey Galt Harpham, *Getting It Right: Language, Literature, and Ethics* (University of Chicago Press, 1992) 17.
2. Ibid., 17.
3. Ibid., 17.
4. Not only does the question have to be explored as to why binary oppositions are such a fundamental part of ethical discourse – why they have not been deconstructed in the way they have been in other discourses – but also in terms of the best ways to engage in their deconstruction. While the essay does not allow for an in-depth examination of these issues, it will become evident that the use of this self/other binary is productive for tracing different lines of inquiry within poststructuralist ethics, but that it ultimately begins to deconstruct itself, and in the end, the opposition is only useful strategically, and by no means is it a static opposition.
5. This essay is an initial inquiry into what I will examine in more detail in my doctoral thesis on contemporary ethics and pedagogy. This essay is a work-in-progress, which brings together the ideas of a number of theorists, examines differences among them, suggests various directions, and poses questions for further analysis.
6. Steven Connor, 'Honour Bound?' Review of *Cultural Pluralism and Moral Knowledge*, ed. Ellen Frankel Paul, Fred D. Miller and Jeffrey Paul; *Cultural Studies and Cultural Value*, by John Frow; *Honor*, by Frank Henderson Stewart; *Ethics, Theory and the Novel*, by David Parker; and 'Narrative and Freedom', by Gary Saul Morson, *Times Literary Supplement* (5 January, 1996) 24–6 (25).
7. Steven Connor, 'Honour Bound?', 25.
8. The ways in which terms like 'self', 'subject', 'individual', 'human', and 'ego', are differentiated or collapsed together at different times and places, and sometimes even within the work of the same theorist, need to be examined in further detail in an extended analysis.

9. James S. Baumlin and Tita French Baumlin, 'Introduction: Positioning *Ethos* in Historical and Contemporary Theory', in *Ethos: New Essays in Rhetorical and Critical Theory*, ed. James S. Baumlin and Tita French Baumlin (Dallas: Southern Methodist University Press, 1994) xi–xxxi (xxiii).
10. Ibid., xii.
11. Ibid., xiii.
12. Ibid., xii.
13. Ibid., xv.
14. Ibid., xviii.
15. Julia Kristeva, 'The Ethics of Linguistics', in *Desire in Language: A Semiotic Approach to Literature and Art*, ed. Leon S. Roudiez, trans. Thomas Gora, Alice Jardine, and Leon S. Roudiez (New York: Columbia University Press, 1977) 23–35 (24).
16. Ibid., 34.
17. Gayatri Chakravorty Spivak, 'Can the Subaltern Speak?', in *Marxism and the Interpretation of Culture*, ed. Cory Nelson and Lawrence Grossberg (Urbana: University of Illinois Press, 1989) 271–313 (307).
18. Robert Con Davis and Davis S. Gross, 'Gayatri Chakravorty Spivak and the *Ethos* of the Subaltern', in *Ethos*, ed. Baumlin and Baumlin, 65–89 (74).
19. Yet I do not want to simplify Foucault's work: it is possible to read him as very interested in the category of the Other. Throughout his corpus he is interested in the Other as a 'limit-experience;' for instance, in the figures of 'the madman', 'the prisoner', 'the homosexual', and especially in terms of the Other of thought.
20. Michel Foucault, *The Use of Pleasure* (1984), trans. Robert Hurley, *The History of Sexuality* 2 (New York: Vintage-Random, 1990) 25.
21. Ibid., 25.
22. Ibid., 26.
23. Ibid., 26.
24. Michel Foucault, 'On the Genealogy of Ethics: An Overview of Work in Progress' (1983), in *The Foucault Reader*, ed. Paul Rabinow (New York: Pantheon Books, 1984) 340–72 (353).
25. Ibid., 27.
26. Ibid., 354.
27. Foucault, *Use*, 27.
28. Foucault, 'Overview', 355.
29. Foucault, *Use*, 27.
30. Ibid., 27–8.
31. Ibid., 32.
32. Foucault, 'Overview', 355.
33. Ibid., 359.
34. Ibid., 359.
35. Ibid., 360, 362.
36. Ibid., 351.
37. Foucault, *Use*, 9.
38. John Rajchman, *Michel Foucault: The Freedom of Philosophy* (New York: Columbia University Press, 1985) 3. Foucault's writing on the

aesthetics of existence and of thought has been traced to Nietzsche, in its emphasis on style and privileging of contingency, but many also trace this model to that of the Baudelarian Parisian dandy.

39. Emmanuel Levinas, *Totality and Infinity: An Essay on Exteriority*, trans. Alphonso Lingis (Pittsburgh: Duquesne University Press, 1969) 47.
40. Ibid., 50.
41. Ibid., 39.
42. Ibid., 41.
43. Ibid., 33.
44. Emmanuel Levinas, 'Time and the Other' (1946–7), trans. Richard A. Cohen, in *The Levinas Reader*, ed. Séan Hand (Oxford: Blackwell, 1989) 38–58 (48).
45. Quoted in Simon Critchley, *The Ethics of Deconstruction: Derrida and Levinas* (Oxford: Blackwell, 1992) 9.
46. Drucilla Cornell, *The Philosophy of the Limit* (New York: Routledge, 1992) 54.
47. Ibid., 55.
48. Ibid., 55.
49. Christopher Norris, *Truth and the Ethics of Criticism* (Manchester University Press, 1994) 44.
50. Ibid., 50.
51. Ibid., 125.
52. Jacques Derrida, 'Violence and Metaphysics' (1964), in *Writing and Difference*, trans. Alan Bass (University of Chicago Press, 1978) 79–153 (125–7).
53. Julia Kristeva, *Strangers to Ourselves*, trans. Leon S. Roudiez (New York: Columbia University Press, 1991) 1.
54. Ibid., 192.
55. Slavoj Žižek, *Tarrying with the Negative: Kant, Hegel, and the Critique of Ideology* (Durham, NC: Duke University Press, 1993) 203.
56. Ibid., 206.
57. Jennifer Gore, 'What We Can Do for You! What *Can* "We" Do for "You"? Struggling over Empowerment in Critical and Feminist Pedagogy', in *Feminisms and Critical Pedagogy*, ed. Carmen Luke and Jennifer Gore (New York: Routledge, 1994) 54–73 (57).
58. Critchley, *The Ethics of Deconstruction: Derrida and Levinas*, 220.

13

The Ethics of the Voice

Steven Connor

In the recent upsurge of interest in ethics among literary and cultural theorists, questions of justice, responsibility and freedom have frequently been framed in terms of the use and abuse, the powers, pleasures, limits and liabilities of the voice. Much of this work is governed by a powerfully assumed, and sometimes theoretically uninspected, negative injunction against the privation of the voice, whether through appropriation or silencing. In the beginning of her study of the borrowing or assumption of female voices by male writers, Elizabeth D. Harvey for example suggests that this literary ventriloquism 'is an appropriation of the feminine voice, and that it reflects and contributes to a larger cultural silencing of women'.[1] Such a judgement is apt to initiate epistemological worries about whether it is possible for a man to know enough about what it is like to be a woman to be able to speak convincingly in a female voice. But the real issue, Harvey insists, 'is not epistemological at all, but ethical and political. It is not whether male poets *can* adequately represent the female voice, but the ethics and politics of doing so.'[2] The ethics and politics of the voice are often presented in terms of a struggle for possession and preservation. Claire Kahane, for example, suggests that the psychoanalytic constitution of hysteria has the struggle for voice both as its theme, and as its mode of operation. Such a struggle occurs not only in the etiology of hysteria prior to the analysis, but also through the analysis itself: 'Ultimately,' Kahane declares, 'Freud's narrative unveiled the voice itself as the passionate object of the hysteric and of psychoanalysis. Who has the voice? Who does what with it? To whom does it belong?'[3] Janet Beizer goes even further than Kahane. In her account, the hysteric must struggle, not only against the loss of the capacity to speak in her own voice, but against the repressive desublimation represented by the idealizing category of hysteria itself, which, in seemingly letting the hysterical body speak for itself, in fact forces a voice on to it.[4]

This privative conception of voice, as something exposed to the ever-present danger of theft, trespass or violation, pervades the politics of voice in feminism, cultural studies, ethnography and postcolonial writing. In this conception, for my voice to issue from another means that my voice can no longer be in my possession. If, by contrast, another forces his voice upon me then it is again impossible for me to speak with my own voice, because the voice of the other must wholly supplant my own. Running through both conceptions, that of the usurpation and of the imposition of voice, is a magical economics, which conceives the quality of the voice, and the exercise or process of voicing as the circulation or manipulation of a vocal substance, which is singular, finite and divisible. The wrong done to the voice is a privative wrong, a wrong done to a right of ownership, and self-ownership; to the right and entitlement to speak with one's own voice.

Curiously, such a concern with the violation of the voice has cohabited with a highly developed suspicion of the claim that the integrity of the self is guaranteed and expressed by the voice. Modern suspicions of the coalition of self and voice precipitate a ventriloquial predicament, and a curriculum of questions such as the following: If I am my voice, why do I yet not fully possess it? If I do not own my own speech, if something or somebody else speaks in my speech, how am I to own myself in it? On the other hand, how am I to speak for another without reducing that other to a theme or vehicle for my own utterance? How may one cede one's speech to another? And how is everyone to speak, in turn, or at once?

We may indeed be struck by the co-operation of the epistemological loosening of the bond between the self and the voice and the tightening of the force of the injunctions against appropriation or abuse of the voice. Such injunctions seem an idealized compensation for what is lost with the suspicion that I do not speak *viva voce* and *in propria persona*.

This essay will offer two forms of explanation for the emergence of what I will call the proprietary thematics of the voice; first of all, a psychoanalytic explanation of the voice in terms of its status as an imaginary object, and, secondly, an accelerated historical sketch of the coming into being of a proprietary conception of voice. This will allow me to broach the possibility of an ethics of the voice which would escape from its proprietary thematics. What, I will ask, if the ethical responsibility to the voice were to become a matter not so much of the duty to assign vocal rights and entitlements, as of a responsibility to its movement, in and as time, in and as the unattributable event of voice? Could this constitute an ethics of the voice, in terms other than the assignment and distribution of voices? I will say that I doubt it; but that it nevertheless might constitute *something* which could perplex those proprietary ethics, and exert upon them the oblique force of an *ethicity* of its own.

THE IDEAL OBJECT

The voice begins, not as property, but as power. The exercise of the voice, and the fantasy that it induces of 'sonorous omnipotence' is 'the body's greatest power of emanation', writes Guy Rosolato.[5] At a point when it is scarcely able to move hand or foot, when it can control neither itself nor its physical environment, the human infant is possessed of a voice which seems to be magically effective across inconceivable distances, bringing nourishment, warmth and company on demand. The voice's capacity to act at a distance, to influence a world outside and beyond itself, comes about, not only as a result of its emanative power, but also from the fact that, unlike seeing, feeling, smelling and tasting, the exercise of the voice results in the production of something separate from the body. This separability of the voice can be a source of intense pleasure, for the voice is thereby available to be moulded and manipulated as a kind of object, for example in songs, chants and cadences. When the voice fails in its purpose of gaining food or attention, it can provide a sort of interim gratification, a hallucination of oral satisfaction.

But the separation of the voice from the body can also take on a puzzling or threatening character. The power of the voice to act on the world derives from its power to become part of that world – which then leads to the possibility that the voice can become alienated from its human source and recoil upon it in persecutory fashion. The strength of the infant's voice is a strength that may return upon it as a horror and a violence, that there is no need to identify prematurely with the castrating voice of the father. The phallic power of the voice, its power to go out beyond the self, is what makes it the very image of castration, of a part-object which has departed from the body and become deposited in the world, thus threatening further partition. Derrida has written of the structure of the *s'entendre parler*, that hearing-oneself-speak which guarantees the phonocentric identification between self and voice. But the experience of the *s'entendre parler* is really best instanced in the familiar modern experience of revulsion and disavowal at the hearing of one's own recorded voice, that mocking, misbegotten twin of the intimate whisper of self-communion.

Human beings have not needed to wait until the advent of recording technologies to experience this alienation, although such technologies have served to dramatize and familiarize the experience. This alienation may in fact originate in the moment in which the infant hears its own cry, and, terrified at its ferocity, is shocked into crying the more. If the baby is terrified by its own crying, it is also pleasurably aroused by and cocooned within the 'toxic envelope' it provides.[6] (Experiments have shown the intensely disorientating effect of depriving a baby of the reassurance provided by this feedback.) The experience of the voice as echo is primary and defining.

The fantasy of the voice as object, capable of an echoic persistence in the world, is answered by an awareness of the fact that the voice is always in passage, and always passing into silence. In its persecutory aspect, the voice seems stubbornly resistant to dissolution. Considered as the object of desire and pleasure, however, it is tenuous and impermanent. This twin apprehension of the menace and impermanence of the voice is enough to initiate a drama of possession and control, centred on the having, holding and even hoarding of the voice as a vocal object. It will not be long before the child learns that even the withholding of the voice can be a gift to be bestowed or a power to be wielded. The fantasy of the voice as a vocal object is so powerful as a sign because it signifies the unencompassability of the voice *as* sign.

This infantile conception of the voice as a quantum, which participates in an economy of less and more, of conservation and loss, is nowhere more clearly and emphatically formulated than in Christian theology, and in particular in the intense reflections on the nature of the *logos* in patristic writings of the second and third centuries. What exercised the early Church Fathers more than any other theological issue was the question of the *homoousia* or cosubstantiality between Father and Son. The Son emanates from the Father as the *logos*, or spoken Word. It is speech which signifies the simultaneous separateness of the Son from the Father, and their continuing participation in each other's nature. The second-century Syrian writer Tatian reproduces from his teacher Justin an early and influential solution to the problem of maintaining this difficult balance, in the metaphor of the voice as a regenerative flame, which makes possible division without diminution or abscission:

> By his mere will the Word sprang forth and did not come in vain, but became the 'firstborn work' of the Father. Him we know as the beginning of the universe. He came into being by partition, not by section, for what is severed is separated from its origin, but what has been partitioned takes on a distinctive function and does not diminish the source from which it has been taken. Just as many fires can be kindled from one torch, but the light of the first torch is not diminished because of the kindling of the many, so also the Word coming forth from the power of the Father does not deprive the begetter of the power of rational speech. I speak and you hear: yet surely when I address you I am not myself deprived of speech through transmission of speech, but by projecting my voice my purpose is to set in order the disorderly matter in you. Just as the Word begotten in the beginning in turn begot our creation by fabricating matter for himself, so I too, in imitation of the Word, having been begotten again and obtained understanding of the truth, am bringing to order the confusion in kindred matter.[7]

The word-voice here is a birth in which otherness has no part: an autistic birth, which can go out without leaving, come from and yet remain with itself. The metaphor of flame creates the voice as an ideal object, with all the powers of emanation and 'sonorous omnipotence' evoked by Rosolato, but without the jeopardy of diminishment represented by the splitting of the voice into autonomous existence, or degradation into the condition of 'disorderly matter'. But the early Fathers are haunted by another, more profane kind of voicing. The parturitive metaphor, which is both borrowed and refused in the idea of a parthenogenetic Word, receives a profanely literal embodiment in the fantasy of ventriloquial utterance; the utterance of the Pythia and the ventriloquial women whose spirit of prophecy, according to Origen and St John Chrysostomos, proceeds from the demon which has taken up residence inside them, and takes the form of a voice that issues from the genitals or anus.[8] This is the voice not as fire or light, but as what we have just heard Tatian refer to as 'disorderly matter'; the cacophony or shit-voice, which is also, in hysterical approximation, the vagitus itself, the terrifying cry of birth that is at once the voice as the rending of a presence from the maternal genitals, and the voice of the genitals as a rending. It is this inarticulate, rent voice, that draws the speaking body into complex, material exchanges and borrowings, and against which the immaterial voicing of the Word is intended to struggle.

This distinction between sacred and profane voice is by no means confined to Christian theology. A similar pattern has been reported in the complex spiritual systems of the West African Dogon people. For the Dogon, the production of voice is bound up in a complex way with the materiality of the person and generative operations of the body: speech is bred in the belly, brewed in the viscera and woven by the larynx.[9] Dogon creation myths focus on the struggle between the twin-spirits Renard and Nommo: where Renard steals the gift of speech from his creator and employs it for the purposes of evil and death, his good and creative twin Nommo breeds life by the warm vapour of his speech.[10] In Dogon mythology, as in patristic theology, the contrast between the living word of Nommo and the dead word of Renard is mapped on to the body. But where Western conceptions centre on a distinction between the oral and the visceral, the divine voice of God and the belly-speech of the demoniac, the operative distinction for the Dogon is between the oral and the nasal. Nasal inflection signifies to the Dogon a form of rotten or putrescent voice. This is explained by Geneviève Calame-Griaule:

> It is called 'putrescent' because it gives the impression that some portion of the sound remains trapped between the nose and the throat without being able to escape; living matter (of which the voice is an example) which gathers without being able to get out into the air, is, according to Dogon conception, bound to putrefy. And everything associated with putrefaction, its most disagreeable manifestation being nauseating smell, is charged with extremely negative meaning for the Dogon, and evokes death irresistibly.[11]

The idea of the corrupt voice here shares a logic with Christian construals of the profane voice delivered by the Pythia or priestess at Delphi. The Pythia derives her name from the fact that her oracle is situated at the spot where Apollo slew a chthonic dragon or python, leaving its body to putrefy in the sun: 'python', and therefore 'Pythia' come from Greek *puthein* meaning to rot or decay. (In Dogon mythology, however, the living voice is female and positively associated with the genitals, where in Christian mythology the genitals are the source of putrefied or demonic speech.) Such religious conceptions of the two kinds of voicing, the divine or living Word that goes forth without division into its progeny and power, and the voice that degenerates into profane and persecutory part-object, mesh with the psychoanalytic ambivalence that I have just outlined. In both cases, there is the attempt to maintain a distinction between the voice as an ideal object, as an emanation from the self which nevertheless retains its qualities of sensitivity and life, and the voice as an excremental, parasitic-persecutory discharge. In the long, slow formation of modern conceptions of the self, the fundamentally autistic theology of the early Christian church, for whom the metaphor of voice was crucial in dramatizing the concept of a going forth that never comes apart, is transferred to an idealism of the self in relation to its voice.

PROPRIETARY VOICE

During the course of the seventeenth and eighteenth centuries in Europe, the operations of the voice became powerfully politicized. The agency of this change is the formation of an ethics of property, which put into place a concept of self related to itself in terms of ownership and possession, and worked to fix and assign the discourse of the self (for example in the coming into being of the idea of authorship), and to textualize voice. The politics of voice is inseparable from this phonographic hunger. The ethical injunction against the reduction of others to the condition of objects suggests the injunction against the theft or misuse of the attributes of the other, and especially of their voice. But it is only as a result of having been thus construed as a possessable and therefore alienable kind of object, that the voice can appear vulnerable to such illegitimate appropriation.

Central to this process is the metaphor of ventriloquism, now newly conceived, not as the voice of the other erupting through the self, as in demonic views of ventriloquism, but as the voice of the self 'thrown' into the other. During the eighteenth century, the use of ventriloquism is conceived as a threat to the state and the socius rather than as a disquieting of the soul or of spiritual authority. The remarkable disquisition of 1772 on the subject of ventriloquism by the Abbé Jean-Baptiste de la Chapelle insists throughout on its dangers: 'In a country in which this artifice was absolutely unknown, and in which credulity had already begun the work of superstition, a sagacious man, an audacious *Ventriloquist*, would be able infallibly to make himself master of all souls, and by this means to be assured of the success of all his ventures.'[12] Charles Brockden Brown, who knew of and perhaps even read la Chapelle's work, carries forward this paranoia into his account of the dangerous, and desocializing powers possessed by Carwin the biloquist in *Wieland*.[13]

During the nineteenth century, the voice comes to be seen less and less as a power acting in, on and through the body, and more and more in terms of what the comfy-sinister law-clerk Wemmick will describe as 'portable property' in Dickens's *Great Expectations*. The voice becomes simultaneously the sign of a person's self-belonging, as that which cleaves most closely to and emanates most unfalsifiably from the self, and, in its detachability from the person, the sign of the self's new mediation through objects. The very notion of the voice as that which is most proper to you comes into being, it appears, in tangled complicity with the idea of the voice as a property, or piece of property. You own yourself (acknowledge, utter yourself) through your *own* voice, which is to say the voice that you own. What theology had fantasized about the word in the second and third centuries, technology began to literalize during the eighteenth, nineteenth and twentieth centuries. The phonographic impulse longs for the reality of a word that can go out without being lost, can be separated from the self without leaving it. The detachable voice is for the first time embodied, rather than merely dreamed of or dissimulated, in technological means, in the talking automata that became popular at the end of the eighteenth century. The actual technologization of the voice was accompanied by its cultural technologization, through a widespread concern with its physiology and attempts to regulate and enhance its workings.

Modern technologies of the voice at once intensify the separability of the voice from the person of which it is supposed to be the indissoluble evidence and provide the physical means to substantiate the phantasmic and metaphorical conception of the voice as a kind of property. A clear parallel seems to suggest itself with the reparative operations of philosophical theories of the voice: the acknowledgement of the separability of the voice from the person consequent upon Derrida's assault upon the phonocentric prejudices of the West both leads to and seems to require the ethical sealing of the compact between the voice and the person, the reassertion of the voice as the self's ideal object or emanation. The law provides a striking parallel. As Jane Gaines has shown, the cultural perception of sound as insubstantial and therefore 'propertyless' has for a long time led to a reluctance to allow the voice to function as a trademark or sign of personhood in the way that images do or to extend to it the protection of the law in the case of misappropriation. During this century, however, a combination of the dematerialization of the idea of property itself and the technological developments that have made possible the fixing of the voice as a material attribute 'have produced the voice as something susceptible to proprietal claims'.[14] The very technological disembodiment of the voice, which loosens its links with the person, makes it possible and necessary for the law to remedy the wrong of misappropriation by restoring the voice to the person.

NUDE VOICE

If legal remedies of the kind described by Jane Gaines offer forms of restitution, then another kind of principle has begun to obtain, in certain philosophical invocations of the ethical destitution of the voice, or of the I in its voice. For Emmanuel Levinas, for example, this destitution or emptying of the self in its vocativity provides an image and enactment of a primordial sociality, prior to all conceptual formulations and mediations. The nudity of the voice, or of the act of primary *saying* accomplished with and through it, is equivalent to the nudity of the face in its ethical encounter with and proximity to the other. In contrast to the oral utopia implied by the work of Walter Ong, Levinas's references to the voice do not promise participation in a community, the intimacy of shared or imparted meanings and values. Discourse promises no coalition of speaking subjects, but rather the revelatory calamity of the subject:

> The relationship of language implies transcendence, radical separation, the strangeness of the interlocutors, the revelation of

> the other to me. In other words, language is spoken where community between the terms of the relationship is wanting, where the common plane is wanting or yet to be constituted. It takes place in this transcendence. Discourse is thus the experience of something absolutely foreign, a *pure* 'knowledge' or 'experience,' a *traumatism of astonishment*.[15]

Levinas insists on the identity between hearing the divine word and being in relation to social Others, and therefore on the fundamental ungraspability of the divine and the human Other:

> To hear the divine word does not amount to knowing an object; it is to be in relation with a substance overflowing its own idea in me.... When simply known, thematized, the substance no longer is 'according to itself.' Discourse, in which it is at the same time foreign and present, suspends participation and, beyond object-cognition, institutes the pure experience of the social relation, where a being does not draw its existence from its contact with the other.[16]

In his explication of the ethics of address in Levinas's work, Jean-François Lyotard emphasizes the stripped condition not of speaking, but of hearing: 'Such is the universe of the ethical phrase: an I stripped of the illusion of being the addressor of phrases, grabbed hold of upon the addressee instance, incomprehensibly.'[17]

More recently, Jean-Louis Chrétien has drawn out from the nudity or exposure of the voice an argument for the primordial relations of promising and being promised as between the self and others:

> The origin of every beginning, the call opening in every call, the voice is nevertheless not primary. Every human voice is a response: every inauguration is on sufferance to and impassioned by an anterior voice, which it hears only in replying to it, which precedes and exceeds it. It speaks only in listening, listens only in replying, and continues to speak only because there is no full and complete reply, no reply possible which would not be, in the most intimate recesses of itself, faulted and belated in relation to what it alone makes audible. The solitary voice utters the proper, but there is no voice that is not irremediably broken by what gives it speech. The nudity of the voice, exposing us body

> and soul to the other, without return, marks the impossibility, immemorially and forever, of transparency, adequation, plenitude, perfection, being.[18]

So, for Levinas and Chrétien, the apparent nudity and destitution of the voice always involve the complexity of an exposure and response to the other. The naked voice is exposed to the impossibility of its nakedness.

This might therefore be to say that the nakedness of this voice is always clothed with a certain figurality. The voice evoked by Levinas and Chrétien is not a phenomenal but a phenomenological voice, that is already recognizable as and implicated in relations of address and rejoinder. It signifies at every moment the inescapability of a *Mitsein*, or being-for-others; signifies itself as the occasion of such a *Mitsein*.

This would be to suggest the metaphoricity of all voice. Against this, Henri Meschonnic has suggested that the force of the voice may lie in its refusal of metaphor. If the speech of the hysteric 'demetaphorises' speech by putting language into the body, then orality can be seen as a counter-hysteria which demetaphorizes language by putting the body into it.[19] The metaphor of the voice seems frequently to be driven by this refusal of metaphor. For the voice is not coincident with speech: rather, it is the body passing into speech. Other invocations of the voice have promised a more exacting recession from the formal to the phenomenal, from the phonemic system of spoken language to the living, unfolding, audible actuality of the production of speech. The title of a recent collection of essays investigating the cultural meanings and powers of the female voice – *Embodied Voices* – emphasizes this promise. The introduction to this collection by its editors, Leslie C. Dunn and Nancy A. Jones, draws a contrast between the pervasive uses of the word 'voice' in feminist writing as 'a metaphor for textual authority' and the 'concrete physical dimensions of the female voice upon which this metaphor was based', promising for its part a return to this 'literal audible voice'.[20]

Such a return brings both subtraction and enrichment. First of all, it subtracts metaphor from the voice; removes from the voice the concept of voice, along with all the values and figural meanings which have accrued to this concept. The voice as a purely sonorous phenomenon must always inhabit the present continuous, must always *be occurring*, at a particular place and time. It arrests and fascinates precisely because it unfolds in and is eroded by the passage of time. This voice then signifies an exposure and elementarity so austere as to furnish no signification whatsoever, not even of its own state. But this subtraction itself yields enrichment and refreshment for the ear accustomed to hearing only conformable voices. In his book *Voice*, David Appelbaum proposes a radical distinction between the civilizing, anthropomorphic power of rational speech, and the primordial, inhuman powers of prephonemic voice, the voice that manifests itself in coughing, laughing and babbling. 'To speak', he concludes, 'is ... to effect the decline of voice.'[21] The ethics of the voice provided by Appelbaum depend upon the evocation of a condition of diverse and generative spontaneity which exists before the articulative, retentive, civilizing powers of speech:

> History is necessarily progressive, a passage from the diversity of voice to the unity of spoken language, persons keeping company together, and the commonwealth. But history points back to a time prior to origin. In prehistory, need rather than desire gave people voice. And need is always diverse, different, dispersing.... In the reborn childhood of humanity, the rebel's childhood, the sounds which voice makes, so fear-provoking to the established regime, are babblings.[22]

In his emphasis on the elementary and inhuman condition of the voice, its resistance to acts of conceptual synthesis and understanding, Jean-François Lyotard's more recent work seems similarly to want to hear an ethical call in the pure phenomenality of sound, a vocality in sonority. In *The Inhuman*, the ethical call of the voice is heard in the course of an essay upon the impoverishment and disarticulation of musical sound, via a reading of a passage of Swedenborg which evokes the relations between listening, obedience and obligation:

> *Auf jemanden hören*, to listen to someone, to lend one's ear to someone, *das ist gehorsam zu sein*, is to be of obedience.... To obey is to *gehorchen*. *Gehören* is not far, to pertain to, to depend on an agency, to fall into a domain, under an authority, a *dominus*. And *zuhören*, to lend one's ear. There is an inexhaustible network linking listening to belonging, to the sense of obligation, a passivity I should like to translate as *passibility* ...

> This obedience is that of spirit to spirit, it is a convocation by another voice, it belongs to what Swedenborg calls 'the correspondence between spirits', to a spiritual message-network; ...man knows nothing, and wants to know nothing of this dependence of the ear on the spirit, of this taking hostage of hearing by the beyond of the body.[23]

Appelbaum, with his interest in organic vocation without voice, and Lyotard, with his emphasis upon the disaccommodation of the I involved in the relation of hearing, both strive to hear a purely phenomenal act of uttering, prior to its formulation as voice, its ascription to a source. Where the voice is always-already speech for Levinas and Chrétien, for Appelbaum and Lyotard, it is always-already *not yet speech*. Does this evocation of the pure and elementary movement of the voice nevertheless point to a way back, or at least aside, from a proprietary ethics of the voice?

In order to answer this question, it is necessary to specify another aspect of the traditional association between the voice and ethical questions of responsibility and obligation. The matter is put at its plainest in the discussion of sound and hearing in Book II of Aristotle's *De Anima*. The difference between sound and voice, writes Aristotle, is a difference between unsouled and ensouled entities: 'Voice is a particular sound made by something with a soul; for nothing which does not have a soul, has a voice.' Having distinguished by means of voice between the ensouled and the unsouled, Aristotle goes on to make a further distinction between the different uses of the voice: 'Not every sound made by an animal is voice (for it is possible to make a sound also with the tongue or as in coughing); but that which does the striking must have a soul and there must be a certain imagination (for voice is a particular sound which has meaning, and not one merely of the inbreathed air, as a cough is).'[24] Thus the concept of voice, and its derivatives – enunciation, discourse, utterance – mark the limits of the ethical. The voice is divided between its articulatory and non-articulatory functions. The ethics of the voice – its association with values, obligations and judgements – are concentrated around the articulate voice. That which has no voice, or which utters inarticulately, has no place in or positive bearing upon ethics. Rather, questions of judgement, goodness and value are borne in upon these inarticulate functions of the voice – in the sense of being deployed against them.

Where, for Aristotle, the voice seems to hold in place the distinction between the animate and the inanimate in general, for us, the voice is much more tightly restricted: possession of the voice, in fact, signifies not the realm of soul or of the animate, but the realm specifically of the human soul. This is made clear by our reluctance in English to use the word 'voice', or correlative terms such as 'utterance', of any other kind of expressive or communicative actions than those performed by human beings. We find it difficult to speak naturally, as Shakespeare apparently still could, of the 'voice of lions' (*Troilus and Cressida*, III, ii, 95).

This restriction of the voice to articulate humans brings about a dramatic narrowing of the scope of ethical community and responsibility. In this economy, relations of ethical obligation are relations only to beings actually or potentially possessed of voices. And what does it mean to be possessed or potentially possessed of a voice? It means primarily to have your sounds heard as a voice, or accorded the respect due to a voice. To give voice, or be capable of giving voice, it is necessary to have been given voice. To count as an ethical partner, one must be a potential interlocutor.

There is no question of a descent below metaphor in this disposition of the voice. The genitivity of the voice, the fact that it is always heard as the voice *of* some ensouled entity or other, is a supplementation of its pure phenomenality. To hear the voice as voice, even in the cough, the sigh, the snigger, or in babble, is to posit it as an expression, or utterance, the intentional passage of meaning from an inside to an outside. It is to take the voice as the outward and visible sign of something hidden. In this sense, there could be said to be no purely phenomenal, no merely corporeal voice. The voice, *qua* voice, is *always* a symbolic sign and property.

Does this make the ethical recourse to the allegedly prehuman or inhuman phenomenality of the voice a simple sentimentality or error? Not necessarily. For the phenomenality of the voice also opens awareness of the uncertainty of its assignment, of the gap between the self and its properties that is revealed by the very necessity of assignment. The voice can only be the sign of the self because it has already come apart from it, and thus may always be able to act as the sign of the self apart from itself. The very history of the coming into being of the idea of the voice as property, in the co-operating senses of characterizing attribute and of owned object, also reveals alternative ways of conceiving the provenance of the voice. This history reveals the persistent problem and astonishment of the dissociated voice, or the voice that does not coincide with itself. It reveals not only the fantasy of sonorous omnipotence, but also the precipitations of voice into the condition of disorderly matter. In such a condition, the possession of voice is not inevitably or permanently restricted to human agents.

During the late classical and early Christian eras, the slow passage of voice into the possession of speaking human subjects was achieved by a move from a demonological to a dramaturgical dispensation, in other words from the experience of voices speaking in and through the self, to the requirement that the self speak as and for itself alone. Our contemporary condition might be said to be that of a resumed demonology. The demoniality developed by the early Church Fathers, especially Tertullian, Origen and Augustine, was a form of exorcistic knowledge. However swarmingly multitudinous they might be, the demons could always be known and shown, made to confess their names and occupations. In contemporary demonology, however, the demon cannot be named and located. We inhabit a condition in which we are visited, traversed and even possessed by voices, desires, agencies which are neither our own, nor can be assigned a name and substantial identity in the world. Pierre Klossowski has explained that the most important feature of a demon is its non-being. The demon borrows us for its purposes, the purpose of affirming non-being against being, but can only do so because our bodies, our words, our artefacts, provide it with a form. Demons are thus dependent upon simulacra. The demon exists in its coming into appearance; it is neither the appearance itself, nor a presence prior to that appearance.[25] A consequence of the breakdown of the old certainties about the distinctions between the human and the inhuman is to release the possibility of hearing voices as other, and the otherness of the voice.

For Levinas the experience of the ethical proximity of the other in the exposure of their vocativity is deeply unsettling. But it is also, as John Llewelyn has argued, held steady by the givenness of the category of the human, to which the ethical is entirely confined.[26] The conception of a renewed demoniality makes it possible to imagine susceptibility and responsiveness to other kinds of voice, emanating from other kinds of source. What cannot speak – cannot be admitted to the parliament of human utterance – can still give and be received as voice.

In previous periods, unattributed voices were attributed to

divine or demonic sources. In our period, in which the experience of the voice separated from its point of origin has become ever more familiar, we may experience the multiplicity of voices as the posing of a question regarding the nature of the source: is this a voice, or a mere sound? Is it ensouled or unsouled? Does it proceed from the kind of entity we call a subject, or Aristotle called a soul? Perhaps this must always fall short of a new ethics of the voice. The voice on the threshold between what belongs to a human subject and what does not belong to, and may not even concern it (and the history of the voice discloses that it always inhabits that threshold) asks a kind of pre-ethical question: is this a matter of voice? meaning – is there to be an ethical relation?

If our polyphonic epoch, of powers and presencings and prosopopoeias, provides no guarantee of our inhabitation of the human, it provides no guaranteed access either to the panvocal inhuman evoked by Don Ihde: 'Yet all sounds are in a broad sense "voices," the voices of things, of others, of the gods, and of myself.... A phenomenology of sound and voice moves... toward full significance, toward a listening to the *voiced* character of the sounds of the World.'[27] The voice, which is to say the question of the voice (who is speaking? is there a voice?) is not the form of, but the provocation to ethical decision. It compels, not obedience, but inquisition. It does not put us back in the midst of the world, but rather into the midst of our questioning of it, and its enquiry of us. Into the midst of the middle voice.

Notes

1. Elizabeth Harvey, *Ventriloquized Voices: Feminist Theory and English Renaissance Texts* (London: Routledge, 1992) 12.
2. Ibid., 12.
3. Claire Kahane, *Passions of the Voice: Hysteria, Narrative, and the Figure of the Speaking Woman, 1850–1915* (Baltimore: Johns Hopkins University Press, 1995) 32–3.
4. Janet Beizer, *Ventriloquized Bodies: Narratives of Hysteria in Nineteenth-Century France* (Ithaca: Cornell University Press, 1994).
5. Guy Rosolato, 'La Voix: entre corps et langage', *Revue française de psychanalyse*, 38 (1974) 76–8.
6. I take this phrase from the work of Didier Anzieu, who argues that the development of the ego depends upon the creation of a number of imaginary containing envelopes. Though generally of a defining

or supportive nature, these envelopes may also become painful or suffocating: see *The Skin Ego*, trans. Chris Turner (New Haven: Yale University Press, 1989) 98–108.

7. Tatian, *'Oratio ad Graecos' and Fragments*, ed. and trans. Molly Whittaker (Oxford: Clarendon Press, 1982) 11.
8. Origen, *Contra Celsum*, trans. Henry Chadwick (Cambridge University Press, 1953) 396–7; *The Homilies of St John Chrysostom, Archbishop of Constantinople on the First Epistle of St Paul the Apostle to the Corinthians*, no translator named, in *A Library of the Fathers of the Holy Catholic Church* (Oxford: John Henry Parker; London: J. G. F. and R. Rivington, 1839) IV, 398–9.
9. Geneviève Calame-Griaule, 'La nasalité et la mort', in *Pour une anthropologie des voix*, ed. Nicole Revel and Diana Rey-Hulmann (Paris: L'Harmattan/Langues d'O, 1993) 23–33.
10. Marcel Griaule, *Conversations with Ogotemmêli: An Introduction to Dogon Religious Ideas* (Oxford University Press, 1965) 18.
11. Calame-Griaule, 'La nasalité et la mort', 25.
12. Abbé Jean-Baptiste de la Chapelle, *Le Ventriloque, ou l'engastrimythe* (London: Chez de l'Etanville; Paris: Chez la Veuve Duchesne, 1772) 339–40.
13. Charles Brockden Brown, *Wieland* and *The Memoirs of Carwin the Biloquist*, ed. Jay Fliegelmann (Harmondsworth: Penguin, 1991).
14. Jane M. Gaines, *Contested Culture: The Image, the Voice, and the Law* (London: British Film Institute, 1992) 119.
15. Emmanuel Levinas, *Totality and Infinity: An Essay on Exteriority*, trans. Alphonso Lingis (Dordrecht: Kluwer, 1991) 73.
16. Ibid., 77–8.
17. Jean-François Lyotard, *The Differend: Phrases in Dispute*, trans. Georges van den Abbeele (Manchester University Press, 1984) 111.
18. Jean-Louis Chrétien, *La Voix nue: phénoménologie de la promesse* (Paris: Editions de Minuit, 1990) 7.
19. Henri Meschonnic, 'L'oralité, poétique de la voix', in *Pour une anthropologie des voix*, ed. Revel and Rey-Hulmann, 83–107, esp. 104.
20. *Embodied Voices: Representing Female Vocality in Western Culture*, ed. Leslie C. Dunn and Nancy A. Jones (Cambridge University Press, 1994) 1.
21. David Appelbaum, *Voice* (Albany: State University of New York Press, 1990) 60.
22. Ibid., 65, 69.
23. Jean-François Lyotard, *The Inhuman: Reflections on Time*, trans. Geoffrey Bennington and Rachel Bowlby (Cambridge: Polity Press, 1991) 178.
24. Aristotle, *De Anima*, Books II and III, trans. D. W. Hamlyn (Oxford: Clarendon Press, 1993) 32, 33.
25. Pierre Klossowski, 'Gide, du Bois et le démon', *Un si funeste désir* (Paris: Gallimard, 1963) 40.
26. John Llewelyn, *The Middle Voice of Ecological Conscience: A Chiasmic Reading of Responsibility in the Neighbourhood of Levinas, Heidegger and Others* (Basingstoke: Macmillan, 1991).

27. Don Ihde, *Listening and Voice: A Phenomenology of Sound* (Athens, OH: Ohio University Press, 1976) 149.

Part V
Bosnia and the Gulag: Literature as Witness

14

Testimony as Art: Varlam Shalamov's 'Condensed Milk'

Leona Toker

In a 1973 discussion of the artistic accomplishments of Solzhenitsyn's Gulag fiction, Victor Erlich echoed Irving Howe's remark on the impossibility of registering a 'purely' literary response to material that presents 'the belated revelation of a long-denied nightmare'.[1] At issue was 'respect for the autonomy of literary criteria' and a recognition that it was impossible to separate the literary analysis of ethically-oriented fiction from its moral–philosophical consideration. Though Erlich concludes that it would be wrong to inhibit one's literary response and to underestimate the heroic writer's actual effectiveness 'out of an excessive distrust of our own motives',[2] the examination of one's motives is as relevant as the examination of the structural and stylistic 'effectiveness' of the works discussed. Studies of the literature of atrocities must involve ethical self-reflexivity, though not necessarily explicit breast-beating. This is particularly true in the case of the literary critical examination of documentary prose – memoirs, autobiographies, and related genres.

The story that I shall discuss here can be *used* as historical evidence and as testimony for the history of ideas. Yet it can also be read for its own sake, that is for the sake of its artistic achievement.[3] The tools used for the analysis of this achievement must, however, take into account the multifunctionality of concentration-camp literature, in particular its ethical orientation.

The theory of works of art as multifunction objects has been developed by Jan Mukařovský (of the Prague Linguistic circle); one of its central points is that the different functions, such as the communicative and the aesthetic, become marked at different stages of reception.[4] While the Gulag still existed and consciousness-raising testimonies about it sought to enlist public opinion in the struggle against forced-labour camps, a sustained literary analysis of such testimonies would, indeed, have appeared callous. Now the situation has changed: the Gulag is no longer news, and the whole complex of issues it raised is now the concern of scholars rather than journalists. After the communicative contents of the memoirs of a particular atrocity have been studied by historians, economists, and sociologists, their artistic merit can become the subject of a literary scholar's uninhibited discourse.

The features that underlie the aesthetic and the consciousness-raising functions of Gulag testimonies are closely interrelated: one cannot do full justice to the communicative significance of documentary prose works without proper attention to their formal traits – nor can one account for the relative artistic merit of these works without taking into account their ethical stance. It has by now become recognized that the form of a literary work has an ethical aspect,[5] as well as that the content of ethically oriented writings may be intrinsically 'implicated in their literary structure'.[6] The ethics of literary form is to a large extent a matter of the textual features (such as focalization, ironies, collocations and temporal deployment of motifs, intertextual links, etc.) that create the conditions for a certain kind of reader response; and such ætiology of reader response is the province of intradisciplinary literary–critical analysis to be performed against an interdisciplinary data background.

The specific features of reader response to survivor memoirs are associated with the specific bi-functionality of documentary prose. One usually turns to such memoirs in quest of facts, of knowledge in 'gift-wrapping',[7] knowledge as 'amenity',[8] even if this knowledge is of the kind that generally we would rather do without. If we are then struck by the literary merit of these texts, we still hesitate whether to regard them as art or just as well-written testimony. This hesitation is, to some extent, a variant of the 'suspicion of fraudulence'[9] that is an integral aesthetic effect of modernist art: is the artist pulling our leg? is this, anyway, art at all? Yet in the case of the literature of atrocities, the terms of such hesitation also involve an anxiety of the kind that stimulated Adorno's provocative remark that it may be 'barbarous' to write poetry after Auschwitz:[10] perhaps aesthetic experience – or any positive reference to it – is inadmissible in the case of accounts of terrible human suffering. However this may be, an initial downplaying of the aesthetic function of such works under the weight of the communicative function is a necessary part of reader response.

Reading works of documentary prose as transparent vehicles for factual evidence amounts to treating them as interchangeable means to an end. The end may be a sociological or historical study, such as, for instance, *Forced Labor in Soviet Russia* by Dallin and Nicolayevsky, or the invaluable books by Robert Conquest. I would not cast aspersions on such a *use* of primary materials. On the contrary, the need for the *use* of survivor memoirs as primary materials has never been as evident as in the days when many KGB archival materials have become available: historians who critique the factual reliability of the limited and subjective first-hand reports and wax enthusiastic over archival statistics are prone to lapse into positions that are almost indecently naive. Another end for which survivor memoirs can be legitimately *used* is exemplified by Terence Des Pres's *The Survivor* (1976), devoted to the structure of survival in the camps in those limited cases when the possibility of survival depended on the prisoner's own strategies and powers of endurance and was not blankly cancelled by external circumstances. A more recent example of such a use of memoirs is Todorov's *Facing the Extreme*, which examines concentration camp testimonies in an attempt to draw ethical conclusions, refine distinctions, evaluate responses, and qualify sweeping statements on guilt and suffering. Both these books were obviously written in response to the authors' urgent ethical need, the need to understand the world in which genocide and concentration camps (Nazi and Soviet) were possible. Both the authors are self-conscious – Des Pres about the para-religious language of his discourse, Todorov about the intuitive character of his distinctions as well as about memories of his young days under a totalitarian regime. Though both Des Pres and, especially, Todorov are literary scholars, the two books belong not to the field of literary study but to that of the history of ideas.

Towards the very end of *Facing the Extreme*, Todorov does, however, offer us three sections of ethically oriented literary criticism – he discusses Primo Levi's heritage, Claude Lanzmann's film *Shoah*, and Gitta Sereni's *Into That Darkness*. He repeatedly emphasizes that these are not merely documentary works but also works of art. The same statement could, in fact, have been made about a number of other materials to which Todorov turns for testimony, prominently including the work of Varlam Shalamov, author of *KOLYMA TALES*.[11] In fact, my case about the bi-functionality of documentary prose is to some extent weakened by my choice of example. It would have been a greater challenge to discuss the bifunctionality of works written by people who were not such conscious artists as this Russian writer. Yet I focus on a story by Shalamov because his artistic achievement has not yet received the recognition it deserves.

Shalamov survived almost two decades of the Gulag. On his release, he explored his camp experience mainly in the genre of the short story. Some of his stories are emphatically autobiographical; others are quite obviously fictional; still others occupy a borderline area between the two. Powerful documentary prose often contains areas of hesitation between what can and what cannot be subject to the procedures of public verification. There is no way of knowing whether Shalamov's 'Condensed Milk'[12] is strictly factual, autobiographical, or whether it presents a fictionalized individual version of what was a typical war-time situation in Soviet hard-labour camps. As a result, the reader has to treat its material as historical testimony but also ask of it the kind of questions that are usually asked of representational art. This two-fold attitude of the reader reflects the double function of the story as a document and as a literary text.

In 'Condensed Milk' a stool pigeon, a geologist by the name of Shestakov, who holds a soft job in a camp office instead of working in the gold mines like most prisoners, organizes a group escape attempt and then leads the fugitives into a prearranged ambush: some of the fugitives are killed, the others are captured and given new prison sentences. The first-person protagonist, who first pretends to accept but ultimately declines the offer to take part in the escape attempt, eventually meets Shestakov in another camp: the agent-provocateur has given state evidence and remained unharmed.

The presence of what are obviously American lend-lease tins of meat and fruit preserves in the camp store (which the protagonist has neither the means nor the permission to use) – sets the story in the early forties, when the Soviet Union was at war with Nazi Germany. At the time, police and camp-guard officers were liable to be sent to the front lines; therefore, in order to prove that they were badly needed in their safe soft berths in the rear, some of them arranged frame-ups that led to new charges against camp inmates and newly extended sentences. As a piece of *historical testimony*, the story presents the mechanics of one provocation of this kind.

As a piece of testimony for the history of ideas, the story may be read as an illustration of Shalamov's blanket condemnation of the quality of moral life in the camps. Unlike Solzhenitsyn who believes that whatever does not kill you can, in principle, ennoble you, Shalamov rejects the redemptive view of suffering; in tune with the Aristotelian belief that a person's character deteriorates as a result of adversity, Shalamov repeatedly states that camp experience generally changed people for the worse.[13] Left at large, Shestakov might have remained an inoffensive geologist rather than a provocateur; and the protagonist might have remained an active and caring intellectual rather than the half-extinguished soul incapable of selfless exertion.

Yet Shalamov makes sure that it should be impossible for the reader to remain content with reducing the story to these types of exemplification. The ironies of his narrative qualify categorical positions and call into question the sweeping diagnoses of what is 'good' or 'bad'. One of the most salient of the techniques that pull the interpretive ground from under our feet is his characteristic ambivalent punchline. Shalamov usually began composing his stories with the first and the last sentences.[14] In 'Condensed Milk' both these sentences emphasize the inner moral predicament of the protagonist rather than the villainy of the outer circumstance. It is the protagonist, more even than Shestakov, who is put on the spot.

The protagonist (or rather what Genette would call the 'focus' in contradistinction to the story's more reflective narrative 'voice'),[15] a rank-and-file political prisoner, is the narrator's former self – for brevity I shall refer to him as 'Shalamov'. The fact that in the text he is not referred to by name leaves it unclear whether the story is representative or directly autobiographical. The first sentence indicates 'Shalamov's' physical and mental condition: 'Envy, like all our feelings, had been dulled and weakened by hunger.'[16] This is what Primo Levi referred to as 'the prescribed hunger',[17] the chronic calorie deficit that was an integral part of the camp authorities' *deliberate* policies: according to the specific reasoning of the Gulag, if a hungry man's rations are further cut for his failure to meet the production quotas, food becomes an incentive for making greater efforts at the work site – thus the Communist state contravened the Marxist analysis of slave labour as economically inefficient because of lack of incentive.[18] Moreover, according to the insights shared also by the Nazis, chronic starvation produces exactly the kind of personality changes described in the story – all emotions are dulled, intellectual activity impeded, and the prisoner's ability to stand up to the authorities is practically cancelled. In *Facing the Extreme*, Todorov refuses to deal with the moral condition of people who have already crossed a certain threshold of suffering.[19] Shalamov leads us beyond that threshold. The experience of people who have reached an advanced stage of dystrophy is different from anything familiar to healthy organisms; hence it can hardly be explained in a discursive manner. It is only the total artistic effect of the text, not the discursive comments and explanations, that can convey, at least in part, the quality of the moral predicament involved. The physical symptoms of this condition are the scurvy sores on 'Shalamov's' legs: his body has already shed all its fats, and has started burning its protein. The brain has been affected as well. In the course of the story, trying to persuade the narrator to flee, Shestakov spouts the famous slogan of the Spanish communist leader Dolores Ibaruri:

> 'Better to die on your feet than live on your knees.' Shestakov pronounced that sentence with an air of pomp. 'Who said that?'
>
> It was a familiar sentence. I tried, but lacked the strength to remember who had said those words and when. All that smacked of books was forgotten. No one believed in books.[20]

The protagonist's failure to place the quotation known to every Soviet schoolchild is a symptom that his brain has already disembarrassed itself of what is not vitally necessary for everyday functioning, namely general memory. Yet the brain is still tenacious of the logistics of survival: the irreversible stage of pellagric dementia is not far behind but has not yet set in. Thinking is a physical effort but not yet an impossible one: 'It was hard to think. For the first time I could visualize the material nature of our psyche in all its palpability. It was painful to think, but necessary.'[21] 'Shalamov' understands not only that the escape attempt is a provocation but also that some benefit may be reaped from it: he intimates that he will join in if Shestakov first gets him some food to help muster his strength. They settle on condensed milk.[22]

At night 'Shalamov' dreams of the treat, for once raising his eyes, as it were, beyond the grim line of the mining-site horizon:

> I fell asleep and in my ragged hungry dreams I saw Shestakov's can of condensed milk, a monstrous can with a sky-blue label. Enormous and blue as the night sky, the can had a thousand holes punched in it, and the milk seeped out and flowed in a stream as broad as the Milky Way. My hands easily reached the sky and I drank the thick, sweet, starry milk.[23]

Almost in tune with Bruno Bettelheim's theory that camp inmates tend to regress to infantility, 'Shalamov' is for a moment almost an infant of the universe, feeding on stellar milk, scooping it with his hands, like snow. Contrary to the traditional associations of night and blackness, the night sky is blue – probably because the action is set in the polar summer with its white nights. Infantility is associated with innocence, and stars with dreams, fate, and lofty aims, yet all such connotations are placed in an ironic perspective by the grotesque ('monstrous') blow-up of the blue-labelled can.

In the evening of the following day, having returned from work, 'Shalamov' eats his two cans of condensed milk. Like his fellow prisoners, we watch him do so. We watch sympathetically, though he does not share the treat with anyone.

One must note here that the portions of text that are mainly accountable for the pleasure we derive from Gulag prose, whether disinterested aesthetic or vicarious pleasure, are usually those dealing not with suffering but with times of reprieve. It would be interesting to ascertain the proportion of the amount of text that these works devote to downright evil, agony, and despair as opposed to recuperation, vitality, attempts to endow *endurance* with meaning, attempts also, in Nietzsche's terms, to turn 'nauseous thoughts about the horror and absurdity of existence into notions with which one can live: ... the *sublime* as the artistic taming of the horrible, and the *comic* as the artistic discharge of nausea of absurdity'.[24] Unlike Holocaust testimonies, Gulag testimonies are rather densely punctuated with accounts of reprieves, as well as with comic plunges and with moments of the sublime. One of the most prominent features of this body of literature is its 'pulsation' method: memoirists do not dwell on hardships uninterruptedly.[25] The literature of atrocities runs the risk of inuring its readers and blunting their emotional response, thus making them re-enact the very callousness its authors attack. To counter the risk of defeating their own purposes, some writers arrange their accounts of atrocities in an escalating sequence, yet the escalation usually ends by producing a cumulatively blunting effect.[26] Most Gulag authors avoid escalation; in their narratives the accounts of suffering alternate with those of reprieves or with informative or analytic passages that act as a foil to the new shocks to come.

Writers have practically no resources for an adequate presentation of the interminable hours of hard, monotonous, and humiliating slave labour. It is therefore practically impossible to imagine what it was like for a starving and sore organism to have to fell trees or load carts for over 12 hours a day, often in the rain, frost, or amid vicious gnats. Literature is more effective with shorter intensities. Thus, in an attempt to convey the sense of hard work at Buna, Primo Levi chooses the day when he has to carry heavy beams which make his whole body ache and which, when thrown off the shoulder, produce the 'ephemeral and negative ecstasy of the cessation of pain'.[27] Very little human communication can take place during hard work; which is one more reason why in Gulag literature much textual space is allotted to lucky respites, smoking- or meal-breaks, days off, and after hours. The action of 'Condensed Milk' takes place entirely in after hours, and at its centre is an all-too-condensed reprieve: 'Shalamov's' staving off the oncoming hunger dementia with the help of a maximally prolonged yet still shortlived treat.

Having finished the milk, 'Shalamov' turns the tables on Shestakov:

> 'You know,' I said, carefully licking the spoon, 'I changed my mind. Go without me.'
> Shestakov comprehended immediately and left without saying a word to me.[28]

'Shalamov' must then face the ethical significance of his conduct:

> It was, of course, a weak, worthless act of vengeance just like all my feelings. But what else could I do? Warn the others? I didn't know them. But they needed a warning. Shestakov managed to convince five people. They made their escape the next week; two were killed at Black Springs and the other three stood trial a month later. Shestakov's case was considered separately ['for legal considerations'].[29] He was taken away, and I met him again at a different mine six months later. He wasn't given any extra sentence for the escape attempt; the authorities played

> the game honestly with him even though they could have acted quite differently.

Then comes the punchline:

> He was working in the prospecting group, was shaved and well fed, and his checkered socks were in one piece. He didn't say hallo to me, (though why not? Two cans of condensed milk are not, after all, such a big deal . . .).[30]

Though the bulk of the story has been working up to the near-orgasmic pleasure of eating condensed milk, the punchline reminds us, among other things, that two cans of condensed milk, blown out of proportion in 'Shalamov's' dream, are, after all, not 'such a big deal'. In a sense, the story is here 'untold', just as the benefit of the extra calories will soon be burnt up. The ironic deflation of the protagonist's minor victory in the struggle for survival places his concerns into perspective. Shalamov frequently pits his own authorial comments against the action of his stories – as if both to express his opinions and to refrain from imposing them upon the reader: his stories test both the attitudes that the reader brings to the text and the ideas that he himself is at times impelled to formulate.[31] The material and structure of the stories amend his authorial diagnoses of the human condition in the camps.

To return to reader response. On being told that after the event Shestakov would not greet 'Shalamov', the reader may think for a moment that Shestakov wishes to avoid the witness of his shameful act. Yet the punchline, 'two cans of milk are, after all, not such a big deal', suggests that Shestakov may be free from shame or remorse; he may just be holding a grudge against 'Shalamov' for double-crossing him. All feelings of guilt and all the need for self-justification that come into play are exclusively 'Shalamov's'.[32] He has led on Shestakov and obtained some food on false pretence; whereas, as the penultimate paragraph tells us with a kind of melancholy sarcasm, the authorities have played fair in this case – they could have used Shestakov and then shot him to cover their tracks.[33]

The ultimate ironic belittling of the two cans of condensed milk reflects 'Shalamov's' residual hankering for a *prima-facie* morality. He has, after all, broken a contract, thus making the will of the other serve the will of his own body. One may counter this by saying that Shestakov was about to use fraud to make 'Shalamov's' will serve his own. In Schopenhauer's ethical system,[34] 'Shalamov's' breaking the contract would be considered legitimate self-defence; yet in Kant's system his breaking of an implicit promise would be *prima-facie* immoral.

Obviously, however, the central *prima-facie* issue lies elsewhere. The real cause of 'Shalamov's' remorse is his failure to prevent Shestakov's deception of five other people – though, all things considered, in his dystrophic condition he had no strength to seek them out. Gilbert Harman notes that, according to contemporary moral conventions, failing to help someone is less bad than deliberately hurting someone.[35] Yet such a convention is hardly acceptable to a person who had been educated in the spirit of supererogation cherished by generations of Russian intelligentsia. One may call to mind how in Dostoevsky's *Crime and Punishment* the conscientious doctor Zosimov, who never fails to come to the sick Raskolnikov and treat him *gratis*, is, from Razumikhin's point of view, a comfort-loving swine – perhaps because he would not give up his last shirt to a friend, only the last but one. The very fact that under the conditions of chronic starvation in the camp extra food is not shared with others suggests that the moral universe in question is radically different from the one created by a century of humanistic education, especially in its Russian version. Sharing a spoonful of condensed milk would require as superhuman an effort as summoning the residue of a goner's energy to seek out and warn the prospective victims of provocation.

The fact that on meeting Shestakov in the epilogue of the story, 'Shalamov' is not averse to greeting him presents a challenge to the reader's semiotic activity. We can infer that he does not expect this stool-pigeon to try to destroy him for having, though tacitly, blown his cover. Shalamov would probably have agreed with Solzhenitsyn that the line separating good and evil runs through each human soul:[36] most of his stories raise the question of the precise location of this line. Shestakov is taking good care of himself: this is made clear by his still possessing his checkered socks and not being reduced to wearing the common camp footrags. After the Black Springs adventure, his socks are still in one piece. The reference to the socks is a realistic part of camp semiotics, but it may also be a submerged allusion to *Crime and Punishment*: when Razumikhin finds Raskolnikov feverish and broke, he brings him a whole second-hand outfit – with the exception of socks. Socks, he says, he could not get. Which means that, up to his change into prison garb, Raskolnikov will be wearing a sock soaked in the murdered old woman's blood: he will be literally treading on blood. In his bid for self-preservation, Shestakov similarly walks over corpses, in checkered socks. Yet Shalamov feels that there is a line that even Shestakov is not prepared to cross: he will not deliberately seek to destroy another person on his own initiative. In ethical theory this is called the principle of the 'double effect': it is bad enough to hurt someone while seeking other goals; but it is still worse to actually aim to injure the other.[37] Thus the acts of both Shestakov, the instrument of the victimizers, and 'Shalamov', the victim, are describable in terms of bad and worse, or bad and less bad. The two have drawn the lines across their souls at different distances from the poles of total saintliness and total evil. And though the dialectical principle of the leap from quantity to quality is here quite obviously effective, the story questions the easy division of people into *us* and *them*.

Some further light on Shalamov's willingness to acknowledge Shestakov despite the latter's treason can be thrown by the diametrically opposite circumstances described in the story 'The Chess Set of Doctor Kuzmenko'.[38] 'Shalamov' and Dr Kuzmenko, formerly a camp surgeon, are about to play chess using a uniquely elaborate set fashioned out of the prison-ration bread that has been chewed and brought to a mouldable condition by the prisoners' saliva. This chess set, whose figures represent historical personages from the Times of Trouble, the period of political turmoil following the death of czar Boris Godunov, was made by the sculptor Kulagin. Two pieces are missing: the black Queen, now lying headless in Dr Kuzmenko's drawer, and the white rook. Driven to the irreversibly lethal stage of dystrophy and dementia, Kulagin started eating his chessmen. It was too late – he should have started earlier; he died after having swallowed the rook and bitten off the head of the Queen. At this point the surgeon makes the following remark:

> 'I did not give the order to get the rook out of his stomach. It could have been done during the autopsy. Also the head of the Queen.... Therefore this game, this match, is two figures short. Your turn, maestro.'
>
> 'No,' I said. 'I somehow don't feel like it any more.'[39]

Why? Obviously not because of tactile squeamishness at the

thought of the clay from which the chessmen have been made. 'Shalamov's' nausea here is, I believe, caused by the sudden realization that there is a moral gulf between him and the intellectual with whom he has just been engaged in a highly meaningful conversation about historical documentation, unsolved mysteries, and prisoners' fates, the person whose attitudes had seemed to be so close to his own. As Bernard Williams notes in *Ethics and the Limits of Philosophy*, one may sense that a person is morally alien to oneself if that person is able to so much as consider certain things as *options*.[40] Surgeons and pathologists are known to be hardened, and, after all, Dr Kuzmenko did not commit the sacrilege of having the missing chess pieces extracted from the corpse, but the way he speaks about it suggests that he must have *considered the option* of doing so. Which makes it impossible for 'Shalamov' to play chess with him, at least not with this particular set. Here the discovery of the qualitative difference in the moral make-up of the two men on the same side of the barricade starkly contrasts with the reluctant discovery of the quantitative nature of the difference between 'Shalamov' and Shestakov, a defector to the other side. Ethics and psychology are usually at odds with each other, but they converge in the complex attitudes conveyed by the endings of 'The Chess Set of Dr. Kuzmenko' and 'Condensed Milk'.

In an article on Paul de Man, Geoffrey Hartman wrote that 'it is impossible to see either fascism or anti-Semitism as belonging simply to the history of ideas: they belong to the history of murder'.[41] The same may be said of Soviet totalitarianism and the Gulag as its notable achievement. The important word in Hartman's remark is 'simply': the atrocities belong both to the history of ideas and to the history of murder. But they are, in addition, associated with a third kind of history, namely the history of individual – or representative – attitudes. The main communicative function of documentary prose is to provide evidence for the history of crime. Its aesthetic function involves 'staging'[42] human experience in such a way as to set a testing ground for the *ideas* that led to the crimes, or failed to prevent them, or were enlisted in the drawing of lessons. At the same time it involves staging human experience in a way that leads to processing and shaping *attitudes* to the material – attitudes of the author as well as of the reader. Attitudes are units of spiritual life that blend psychological drives and moral–ideological commitments. They are about the only aspect of life in concentration camps that can be understood and re-enacted by those who have not shared the experience. They precede the formation of ideas, exceed ideas in complexity, and lag behind them in their degree of crystallization. They are therefore more amenable to adjustment, to perfectibility; they are more fluid, and more liable to fall between the conceptual frameworks of philosophical disciplines.[43] Processing and transforming our own attitudes is what makes reading literature, including the best works of documentary prose, an *ethical* as well as an aesthetic experience, *ethical* in the narrower, evaluative meaning of the word.

Notes

1. Victor Erlich, 'The Writer as Witness: The Achievement of Aleksandr Solzhenitsyn', in *Aleksandr Solzhenitsyn: Critical Essays and Documentary Materials*, ed. John B. Dunlop, Richard Haugh and Alexis Klimoff (New York: Collier Macmillan, 1973) 19.
2. Ibid., 16–17.
3. Schopenhauer wryly remarked that Kant's practical imperative – to treat people not as means only but as ends in themselves – is 'very suitable for those who like to have a formula that relieves them from all further thinking': indeed, it does not provide all the answers. Arthur Schopenhauer, *The World as Will and Representation*, trans. E. F. J. Payne (New York: Dover, 1969) I, 349. According to Todorov's recent comment, 'at times individuals must inevitably be treated as a means' yet they should 'not be considered solely that' (Tzvetan Todorov, *Facing the Extreme: Moral Life in the Concentration Camps*, trans. Arthur Denner and Abigail Pollak [New York: Holt, 1996] 158). If we replace 'individuals' by 'individual texts' in this formulation, we shall say that literary texts may perform varied functions for different interpretive communities and for individual readers, but they should also be granted individual attention for their own sake.
4. Jan Mukařovský, *Aesthetic Function, Norm and Value as Social Facts*, trans. Mark E. Suino (Ann Arbor: University of Michigan Press, 1970) 1–9. For a more detailed application of this theory to documentary prose, see Leona Toker, 'Toward a Poetics of Documentary Prose – from the Perspective of Gulag Testimonies', *Poetics Today*, 18 (1997) 187–222.
5. See, in particular, Wayne Booth, *The Company We Keep: An Ethics of Fiction* (Berkeley: University of California Press, 1988); Martha Nussbaum, *The Fragility of Goodness: Luck and Ethics in Greek Tragedy and Philosophy* (Cambridge University Press, 1986); and Cora Diamond, *The Realistic Spirit: Wittgenstein, Philosophy, and the Mind* (Cambridge, MA: The MIT Press, 1991) 367–81.
6. Berel Lang, *Act and Idea in the Nazi Genocide* (University of Chicago

Press, 1990) 120. See Shoshana Felman and Dori Laub, *Testimony: Crises of Witnessing in Literature, Psychoanalysis, and History* (New York: Routledge, 1992) on verbal responses to the accounts of atrocity as (second- or third-degree) testimony to one's own response to the testimony of others.

7. Heather Dubrow, 'The Status of Evidence', *PMLA*, 111 (1996) 7–20 (16).
8. Bernard Harrison, *Inconvenient Fictions: Literature and the Limits of Theory* (New Haven: Yale University Press, 1991) 1–8.
9. Stanley Cavell, *Must We Mean What We Say? A Book of Essays* (Cambridge University Press, 1976) 188–9.
10. T. W. Adorno, *Noten zur Literatur III* (Frankfurt/Main: Suhrkampf, 1965) 125.
11. I capitalize the title in order to distinguish Shalamov's main triptych of story cycles (which has still not been published in the structure intended by the author) from the existing publications by John Glad (Varlam Shalamov, *Kolyma Tales*, trans. John Glad [Harmondsworth: Penguin, 1994]), I. P. Sirotinskaya (Varlam Shalamov, *Kolymskie rasskazy*, ed. I. P. Sirotinskaya [Moscow: Sovremennik, 1991] and *Kolymskie rasskazy v dvukh tomakh*, ed. I. P. Sirotinskaya [Moscow: Russkaya kniga, 1992]), and Mikhail Geller (Varlam Shalamov, *Kolymskie rasskazy*, ed. Mikhail Geller [3rd edn, Paris: YMCA Press, 1985; 1st edn, London: Overseas Publications Interchange, 1978.]).
12. Varlam Shalamov, 'Condensed Milk' *Kolyma Tales*, trans. John Glad (Harmondsworth: Penguin, 1994) 80–5.
13. See Todorov, 32–43; V. Yakubov, 'V kruge poslednem: Varlam Shalamov Aleksandr Solzhenitsyn' (In the last circle: Varlam Shalamov and Aleksandr Solzhenitsyn), *Vestnik Russkogo Khristianskogo Dvizheniya*, 137 (1987) 156–61; Anna Shur, 'V. T. Shalamov i A. I. Solzhenitsyn: Sravnitel'nyj analiz nekotorykh proizvedenii' (V. T. Shalamov and A. I. Solzhenitsyn: A comparative analysis of some works) (*Novyi zhurnal* [*The New Review*, New York] 155 (1984)) 92–101.
14. See Varlam Shalamov, 'O moei proze' (On my prose), *Novyi mir*, 12 (1989) 58–71.
15. Gérard Genette, *Narrative Discourse: An Essay in Method*, trans. Jane E. Lewin (Ithaca: Cornell University Press, 1980) 186–9.
16. Shalamov, 'Condensed Milk', 80.
17. Primo Levi, *If This is a Man/The Truce*, trans. Stuart Woolf (London: Abacus, 1990) 42.
18. See Robert Conquest, *The Great Terror: A Reassessment* (Oxford University Press, 1990) 332.
19. Todorov, *Facing*, 38–9.
20. Shalamov, 'Condensed Milk', 82.
21. Ibid., 83.
22. In his later years Shalamov was a vegetarian.
23. Shalamov, 'Condensed Milk', 83.
24. Friedrich Nietzsche, 'The Birth of Tragedy', *Basic Writings of Nietzsche*, trans. and ed. Walter Kaufman (New York: The Modern Library, 1968) 1–144 (60).

25. Cf. Alexander Wat, *My Century: The Odyssey of a Polish Intellectual*, foreword by Czesław Miłosz, trans. Richard Lourie (New York: Norton, 1990) 200–201: 'Let's go back to the cell. If I keep launching into digressions and often needless rationalizations, it's not only the result of my bad habits or my literary failings, but also because it's not easy in the least to return to prison voluntarily. To return to prison after twenty-five years by the faithful exercise of memory involves my entire being and is almost a physical act; it requires the greatest concentration I am capable of, and I'm already so much older now, so much more devastated.'
26. Precisely this effect is explored, through the use of escalation, in Jerzi Kosinski's *The Painted Bird*.
27. Levi, *If This is a Man*, 73.
28. Shalamov, 'Condensed Milk', 84.
29. Amended translation.
30. Shalamov, 'Condensed Milk', 84–5. Amended translation.
31. Cf. Wolfgang Iser, *The Act of Reading: A Theory of Aesthetic Response* (Baltimore: Johns Hopkins University Press, 1974) 68–79, and Bernard Harrison, *Inconvenient Fictions*, 1–8, on literature as a testing ground for ideas.
32. Some writers on camp life consider it a moral universe with its own specific semiotics; others regard it as a field in which tendencies at work in the society as a whole reach a kind of diabolical crystallization. Shalamov explicitly leaned to the latter position and made a number of on-record comments on the shift in the scales: explicitly, indeed, he speaks of his feelings as more or less 'normal' in quality though weaker in intensity. The punchline, however, suggests the opposite: the shift has occurred not only in the quantitative specificity of the emotion but also in the quality of the attitude: the tinge of remorse has been redirected from the failure to seek out and warn the victims of the provocation to the double-crossing of the agent provocateur (himself a double-crosser *ex officio*).
33. Shestakov is the namesake of the author of Stalinist high-school history books. His name may have been chosen in order to evoke the covering up of the past, the massive rewriting of history, and the falsification of records – but for all we know the name may also be authentic.
34. Schopenhauer, *The World as Will and Representation*, 334–50.
35. Gilbert Harman, *The Nature of Morality: An Introduction to Ethics* (New York: Oxford University Press, 1977) 111.
36. Aleksandr Solzhenitsyn, *The Gulag Archipelago: An Experiment in Literary Investigation*, trans. Thomas P. Whitney (New York: Harper and Row, 1975) II, 615–16.
37. See Harman, *The Nature of Morality*, 58.
38. Varlam Shalamov 'The Chess Set of Doctor Kuzmenko', *Kolymskie rasskazy*, ed. I. P. Sirotinskaya (Moscow: Sovremennik, 1991) 456–9.
39. Shalamov, 'The Chess Set of Doctor Kuzmenko', 458–9 (my translation).
40. Williams notes that in order for people to be able to rely 'on not being

killed or used as a resource, and on having some space and objects and relations with other people they can count as their own', certain motivations must be encouraged, 'and *one* form of this is to instill a disposition to give the relevant considerations a high deliberative priority in the most serious of these matters, a virtually absolute priority, so that certain courses of action must come first, while others are ruled out from the beginning. An effective way for actions to be ruled out is that they never come into thought at all, and this is often the best way. One does not feel easy with the man who in the course of a discussion of how to deal with political or business rivals says, "Of course, we could have them killed, but we should lay that aside right from the beginning." It should never have come into his hands to be laid aside' (Bernard Williams, *Ethics and the Limits of Philosophy* [Cambridge, MA: Harvard University Press, 1985] 185).

41. Geoffrey Hartman, *Minor Prophesies: The Literary Essay in the Culture Wars* (Cambridge, MA: Harvard University Press, 1991) 131.
42. Wolfgang Iser, *The Fictive and the Imaginary: Charting Literary Anthropology*, (Baltimore: Johns Hopkins University Press, 1993) 296–303.
43. Martha Nussbaum, *The Fragility of Goodness*, 13, 32, and *Love's Knowledge: Essays on Philosophy and Literature* (New York: Oxford University Press, 1990) 143–5.

15

Cosmopolitanism as Resistance: Fragmented Identities, Women's Testimonial and the War in Yugoslavia

Anne Cubilié

In this essay I would like to suggest a broadening of the category of 'testimonial' literature. Works such as Elma Softić's *Sarajevo Days, Sarajevo Nights* and Slavenka Drakulić's *The Balkan Express* embody a progress, from the writings of Holocaust survivors, through texts by survivors of State terror and oppression in Latin America in the 1970s and 1980s, to the position of survivors of the warfare that recently overtook the former Yugoslavia. Increasingly, such testimonials participate in a dialogue both with the history of the genre itself, and with human rights organizations and international (especially Western) opinion that might be swayed towards political intervention. Human rights discourses, however, typically rely upon universalist assumptions about the basic sameness of human bodies, and are in tension with the individual experiences of trauma that victims experience. Witnessing is one of the primary imperatives of the testimonial, and this is crucial to much human rights work. But while human rights work moves to stabilize the testimonial discourse at all times, insisting on the transparent authenticity of the singular experience of suffering, testimonial literature itself refuses such easy moves toward the naturalizing of experience. Instead, it draws attention to the fragmentary nature of memory, experience, identity and the literary – out of which a witnessing voice can be sutured together.

To recuperate bodies that have gone from being full citizens of civil and political life to being illegally removed from it, as difficult as this might be, is easier than granting such full citizenship to bodies that for specific structural reasons, such as the relationships of power and domination often inherent between different sexes and races, have never fully enjoyed it. As is clear from the United Nations Universal Declaration of Human Rights, human rights as they are constituted today, although always in a process of change, have dealt with this by rhetorically enacting the universal individual and then attempting to provide some guidelines on the structure of social and cultural life through which the 'playing field' will be made more equal. But this is only half a solution.

Women, and other bodies feminized by totalitarian violence, must be deconstructed as juridical subjects in order for the state to justify not the 'random' outbreaks of violence against them but the systematic internment and murder of individuals who as universal humanist subjects have human rights.[1] By excluding certain bodies from the juridical discourse of human rights, violent States can maintain the facade of civilization while enacting mass murder. Testimony, having developed an increasingly sophisticated discourse both with previous violent events, and with interventionist human rights groups and structures, plays a growing role in re-appearing these excluded bodies and voices.

It is in the tension between the assumption of the always/already private and juridically recognizable body of humanism and the inability of humanist, rights-based discourses to protect so many bodies around the globe that one of the great problems of a rights-based juridical theory surfaces. Torture and abuse happen within the private spaces of the home as well as in those of the State and in public spectacles involving the police and the military; but in all instances they happen because the bodies that are being acted upon are not fully subjects and therefore not bodies at all. They are not the (universal individual) body that is juridically recognizable. The self-conscious theatricality of memory and narrative performed in testimonial literature, by contrast, creates not the universal subject/narrator, but a gendered subject/narrator who is aware of the necessity of her own instability. The paradox inherent in the act of using language to witness one's banishment from a juridical field comprised by the same language is overridden by the need for visibility and subjecthood.

Language, as a site of resistance, is a focus of all of these accounts of survival and witnessing.[2] To be one's own witness is fundamental in perceiving oneself as a subject within the juridical field. The ability to speak and to act for oneself, which is so important and contested a position for the narrators of these testimonials, is a resistant act necessary to their survival. These moments are not constant, but as they punctuate the totalitarian concentrationary universe, they become important and remembered links in the attempt to rebuild a history and narrative within which the individual-as-subject, and therefore as person, can begin to exist again. From these kernels of memory comes the narrative of the testimonial, performed as oral or written event for the witness/survivor as well as the witness/audience – crucial to the rebuilding of the survivor's 'internal witness'.[3] This performative act of memory does not construct a unified narrative of the historical event, but instead functions as the truth of witnessing experiences whose truths can never be known.

As James Young notes, '[t]he Holocaust survivor who continues to testify in narrative seems to have intuited the paradoxical knowledge that even though his [*sic*] words are no longer traces of the Holocaust, without his words, the Holocaust takes no form at all'.[4] Young concludes that the criticism of such literature should be 'life-affirming'. That is, that we should read it not only as the narrative of a traumatic event or as a textual product, but in a way that is synergistically connected with the larger project of furthering our understanding of our lives in the world.

Dori Laub, referring to the Holocaust, states that

> [t]he perpetrators, in their attempt to rationalize the unprecedented scope of the destructiveness, brutally imposed upon their victims a delusional ideology whose grandiose coercive pressure totally excluded and eliminated the possibility of an unviolated, unencumbered, and thus sane, point of reference in the witness.[5]

From this, he concludes that there could be no witness to the Holocaust from within the event itself. Thus, the attempt to rebuild the 'internal witness' through testimony results in the doubled role of testimony as the political act of witnessing an event that has been radically denied and the 'private' necessity to rebuild one's historical link to the experience by recounting one's memories of it in front of a witness – language and representation serve to give substance and 'reality' to an experience that no longer exists or seems real. The compulsion of some survivors to tell their stories over and over again is an act of resistance against this 'delusional ideology' that denies the survivor's memories of her/his experience.

To oppose the fascist imaginary, and to replace its delusional history with the history and memories of one's own experience, it is necessary for survivors to reclaim for themselves the position of juridical subjects who have the right to speak and to be heard and to be free from violence. Thus, testimony must acknowledge the paradoxical need to speak and to witness, both for oneself and for others who may not have survived, while maintaining the awareness of an essential inability to communicate the experience.

The testimonies of survivors of other experiences of human rights abuse are substantially similar in their difficulties with language, memory and history to the testimonies of Holocaust survivors. As Young notes:

> The aim of an inquiry into 'literary testimony' is rather to determine how writers' experiences have been shaped both in and out of narrative. Once we recognise that the 'facts' of history are not distinct from their reflexive interpretation in narrative, and that the 'facts' of the Holocaust and their interpretation may even have been fatally interdependent, we are able to look beyond both the facts and the poetics of literary testimony to their consequences.[6]

Thus, Young proposes a self-reflexive criticism that seeks to understand 'the ways our lives and these texts are inextricably bound together'.[7] I would suggest, further, that there is value in reading the testimonies of Holocaust survivors alongside those of survivors of more recent state-sponsored human rights abuses. In doing this, I am not trying to suggest either a continuum of traumatic experience or a relativistic levelling of witnessing into universal norms, but rather that the genre of testimonial and the imperative to testify are culturally bound to a developing moment in which our understandings of bodies and subjects and their juridical positions is deeply in flux.

Unlike the authors of Holocaust testimonial, survivors of the war in Bosnia, such as Softić and Drakulić, are writing after the Universal

Declaration of Human Rights, and are aware of the existence of human rights as a juridical discourse, administered through the United Nations, that attempts to formulate international guidelines for the behaviours of States toward their subjects/citizens. As such, their projects bear with them from the outset the imperative not just to bear witness to past murders but to intervene into ongoing situations of abuse. These authors know the crucial political role their testimonies can play.

Throughout the course of the war in Yugoslavia, the response by the European and American political community, both at the level of the State and internationally (NATO and the UN) was one of paralysis, appeasement, and reluctant engagement. Any commitment to an international community of shared ideals and common interests was discarded at the first hint that armed engagement might be necessary to end the genocide and ethnic partitioning of former Yugoslavia. News media reflected this same paralysis of ethical engagement. Despite the fact that the war was thoroughly covered by world media since the beginning, including film of concentration camps, starving inmates and piles of bodies (deliberately recalling the Holocaust) public opinion was not mobilized to such an extent that governments felt compelled to commit large numbers of troops to potentially life-threatening situations.

The discourse of international 'cosmopolitanism' versus 'primitive, bloodthirsty, fundamentalist ethnic division' was engaged in by both the Western media and war resisters within the former Yugoslavia, and was exemplified by the iconic role played by Sarajevo. Sarajevo, with its diverse, multi-ethnic and multi-religious communities, living as neighbours and intermarrying, came to signify, through the mass media, an idealized vision of the potential Western communities of the future. As the city was besieged, this vision of Sarajevo also became an important tool for the activists trying to encourage relief efforts and military intervention by Western governments and citizens that would help to save lives, stop the war and restore order to the region. However, as it became clear that nothing would be done to stop the war, and that instead we had all become front-row spectators to the massive destruction and murder, this vision of Sarajevo as all that was ideal in 'civilized' culture became linked to an idea of unstoppable downfall. The ethical paralysis brought on in the mass media and Western governments by such spectatorship took the form of a voyeuristic fascination with what came to be seen as an example of the inevitable march of the destructiveness of human nature. Such fatalism, of course, is an excellent excuse for non-involvement, but what is also interesting is the way that exhaustive media coverage – including death camps, complicity by UN troops, the persistent shelling of Sarajevo – failed to fulfil the promise that documentary witnessing seems to have held since the Holocaust. Being witness to such violences, and bearing the slogan 'never again' in mind, was hopefully to provide the key to preventing such events. What the mass documentary witnessing, by the Western media and other observers, proved instead was that witnessing such violence was not enough to mobilize an empathic response from the massed citizens of Europe and the United States that would cause them to feel the vital necessity of intervening to stop the warfare.

The various media and organizations that work to prevent and contain such radical violences have, therefore, increasingly relied on eyewitness accounts and testimonial as avenues of intervention. The personalized account of trauma, with its claims to a truth of individual experience, is powerful and difficult to deny. In contrast to the faceless unaccountability of governments and state agencies, testimonial provides the voice of the individual survivor/witness. As both Laub and Young suggest, however, testimony itself is not separate from this historical moment. To the extent that testimony as a personal and political act is imbricated within the panoptical systems of national and multi-national state and corporate control, it faces the same untenable paradox as the authorial 'I' in much testimonial literature. By using language as the mode of entry and intervention into the social and juridical fields from which they have been excised, survivors must accept implication within the totalitarian cultural field responsible in part for their abuse.

These survivors are also painfully aware of the role torture and disappearances play in reinforcing state oppression through terror and fear. Their writings, therefore, must address this terror as an ongoing attack against the peoples of the nations in which it is being experienced. Yugoslavian writers such as Softić and Drakulić, whose work was being published while the war was still underway, are aware that their work could play an important role in organizing international opinion against the war. These are not works of propaganda in any way; instead they are intellectual and artistic interventions into the vast, universalizing field of discourses about the war that speak in terms of troop movements, attack and defence, and groups of people defined only through a collective attribute such as ethnicity, gender or death. Unlike the writings of women who were imprisoned in concentration camps, or have been victims of a debilitating trauma, such as torture, Softić's and Drakulić's testimonial writing serves as a way for them to maintain – during the event itself – a (sometimes tenuous) voice and identity through which to resist oppressive state discourses.

Sarajevo Days, Sarajevo Nights is a collection of journal entries and letters to friends that Elma Softić wrote while living in Sarajevo from 8 April 1992 to 23 June 1995. Translated by Nada Conić and published in English in 1996, these writings form a testimonial to Softić's experiences during the Serbian siege. Having made friends through ham radio contact maintained between the Jewish Community Centres in Sarajevo and Zagreb during the siege, Softić wrote them letters which began to be published in Croatia and, along with her diary entries, appeared in book form in Zagreb in 1994. As a teacher and intellectual, Softić experiences the siege through the lens of continual self-critique, and documents the ways in which identity is shaped and altered by the changing affiliations, pressures and discourses of the war. Similarly, Slavenka Drakulić's *The Balkan Express* was written between April 1991 and May 1992 and concerns the author's experiences of the way in which the war changed, or put pressure on, her various identities as a journalist, a Yugoslavian, a Croatian, a woman and an exile. Several of her chapters were originally published in various magazines and newspapers before she determined to gather them together and produce a book.

These texts function as testimonials not just because of the material conditions through which they were produced, but because they speak to the pressures placed on individuality through the experience of trauma and to the ways in which community affiliations can be formed to resist such pressures. Like many of the testimonials that have been written by survivors of previous events of genocide and mass murder, these texts also focus on witnessing not just the authors' experiences but the lives and deaths of other people who have not survived, and by giving voice to the memories of these other people Softić and Drakulić find a powerful ground from which to resist and to rebuild their own identities as particular individuals.

The Holocaust serves as a foundational event for both authors. While neither makes claims for the commensurability of their own experiences with the events of the Holocaust, both Softić and Drakulić reflect upon the irony of the spatial and temporal proximity of the two events. And both authors reflect upon the importance of the filmic and the televisual in shaping their own identities as they are caught up in the war, as well as the response to the war by the rest of the world. The understanding that we have of the Holocaust is mediated through numerous films, and the ghosts of many fictional accounts of World War II haunt the present writings of Drakulić and Softić as much as do the Holocaust documentaries.

Drakulić begins her book with a quotation from the film *Shoah* and ends it with five chapters that work as a series, the first of which returns to this opening quotation. From this, she moves in the next chapter to a consideration of the Holocaust as an event which marks the ways in which genocide will always, rather than never, happen again while the cultural and social grounds that produced it remain intact. The following two chapters weave events of the war, the sniper murder of two lovers from different ethnic groups (one Muslim and one Serbian) trying to escape Sarajevo, and the destruction of the Old Bridge of Mostar, into metaphors that represent the massive destruction of war as it obliterates the mythic foundations upon which cultures and identities depend. From this, Drakulić moves to her final chapter, which is a complex consideration of the way Sarajevo has become, for observers, the central metaphor of the destructiveness of the war and of the fight between cosmopolitan diversity and murderous fundamentalism. Witnessing, finally, is not enough for Drakulić, and in fact can be the worst form of collaboration with murder if it is not combined with action. Thus, her testimony ends with a crisis of witnessing not just for herself, but for all of the observers, well intentioned or not, of the war in the former Yugoslavia.

The quotation from *Shoah* which provides the epigraph to her book is taken from a dialogue between the filmmaker, Claude Lanzmann, and a villager from Treblinka about what it was like to work a field that bordered the death camp. In response to Lanzmann's question about whether the man being spoken of was bothered by working within hearing of the screams from the camp, the villager replies: 'At first it was unbearable. Then you got used to it.' Drakulić returns to this, asking:

> What had a Pole to do with the fact that Germans were killing Jews? So we all get used to it. I understand now that nothing but this 'otherness' killed Jews, and it began with naming them, by reducing them to the other. Then everything became possible.... For Serbians, as for Germans, they are all others, not-us.

She goes on to name a continuum of othering and collaboration – for herself refugees are others, for Europe it's the Balkans, for the USA it's a European problem, etc:

> I don't think our responsibility is the same,... all I'm saying is that it exists, this complicity: that out of opportunism and fear we are all becoming collaborators or accomplices in the perpetuation of war.[8]

The problem, for Drakulić, is that 'our defense is weak' in the face of this 'othering' because it is caused by a central crisis of identity formation. How can we constitute ourselves as individuals without recourse to perceiving other people as 'other', as separate from ourselves? Yet for her this seems to be the beginning of the slippage that leads to violence. Her answer lies in the form of the book itself: in her embrace of identity and voice as fragmentary and constituted through a diversity of affiliations and experiences, and in her call for a continual self-awareness and critique of the ways we are all, as witnesses, implicated in violent acts, even while witnessing is an important first step in resistance.

Drakulić goes on to argue that the post-Holocaust credo, 'never again', has become perverted through the very mechanisms that were meant to prevent the recurrence of such events. Witnessing is a complex political position, and while for survivors to tell their stories after their return from a death camp or torture chamber is a powerful intervention into the totalitarian discourses that have sought to erase them from the field of discourse as well as the human community, documentary witnessing of an ongoing genocide is not, in itself, an interventionist act:

> Day after day, death in Bosnia has been well documented.... [F]ifty years ago this is how the Jews suffered; now it's the Muslims' turn. We remember it all, and because of that memory we have the idea that everything has to be carefully documented.... [G]enerations whose parents swear it could

> never happen again, at least not in Europe, precisely because of the living memory of the recent past. What, then, has all the documentation changed? ... [T]he biggest change has happened within ourselves: the audience, spectators. We started to believe this is our role, that it is possible to play the public, as if war is theater.... To watch war from so near and in its most macabre details makes sense only if we do so to change things for the better. But today, nothing changes. Documentation has become a perversion, a pornography of dying.[9]

The line between spectatorship and voyeurism is very fine, and both contain an erotic attachment to the object being viewed. Neither the spectatorial nor the voyeuristic position is one of equitable exchange between the viewer and the viewed, and the power of the active gaze rests with the viewer. Mediated through the technology of the camera, the murdered, dying, broken bodies become objects of spectatorial interest, but they have no power within themselves to demand an active response that would change their status to that of a person who also holds power and can make demands for equal footing as an individual with rights. Drakulić calls for a spectatorial position that is self-critical, that can 'change things for the better', otherwise such documentation is a form of complicity that engages the erotics of murder and warfare and authorizes it to continue, in order to continue the voyeuristic pleasure of the viewer.

Such self-critique, however, is not enough to stop the war. For the witness to be aware of the perils of witnessing as well as the continuing imperative to witness leads Drakulić in her final chapter into the danger of a nihilistic impasse. As a journalist, as well as a refugee, she herself is implicated within the discourse of documentation which she critiques. She recognizes that '[m]y words – any words – have no real meaning'. Faced with silence as the only other option, witnessing must necessarily perform this crisis and inadequacy as part of the testimonial process. Stating that '[f]inally, all we have achieved with words is to establish Sarajevo as a metaphor for tragedy', the impotence of language to effect change overwhelms the end of her text. Language, and witnessing, are bound up, in her text, with the position of Sarajevo as the metaphor for cosmopolitan culture, and ultimately all are lost in the face of the relentless onslaught of nature. Winter, with the spectre of death through starvation and cold, defeats her words, and is itself a metaphor for the triumph of the 'primitive' erotics of warfare and genocide over the 'civilized' cosmopolitanism of language and culture. Such an ending performs the crisis of witnessing, but Drakulić's text remains resistant to the extent that it has been written and published. It remains an act of memorial and of witnessing that contains in its form as well as its content possibilities for resistance to hegemonic discourses of otherness and violence.

Softić's testimony contains very similar concerns over language, witnessing, and the documenting of the war. In reflecting upon her reasons for becoming a teacher, when she was drawn to becoming a war correspondent, she states that teaching held for her the promise of creation as opposed to the ethically compromised position of the correspondent who searches out and documents slaughters to which she/he has no connection. The crisis of language, also, is just as present for Softić as it is for Drakulić and other testimonial authors. Her text embraces the paradox of the inadequacy of language to convey such trauma while recognizing it as the only vehicle for doing so:

> I'm sharing with you all these wearisome and perhaps unedifying reflections in order to convince you that this is not the materialization of my despair or my bitterness. This is my need to recapitulate my wartime experience, and for that I require a listener, not a conversational partner, just a listener. For you and I cannot discuss this war. Nowadays we inhabit different worlds, you and I. We do not understand each other and in certain matters we will not only never understand each other, but there will also be times when we won't be able to communicate at all because we will be speaking different languages. Nevertheless, that does not diminish my need and my duty to tell you something about this war.[10]

Witnessing needs a spectator, a 'listener', for the act to occur, and as much as Drakulić is sceptical of the spectatorial position, Softić acknowledges its importance to the performance of witnessing. The understanding is by necessity fragmentary and incomplete, but this is itself integral to the act of testimony as it refutes the possibility of building complete narratives and solid truths through which readers can integrate such traumatic experiences into their own historical narratives.

Both Softić and Drakulić are aware of being, themselves, prey to hegemonic ethnic and nationalist discourses, and sometimes take refuge in the very universalism they critique. This universalism, however, moves quickly toward an embrace of the ways in which identity is discontinuous and fragmented, rather than consistent, as the best ground from which to speak and understand their situation. Thus, Drakulić mourns the loss of coherent identity, of the fiction of the cohesive self, in a chapter that moves from her feelings of separation as an exile in Paris in December 1991, to her retreat into the most basic recognition of all bodies of persons as human, to a loss of recognition of a familiarity with her own body.

The passage begins with Drakulić's recognition of the vast gulf that separates her from people outside the war zone, in the 'normative' world, who have not experienced the physical and psychic traumas enacted by the war. Traumas that she does not recognize herself until she is confronted with the 'normative' world.

> It seemed to me I was almost floating, not touching the pavement, not touching reality; as if between me and Paris there stretched an invisible wire fence through which I could see everything but touch and taste nothing – the wire that...kept me imprisoned in the world from which I had just arrived. And in that world things, words and time are arranged in a different way....In a Europe ablaze with bright lights getting ready for Christmas I was separated from Paris by a thin line of blood: that and the fact that I could see it, while Paris stubbornly refused to.[11]

The experience of war is carried within her beyond the war zone. It enacts an alienation from the facades and rituals of cosmopolitan and intellectual life. Because in the world of war 'things, words and time are arranged in a different way', Drakulić cannot bring with her into the 'normative' world the language of her experience. A gap exists between the memory of her experiences and the language through which she can express those experiences. Instead, it is sensory experience that keeps her trapped in the alienating loop of memory. The experience of her body overrides that of her intellect; she cannot bridge the gap, but in recognizing it, she can attempt to suture over the chasm – recognizing in herself the role of witness. It is not just the fact of her alienation that is important, her separation from the normative world 'by a thin line of blood', but the fact that she sees and recognizes the importance of her role as witness as the cause of her alienation, while the other potential witnesses and actors around her 'stubbornly' refuse to do so. As with so much testimonial literature, a central crisis of Drakulić's experience is the inadequacy of language to convey what seems so unreal, even to her.

This crisis over language, and over identity, is crystallized for Drakulić by the visual. Seeing a picture of a dead family beside a destroyed house in the newspaper, she represses it, only to have it return to her memory, floating up through her consciousness, when a cut on her finger she had thought closed comes open again, spilling blood into her bath water. It is not just the return of the repressed, the fear of death, that this moment enacts for her, but the destruction of her own fiction of coherent identity. This is the wound that comes unsutured, bleeding into the present reality of her physical comfort and safety in Paris. In the face of the terror of such a wound, such fragmentation, the imperative to witness, to give voice to the dead and to the 'blood' that Paris 'stubbornly refuses to see', becomes crucial. Remembering the picture, she realizes that

> [t]heir smashed skulls canceled out my own effort to live. The naked brain on the grass is no longer death, horror, war – it eludes any explanation or justification, it makes no sense at all. You ask yourself how it is possible to live in a place where things like that are happening. I know I should have asked myself at this point whether the murdered people were Croats or Serbs and who killed them; perhaps I should have felt rage or a desire for revenge. But as I gazed at the dark gaping hole, at the blood-caked pulp, I only felt an unspeakable revulsion towards humankind. The naked brain is stronger than such questions, it is the evidence that we are all potential criminals.... In the face of the picture of a naked brain all human values are simply reduced to nothing.[12]

It is not the sight of a head split open with brains spilling out that appals Drakulić. What she experiences is the death of 'human values'. She finds herself unable to take recourse in the national and ethnic constitutions that would enable her to distance herself from these bodies by labelling them 'other/enemy', thus allowing her to participate in discourses of 'rage, or the desire for revenge'. Her language here reads as slightly disingenuous precisely because she takes refuge in the universalist identity of the human as an alternative to the identities which are proffered by the material conditions of her life and the context of the photograph. The materiality of the brain, as the basic substance that weds the body and the self to make a person, disrupts all other identity formations for Drakulić. This overly 'civilized' response by Drakulić to the 'naked brain' is, however, symptomatic of the trauma to her own identity that has been enacted by her experiences of the war and which has surfaced at the sight of the photograph.

Following on this passage, Drakulić herself becomes aware of the rupture this has enacted in her identity. Overcome with a feeling that her body has suddenly become alien to her, she states:

> It must have been a momentary death of sorts, a revulsion, a recoiling from the body I could no longer feel as mine.... I squeezed the cut on my finger as if trying to prove to myself I was still alive.... This body was no longer mine. It had been taken over by something else, taken over by the war. I had thought that the death of the body was the worst thing that could happen in war; I didn't know that worse was the separation of self from the body, the numbness of the inner being, extinction before death, pain before pain.[13]

This moment of misrecognition, of the recognition that the body one sees in the mirror, or in front of one's eyes in the bath, is not the body one had always taken for granted, but is instead alien, seemingly an other even to the self contained within the body, is a crisis enacted in most testimonial literature by survivors of trauma. It is both a moment that crystallizes for the survivor the absolute separation between the world of the war/concentration camp/torture chamber and the world of normative society and a moment that enacts the crisis of language that is at the heart of testimonial literature.

Language will never be able to bridge the separation represented through the incommensurability of these two bodies that must – to maintain the fiction of coherent identity crucial for the construction of the self – occupy the same space at the same time and yet can never do so. This realization is the 'momentary death', the 'extinction before death, pain before pain', that Drakulić experiences. Like many testimonial authors, she sutures over the wound exposed through this moment with the imperative to witness. As she states in her introduction, 'as the war came closer the urge to write about it and nothing else grew stronger and stronger. I ended up writing a book because, in spite of everything, I still believe in the power of words, in the necessity of communication. This is the only thing I know I believe in now.' Although her text compulsively documents the way in which the experiences of war overtake 'the inner self until one can scarcely recognize oneself any longer', this loss of recognition results, for Drakulić, in the need to witness both the process itself and the lives and deaths of others with whom she has come into contact.[14]

Elma Softić also writes of experiencing such a disruption of identity, although hers occurs while she is still an 'inmate' of Sarajevo. She writes of watching the television and seeing:

> [b]eneath the azure sky of Barcelona – the Olympics. The twenty-fifth in the series began the twenty-fifth of July, 1992. I don't know how it came about, but we had electricity and we managed to watch the opening ceremonies. All those people in the audience seemed to me to come from another planet. The first reaction I had, when I saw the packed stadium, was dread, because it occurred to me – what if a shell lands! And once this ghastly anxiety lodged itself within me at the first sight of the stadium, there was no longer anything that could drive it out of me. Not the whole beautiful, fashionable, joyous and contented crowd. Not the overjoyed participants in their colourful uniforms, not the glamorous performance, not the spectacular divas singing arias from popular operas.
>
> And here: death, starvation, horror. Yes, once upon a time there were Olympics in Sarajevo.[15]

One of the things that marks the horror of this war for Softić is not just the yawning gulf that separates her within the war from the 'normative' world of non-war, but also the bizarre proximity of these two worlds. Through the technology of telecommunications, not only does the outside world have unprecedented access to the intimate daily details of the carnage, but the people trapped within the war have the possibility of viewing both the gross detail of destruction as they themselves are experiencing it and the simultaneous world of experience outside the boundaries of the war zone where life is continuing in the most normative way, as though the horrors and traumas suffered by the people within the war were indeed happening on another planet. At this moment, she forcefully realizes the absolute incommensurability of experience that separates her from the world in which the Olympics is taking place. While toward the end of her text Softić will state that 'I myself have changed so much that in the autobiographical film which was playing in my mind I had the greatest difficulty recognizing myself',[16] here it is not Softić that is the alien, but all of us, the inhabitants of the world outside the circle of traumatic experience. Our world is built on fictions of stability, boundaries and narrative coherence, the promise of which, for Softić, has so disastrously been proved false.

The Holocaust haunts Softić's text as it does Drakulić's. For Softić, the Holocaust is composed of memories, documentary knowledge, and the media representations that resonate through European and American culture. The experiences she has of Sarajevo under siege, a 'giant concentration camp', are haunted by images of World War II. Thus:

> [i]n the Jewish Community Centre, bedlam. People have been coming to see whether they're on the departure list. It's a scene out of a movie: Paris, World War II, the Germans at the city gates, shadowy corridors and stairways packed with desperate people waiting for a visa to Lisbon or to who knows what more fortunate destination. That's how it was in the centre...[17]

The difficult conjunction of her perceived reality and the reality that is presented through media such as news broadcasts and film permeates Softić's text and provides opportunities for her to destabilize and reread seemingly fixed or coherent narratives. Thus, the powerful image of bombs falling over the Olympic stadium at Barcelona and the lines of desperate people in Sarajevo seen as the doomed Jewish populations of World War II are powerful metaphors for the inability of narrative to temporally contain moments of history. At the same time that satellite hook-ups permit the citizens of Sarajevo to watch the siege that they are experiencing on their television sets (when the electricity is working), media representations of past events like the Holocaust provide powerful moments of cultural *déjà vu*. Softić's text becomes not just a testimonial of her experiences in Sarajevo, but a fragmentary witnessing to visions of past and possible future wars and genocides. This widens the spectrum of implication for the readers of her text, as they are witness not just to her testimony, but to past genocide and the threat of future violences which could engulf them.

Both Softić and Drakulić figure their testimony as a form of resistance to the 'normalization' of war. Similarly, they oppose the totalitarian discourses of nationalism with a discourse of cosmopolitanism, exemplified by the metaphor of Sarajevo, that values diversity and difference over the 'primitive' and 'regressive' consolidations of nationalism. Softić writes that

> [n]ationalism is the most serious form of disturbance of the consciousness of values. The person who is happy and content only when he lives in a ghetto where everyone is the same, ... that person is definitively lost to culture and civilization, to the world and the future – in a word, to humanity.... What's happened to my, *my* Sarajevo?[18]

She opposes not just the nationalism of the Serbs, but the nationalisms that the people within Sarajevo are falling into as well under the pressure of the war. To participate in nationalist discourse, for Softić, is to stop participating in the human race. While she opposes the consolidation of sameness constructed through nationalism, she offers a universal sameness of humanity founded on the recognition and enjoyment of differences.

Drakulić also writes against the sameness of nationalism, stating that

> the war is... reducing us to one dimension: the Nation. The trouble with this nationhood, however, is that whereas before, I was defined by my education, my job, my ideas, my character – and, yes, my nationality too – now I feel stripped of all that. I am nobody because I am not a person any more. I am one of 4.5 million Croats.... [J]ust as in the days of brotherhood-unity, there is now another ideology holding people together, the ideology of nationhood.[19]

For Drakulić, also, to lose one's differences from other people is to no longer be a person, or as Softić figures it, a member of 'humanity'. By writing her testimony, Drakulić asserts her own individuality in the face of this hegemonic nationalism, while speaking for those others who can no longer speak for themselves.

Although it is impossible for her to place herself outside the ideology, she can resist it through her text, especially in her embrace of fragmentary rather than cohesive formations of identity.

Softić and Drakulić, like many testimonial authors before them, refuse the stabilizing (authenticating) moves that autobiography claims and that international agencies such as Amnesty International rely on when they use testimonial as an interventionist tool. These authors posit survival as much in accepting and balancing discontinuity as in rebuilding a continuous identity and narrative history.[20] The survivors, again and again, insist on both the actuality of their experience and its phantasmic nature, so that they themselves are no longer sure what was real and what was not. For these women, however, this very inability to tell the difference is somehow the essence of their experience. Rather than erasing the experience from history (as fascism hopes) they reclaim this instability as the 'truth' of their experience.

While testimonials call to the carpet the ethical bankruptcy of Western humanist ideals and the engines of international human rights law, at the same time they refuse to let go of the belief in the necessity for just such an international, cosmopolitan community. Thus these testimonials, like those from other genocides and armed struggles in the past, both resist the dehumanizing, authoritarian discourses under which the authors suffered, and recognize the need for a voice within the very systems of the law and culture which have let them down. Unlike previous testimonials, however, those such as Softić's and Drakulić's can take place from 'within the event itself', as Dori Laub constructs it. Aside from the difference in scope between the Holocaust and the war in former Yugoslavia, mass media technology makes possible an unprecedented perspective for the people trapped and trying to survive within the event, one which both breaks and reinforces the field of the 'concentrationary' perspective.

Testimonial literature is both a contested term and an emerging genre. Softić and Drakulić are not survivors of the most immediate and extreme attack on their bodies that a death camp or torture signifies. Instead they are writing both from within the war and from a position where their writings are read by outsiders to the event while they themselves are still experiencing it. This creates the opportunity for them possibly to help intervene into the ongoing event by organizing resistance to it in the West, where their work will be read. By employing a discourse of 'cosmopolitanism' to oppose nationalism, and by telling stories of the ways community affiliations are formed that resist such monolithic formations of identity, they lay claim to a human universality which paradoxically resides in the appreciation of differences. Such a conception of universality could provide the possibility for a different, and perhaps more effective, form of human rights discourse, not founded on the universal sameness of all bodies.

Notes

I would like to thank Alejandro Yarza and Dominic Rainsford for their helpful comments on earlier versions of this essay.

1. The relationship between the torturer and the person being tortured typically comes to be constructed as a gendered relationship between men and women, with the (male or female) victim occupying the position of the woman whose body is controlled, penetrated and emasculated. See Ximena Bunster-Burotto, 'Surviving Beyond Fear: Women and Torture in Latin America', in *Women and Change in Latin America*, ed. June Nash and Helen Safa (South Hadley, MA: Bergin and Garvey, 1985), Elaine Scarry, *The Body in Pain: The Making and Unmaking of the World* (New York: Oxford University Press, 1985), and Jean Franco, 'Gender, Death and Resistance: Facing the Ethical Vacuum', in *Fear at the Edge: State Terror and Resistance in Latin America*, ed. Juan Corradi, Patricia Weiss Fagen and Manuel Antonio Garretón (Berkeley: University of California Press, 1992).
2. Representative texts include Holocaust works such as Charlotte Delbo, *Who Will Carry the Word?* in *Theatre of the Holocaust*, ed. Robert Skloot (Madison: University of Wisconsin Press, 1982), Sara Nomberg-Przytyk, *Auschwitz: True Tales From a Grotesque Land* (Chapel Hill: University of North Carolina Press, 1985), Margarete Buber-Neumann, *Milena: The Story of a Remarkable Friendship* (New York: Seaver Books, 1988), and Latin American works such as Alicia Partnoy, *The Little School: Tales of Disappearance and Survival in Argentina* (Pittsburgh: Cleis Press, 1986), *Information for Foreigners*, in *Information for Foreigners: Three Plays by Griselda Gambaro*, trans. and ed. Marguerite Feitlowitz (Evanston, IL: Northwestern University Press, 1992), and Rigoberta Menchú, *I, Rigoberta Menchú: An Indian Woman in Guatemala*, trans. Ann Wright, ed. Elisabeth Burgos-Debray (New York: Verso, 1984).
3. Shoshona Felman and Dori Laub, *Testimony: Crises of Witnessing in*

Literature, Psychoanalysis, and History (New York: Routledge, 1992), Chapter 3.

4. James Young, *Writing and Rewriting the Holocaust: Narrative and the Consequences of Interpretation* (Bloomington: Indiana University Press, 1990) 38.
5. Felman and Laub, *Testimony*, 81.
6. Young, *Writing and Rewriting the Holocaust*, 39.
7. Ibid., 192.
8. Slavenka Drakulić, *The Balkan Express: Fragments from the Other Side of War* (New York: Norton, 1993) 144–5.
9. Ibid., 149–50.
10. Elma Softić, *Sarajevo Days, Sarajevo Nights*, trans. Nada Conić (Saint Paul, MN: Hungry Mind Press, 1996) 90.
11. Drakulić, *Balkan Express*, 42–3.
12. Ibid., 47.
13. Ibid., 48.
14. Ibid., 4.
15. Softić, *Sarajevo Days, Sarajevo Nights*, 62.
16. Ibid., 168.
17. Ibid.
18. Ibid., 50.
19. Drakulić, *Balkan Express*, 51.
20. Laub's chapters, in *Testimony*, also contain suggestions that some survivors perceive their identities as more a balancing of discontinuities than an unbroken narrative.

Select Bibliography

Antczak, Frederick J., ed., *Rhetoric and Pluralism: Legacies of Wayne Booth* (Columbus: Ohio State University Press, 1995)
Bauman, Zygmunt, *Postmodern Ethics* (Oxford: Blackwell, 1993)
——, *Life in Fragments: Essays in Postmodern Morality* (Oxford: Blackwell, 1995)
Bell, Michael, *Literature, Modernity and Myth: Belief and Responsibility in the Twentieth Century* (Cambridge University Press, 1997)
Benhabib, Seyla, *Critique, Norm and Utopia* (New York: Columbia University Press, 1986)
——, *Situating the Self: Gender, Community, and Postmodernism in Contemporary Ethics* (New York: Routledge, 1992)
Bernasconi, Robert and David Wood, eds, *The Provocation of Levinas: Rethinking the Other* (London and New York: Routledge, 1988)
Bernstein, Richard J., *The New Constellation: The Ethical–Political Horizons of Modernity/Postmodernity* (Cambridge: Polity Press, 1991)
Booth, Wayne C., *The Company We Keep: An Ethics of Fiction* (Berkeley: University of California Press, 1988)
Card, Claudia, ed., *Feminist Ethics* (Lawrence: University of Kansas Press, 1991)
Chanter, Tina, *Ethics of Eros: Irigaray's Rewriting of the Philosophers* (London: Routledge, 1995)
Connor, Steven, *Theory and Cultural Value* (Oxford: Blackwell, 1992)
Cornell, Drucilla, *The Philosophy of the Limit* (New York and London: Routledge, 1992)
Critchley, Simon, *The Ethics of Deconstruction: Derrida and Levinas* (Oxford: Blackwell, 1992)
Derrida, Jacques, 'Afterword: Toward an Ethic of Discussion', trans. Samuel Weber, in Gerald Graff, ed., *Limited Inc.* (Evanston, IL: Northwestern University Press, 1988) 111–60
——,'"Eating Well", or the Calculation of the Subject: An Interview with Jacques Derrida', trans. Peter Connor and Avita Ronell, in Eduardo Cadava, Peter Connor, and Jean-Luc Nancy, eds, *Who Comes After the Subject?* (New York: Routledge, 1991) 96–119
——, *The Gift of Death*, trans. David Wills (Chicago and London: University of Chicago Press, 1995)
——, *Adieu à Levinas* (Paris: Galilée, 1997)
Diprose, Rosalyn, *The Bodies of Women: Ethics, Embodiment and Sexual Difference* (London: Routledge, 1994)
Eaglestone, Robert, *Ethical Criticism: Reading after Levinas* (Edinburgh University Press, 1997)
Furrow, Dwight, *Against Theory: Continental and Analytic Challenges in Moral Philosophy* (London: Routledge, 1995)
Gatens, Moira, *Imaginary Bodies: Ethics, Power, and Corporeality* (New York: Routledge, 1995)

Hadfield, Andrew, Dominic Rainsford and Tim Woods, eds, *The Ethics in Literature* (Basingstoke: Macmillan; New York: St Martin's, 1998)

Harpham, Geoffrey Galt, *Getting It Right: Language, Literature, and Ethics* (University of Chicago Press, 1992)

——, 'Ethics', in *Critical Terms for Literary Study*, ed. Frank Lentricchia and Thomas McLaughlin, 2nd edn (University of Chicago Press, 1995) 387–405

Hartman, Geoffrey H., 'Is an Aesthetic Ethos Possible? Night Thoughts after Auschwitz', *Cardozo Studies in Law and Literature*, 6 (1994)

Krieger, Murray, 'In the Wake of Morality: The Thematic Underside of Recent Theory', *New Literary History*, 14 (1983–84) 119–36

Kristeva, Julia, *The Black Sun: Depression and Melancholia*, trans. Leon S. Roudiez (New York: Columbia University Press, 1989)

——, *Strangers to Ourselves* trans. Leon S. Roudiez (New York: Columbia University Press, 1991)

Leavis, F. R., *The Living Principle: 'English' as a Discipline of Thought* (London: Chatto and Windus, 1975)

Lentricchia, Frank, *Criticism and Social Change* (University of Chicago Press, 1983)

Levinas, Emmanuel, *Totality and Infinity: An Essay on Exteriority*, trans. Alphonso Lingis (Pittsburgh: Duquesne University Press, 1969)

——, *Otherwise Than Being, or Beyond Essence*, trans. Alphonso Lingis (The Hague: Martinus Nijhoff, 1981)

——, 'Ethics as First Philosophy' (1984), in Séan Hand, ed., *The Levinas Reader* (Oxford: Blackwell, 1989) 75–87

——, *Ethics and Infinity: Conversations with Philippe Nemo*, trans. Richard A. Cohen (Pittsburgh: Duquesne University Press, 1985)

Llewelyn, John, *Emmanuel Levinas: The Genealogy of Ethics* (New York: Routledge, 1994)

Lockridge, Laurence S., *The Ethics of Romanticism* (Cambridge University Press, 1989)

MacIntyre, Alasdair, *A Short History of Ethics* (London: Routledge and Kegan Paul, 1967)

——, *After Virtue* (Notre Dame, IN: University of Notre Dame Press, 1988)

Miller, J. Hillis, *The Ethics of Reading: Kant, de Man, Eliot, Trollope, James, and Benjamin* (New York: Columbia University Press, 1987)

Murdoch, Iris, *Metaphysics as a Guide to Morals* (London: Chatto & Windus, 1992)

Nehamas, Alexander, and others, 'Art and Ethics: A Symposium', *Salmagundi*, 111 (Summer 1996) 25–145

Norris, Christopher, *What's Wrong with Postmodernism? Critical Theory and the Ends of Philosophy* (Hemel Hempstead: Harvester, 1991)

——, *The Truth about Postmodernism* (Oxford: Blackwell, 1993)

——, *Truth and the Ethics of Criticism* (Manchester University Press, 1994)

Nussbaum, Martha C., *Love's Knowledge: Essays on Philosophy and Literature* (New York: Oxford University Press, 1990)

——, *Poetic Justice: The Literary Imagination and Public Life* (Boston: Beacon Press, 1995)

Oliver, Kelly, ed., *Ethics, Politics and Difference in Julia Kristeva's Writings*

(New York: Routledge, 1993)
Parker, David, *Ethics, Theory and the Novel* (Cambridge University Press, 1994)
—— Jane Adamson and Richard Freadman, eds, *The Ethics of Literary Theory: Politics, Postmodernism, and Philosophy in Contemporary Critical Theory* (Cambridge University Press, 1998)
Peperzak, Adriaan T., ed., *Ethics as First Philosophy* (New York and London: Routledge, 1995)
Putnam, Hilary, *Reason, Truth and History* (Cambridge University Press, 1981)
Rainsford, Dominic, *Authorship, Ethics and the Reader: Blake, Dickens, Joyce* (Basingstoke: Macmillan; New York: St Martin's, 1997)
Rorty, Richard, *Contingency, Irony, and Solidarity* (Cambridge University Press, 1989)
Rose, Gillian, *The Broken Middle: Out of Our Ancient Society* (Oxford: Blackwell, 1992)
Siebers, Tobin, *The Ethics of Criticism* (Ithaca, NY: Cornell University Press, 1988)
——, *Cold War Criticism and the Politics of Skepticism* (New York: Oxford University Press, 1993)
Singer, Peter, ed., *A Companion to Ethics* (Oxford: Blackwell, 1991)
Smith, Barbara Herrnstein, *Contingencies of Value* (Cambridge, MA: Harvard University Press, 1988)
Toker, Leona, ed., *Commitment in Reflection: Essays in Literature and Moral Philosophy* (New York: Garland, 1993)
Tong, Rosemarie, *Feminine and Feminist Ethics* (Belmont, CA: Wadsworth Pub. Co., 1993)
Williams, Bernard, *Ethics and the Limits of Philosophy* (London: Fontana, 1985)
Woods, Tim, 'The Ethical Subject: The Philosophy of Emmanuel Levinas', in Karl Simms, ed., *Ethics and the Subject* (Amsterdam: Editions Rodopi, 1997) 53–60
Wyschogrod, Edith, *Saints and Postmodernism: Revisioning Moral Philosophy* (Chicago and London: University of Chicago Press, 1990)

Index